I0814539

"This is a desperately needed book. As a male survivor of childhood sexual abuse—and now professor of theology and practicing therapist—this book is a double blessing of the highest order. The words on every page are pastorally sensitive, clinically wise, eminently researched, and brimming with survivor testimony. Too often, the topics of sexual abuse and trauma healing are either overlooked or sensationalized, rather than approached with God's kindness, bold care, and radical hope. This book does justice to the topics and should be standard reading for all faith-based caring professionals."

Preston McDaniel Hill, professor of integrative theology and co-chair of integration at Richmont Graduate University

"*Freedom to Heal* is a must-read for Christian, faith-based therapists and others who seek to fuse evidence-based approaches and recognized best practices with a spiritually integrated, theologically informed perspective on therapeutic treatments of adult survivors of childhood sexual abuse (CSA). This book treats a range of major topics in clinical treatments of CSA with great sensitivity, care, and depth of insight. While acknowledging the profound damage CSA can cause, the authors invite readers to the possibility of healing, and even flourishing, as outcomes in the lives of people who have experienced CSA."

Yvonne Zimmerman, dean of academic affairs and religious studies at Clarke University in Dubuque, Iowa, and author of *Other Dreams of Freedom: Religion, Sex, and Human Trafficking*

"As both a survivor and advocate, I found *Freedom to Heal: A Christian Clinician's Guide to Treating Child Sexual Abuse* to be a much-needed resource for both survivors and the faithful helpers who walk the healing road with us. Loaded with deeply researched tools and insights for clinicians, intertwined with the biblical story and drenched in empathy for survivors, *Freedom to Heal* covers the rugged ground associated with child sexual abuse while keeping readers on the middle path that can ultimately lead to freedom for those who have been victimized."

Nicole Braddock Bromley, author of *Hush: Moving From Silence to Healing After Child Sexual Abuse* and executive director of OneVOICE

"Most pastors are not trained therapists, yet we often find ourselves operating in that role. Educating ourselves in a researched, trauma-informed way is vital to properly caring for hurting people, and *Freedom to Heal* is an incredibly powerful and practical resource for every pastor as we walk alongside others toward healing and wholeness."

Jay Pathak, national director of Vineyard USA

"It's rare for authors to take spiritual integration, research, and clinical expertise seriously. This combined with the sharing of their own personal stories make this a wonderfully informative read. I will certainly be recommending it to clients."

Eric M. Brown, assistant professor in the department of psychiatry at Boston University Chobanian and Avedisian School of Medicine

"*Freedom to Heal* is a vital resource for anyone supporting survivors of childhood sexual abuse. This compassionate and evidence-informed guide integrates theological wisdom with clinical best practices, offering a practical path toward healing. The authors skillfully combine their personal experiences, extensive research, and therapeutic insights to provide a clear and hopeful approach to trauma care. It is a must-have for those committed to helping survivors move beyond recovery and toward a life of flourishing."

Jamie Aten, cofounder of Spiritual First Aid, founder and codirector of the Humanitarian Disaster Institute, Blanchard Chair of Humanitarian and Disaster Leadership, and co-coordinator of the Trauma Certificate Program at Wheaton College

"We each are much more than the worst thing that ever happened to us. Schultz, Estabrook, and Dell have applied this truth to childhood sexual abuse. Yes, people accept that they have been victimized. And they also practice leaning into the *ands*: *and* God has redeemed their suffering, *and* they are attached to God, *and* they have the possibility of forgiving and experiencing post-traumatic growth. The stories, examples, and clinical interventions of this book make it come alive. A well-rounded approach to treatment!"

Everett L. Worthington, Jr., professor emeritus at Virginia Commonwealth University

"With plenty of clinical 'chops,' Schultz, Estabrook, and Dell boldly delve into the holiness and humanity of healing from sexual trauma. Drawing on their personal experience on both sides of the process, the trio invites and supports the reader in honoring the spiritual components of freedom while providing sound scriptural support. This work serves as a validation for clinicians and clients longing for their souls to experience healing."

Mandi Pierson, licensed independent social worker-supervisor and cofounder of Porchlight

"The authors have taken an original approach to the critical work of healing childhood sexual abuse. They weave together contemporary psychoeducation, beautiful narratives, and thoughtful, practical interventions for every step of trauma recovery counseling. This is a book I'll return to again and again as I work with survivors of CSA."

Clair Miller, mental health therapist at Optimum Joy Clinical Counseling

A CHRISTIAN CLINICIAN'S GUIDE TO TREATING CHILD SEXUAL ABUSE

FREEDOM TO HEAL

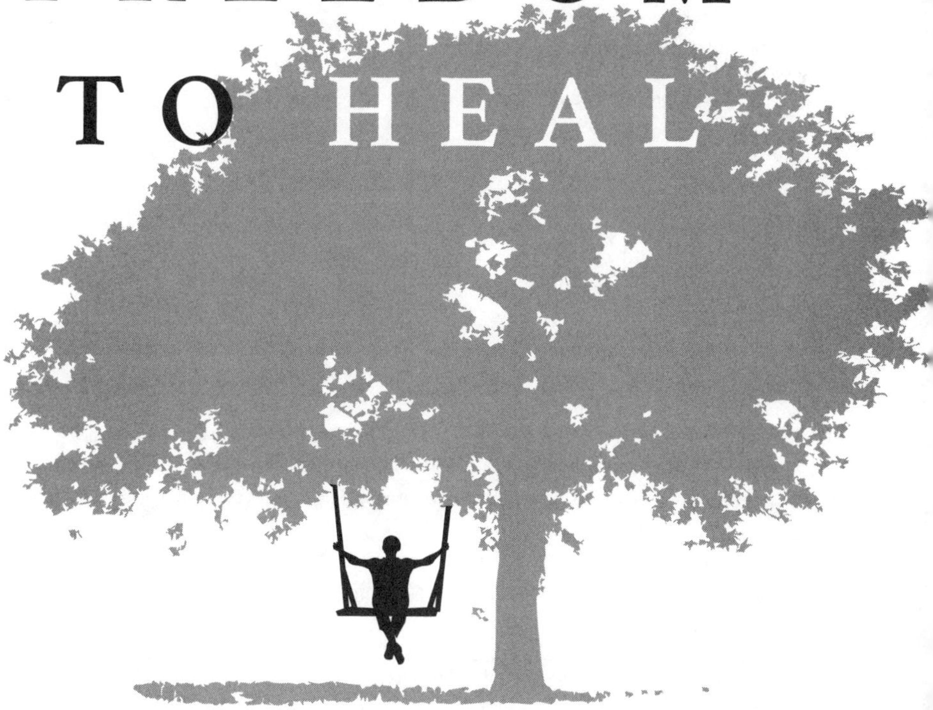

TAMMY SCHULTZ, HANNAH ESTABROOK & ADAM DAVID DELL

An imprint of InterVarsity Press
Downers Grove, Illinois

InterVarsity Press
P.O. Box 1400 | Downers Grove, IL 60515-1426
ivpress.com | email@ivpress.com

Expanded Edition © 2025 by Tamra Mae Schultz, Hannah Ruth Estabrook, and Adam David Dell.

First Edition © 2012 by Tamra Mae Schultz and Hannah Ruth Estabrook

All rights reserved. No part of this book may be reproduced in any form without written permission from InterVarsity Press.

InterVarsity Press® is the publishing division of InterVarsity Christian Fellowship/USA®. For more information, visit intervarsity.org.

Scripture quotations, unless otherwise noted, are from the New Revised Standard Version, Updated Edition. Copyright © 2021 National Council of Churches of Christ in the United States of America. Used by permission. All rights reserved worldwide.

While any stories in this book are true, some names and identifying information may have been changed to protect the privacy of individuals.

The publisher cannot verify the accuracy or functionality of website URLs used in this book beyond the date of publication.

Cover design: Faceout Studio
Interior design: Jeanna Wiggins

ISBN 978-1-5140-0751-8 (print) | ISBN 978-1-5140-0752-5 (digital)

Printed in the United States of America ♾

Library of Congress Cataloging-in-Publication Data

Names: Schultz, Tammy, 1963- author. | Estabrook, Hannah, 1983- author. | Dell, Adam David, 1984- author.
Title: Freedom to heal : a Christian clinician's guide to treating child sexual abuse / Tammy Schultz, Hannah Estabrook, and Adam David Dell.
Description: Downers Grove, IL : IVP Academic, [2025] | Includes index.
Identifiers: LCCN 2024038205 (print) | LCCN 2024038206 (ebook) | ISBN 9781514007518 (cloth) | ISBN 9781514007525 (ebook)
Subjects: LCSH: Adult child sexual abuse victims–Pastoral counseling of. | Adult child sexual abuse victims–Rehabilitation. | Caring–Religious aspects–Christianity.
Classification: LCC BV4463.5 .S38 2025 (print) | LCC BV4463.5 (ebook) | DDC 261.8/3272–dc23/eng/20241001
LC record available at https://lccn.loc.gov/2024038205
LC ebook record available at https://lccn.loc.gov/2024038206

33 32 31 30 29 28 27 26 25 | 12 11 10 9 8 7 6 5 4 3 2

To my mom.

Thanks for teaching me to pray.

Look at what you started!

To Hannah and Adam.

It has been an honor to cowrite together.

I love you both dearly.

TAMMY SCHULTZ

To my mom,

who is grandmother to so many oak trees.

Thank you for nurturing my gifts.

HANNAH ESTABROOK

To survivors of childhood sexual abuse and

those caring for such precious souls.

My sincere gratitude to *Tammy and Hannah*

for welcoming me into this project.

You exemplify posttraumatic growth.

You are part of the redemptive

"and" in my story.

I love you.

ADAM DELL

CONTENTS

INTRODUCTION

Just as every survivor has a story, *Freedom to Heal: A Christian Clinician's Guide to Treating Child Sexual Abuse* was also birthed in narrative. Years ago, Hannah and Tammy traveled to South Korea to speak at a sexual abuse conference. At the end of the conference, a poised and elegant woman lingered, waiting to talk with us. With hesitation, she looked around to ensure that no one could hear, and then, with her gaze fastened to the floor, she spoke in a hushed tone. A trusted and much-loved leader in her church had sexually violated her when she was a teenager. With the aid of a trusted translator, she explained that she would never confront this loved elder because this would bring dishonor to the church. During that week, we were deluged with many more sad stories of child sexual abuse (CSA) experienced by Korean women attending the conference.

After the conference, on our flight from South Korea to Germany, Hannah scribbled a downpour of ideas in a soft, red leather journal as we talked, dreamed, and prayed. The writing journey of the first edition of this text on CSA commenced. Specifically, the primary purpose of this text would be to serve as a trusted roadmap for clinicians and caregivers walking alongside adult survivors of CSA.

Under the broader umbrella of sexual trauma, there are two groups: adult survivors of CSA and adult survivors of sexual assault (ASA). There are overlapping mental health effects and neurobiological outcomes for both groups. However, there are also distinctions (Rowland et al., 2024). In our efforts to complete a distinctively Christian and clinical guide, we elected to focus singularly on adult survivors of CSA to narrow the focus and make this project attainable. Indeed, more research is needed on the topic of ASA. Moreover, many individuals who experience CSA often *also* later experience ASA (Rowland et al., 2024).

In 2022, we invited Adam to join us in the significant revision of this book. Adam served as an active-duty psychologist with the United States Air

Force. In his military career, he accumulated training and real-world experience in offering numerous empirically supported therapies for military members and civilians who survived childhood and adulthood traumas. We asked him to coauthor based on his clinical and teaching experience concerning CSA survivors, his personal, powerful story of CSA that he regularly shares with military and civilian audiences, and because we love and admire Adam.

Mental health research, clinical experience, and spiritual integration deeply matter to many faith-based clinicians as they journey with CSA survivors. Thus, we discuss the integration of theology, mental health approaches, and Christian-accommodated practices throughout this edition. We begin with the sullied story of an Israelite princess who was raped. The threads of her narrative are woven into each chapter. Years ago, when we first read Tamar's story in 2 Samuel, we were undone by how God so astutely understood and described the ways abuse impacted every aspect of her being. Without an excess of words, Scripture reveals that he sees and understands the imprint of sexual violation that crosses culture and class. We also include Tamar's story as an invitation to clients *and* clinicians to contend with the God who permits such violence.

We decided to also draw chapter portions from the reservoir of our own stories. The bittersweet waters we have swallowed remind us that this text was set in motion long before we met. We are three individuals born in different generations, growing up in other countries, each impacted by CSA in our lives. Coincidence? Hardly. As children with tiny hands and hearts, we each emerged from the rubble of CSA, tragically primed for the work God prepared for us to embark on. It would be paramount to share sips of God's grace poured out in our lives with our readers.

Still, despite all our combined experiences, personal opinions alone would be insufficient, as we intend this to be substantially a research-based endeavor for veteran clinicians, counselors in training, and other caregivers who bear witness to stories of individuals who have been sexually violated. With the increased global attention on CSA, there has been a more comprehensive, empirical focus on CSA. Thus, we have sifted through the rivers of research, panning for gold. In this second edition, we have intentionally incorporated evidence-based interventions into each chapter with greater emphasis on practical and clinical considerations as we walk in the direction of hope and healing. We have also provided more hope-imbued perspectives and interventions focusing on flourishing.

While we hold evidence-based approaches in high regard, we also acknowledge their limitations. There are times when manualized approaches offer the illusion of certainty. We understand that well-being is not a simple equation of three steps or stages. Therefore, the goal of healing in this edition extends beyond the cessation of symptoms. It is about thriving, about being freed up to love others and to love God. We firmly believe that those marred by tragedy can also be destined for triumph.

Almost two decades have passed between Hannah's and my (Tammy) plane ride from South Korea and the gift of Adam joining the writing of this second edition. We have journeyed through forests of gloom and heard one more story about a famous Christian leader molesting a trusting teenager. The #MeToo and #ChurchToo movements that occurred have increased the onslaught of abuse stories shared by survivors worldwide. We have met with many more brave survivors who have entrusted their stories to each of us, which has continued to inform us and, at times, move us to tears.

Hannah has worked in varied settings where she journeyed primarily with survivors of sex trafficking. She is a well-known speaker in sex trafficking leadership circles across Ohio and is connected with municipal and state elected officials and influential leaders in the Ohio faith and clinical communities. She regularly responds to requests from clinicians and clergy alike concerning resources to better understand sexual trauma and care for survivors. Adam worked in military and civilian settings, including hospitals, private practice, integrated behavioral health, and multidisciplinary settings over the past twenty years. He is trained and experienced in offering the following therapies for survivors of CSA: prolonged exposure (PE), concurrent treatment of PTSD and substance use disorders using prolonged exposure (COPE), Cognitive Processing Therapy (CPT), Eye Movement Desensitization and Reprocessing (EMDR), and Written Exposure Therapy (WET). My therapy work (Tammy) with survivors has continued over many decades in community mental health centers, private practice, and college counseling centers. As the co-coordinator of the trauma certificate program at Wheaton College, I have also learned from numerous brave conference attendees and students who have shared their stories with me over the years. Moreover, each chapter of this book has been read by students in my Wheaton College Introduction to Trauma class. It has been such a privilege to hear from these dear students and make revisions based on their wise feedback prior to sending it off to our publisher.

Freedom to Heal is designed to be a go-to resource for faith-based therapists, medical professionals, clinicians in training, pastoral counselors, foster parents, teachers, and student life professionals on university campuses hungry for theologically informed principles and evidence-based approaches to use with adult survivors of CSA. The reader will find additional clinical resources at the end of each chapter and in the "Children's Corner," where we share children's books that focus on a theme from the chapter for children (and adults) to grasp. Sometimes complexities are more aptly understood when spoken in the language of children.

A FEW CAVEATS

No two alike. During a deposition, a defense attorney asked me (Tammy) why my client, who had experienced years of abuse by a trusted caregiver, did not exhibit every posttraumatic stress disorder (PTSD) symptomatology. His question reflected a one-size-fits-all perspective. People who are sexually abused do not react in carbon-copy ways. They are a heterogeneous group. This means no two survivors are exactly alike. Diversity of abuse ensures diversity of aftermath effects of abuse. As psychiatrist Frank Putnam (2003, p. 269) explained,

> Childhood sexual abuse is a complex life experience. . . . This diversity alone ensures that there will be a range of outcomes. . . . Thus sexually abused children constitute a very heterogeneous group with many degrees of abuse about whom few simple generalizations hold.

A review of research on CSA reveals significant consistency among trauma clinicians and researchers regarding the most common negative aftereffects. Yet differences are apparent as well. The age of the victim; the severity of abuse; the nature of the relationship with the perpetrator; the response of caregivers and significant others; personality factors; support system; relationship with God; family dynamics; use of force, aggression and grooming; number of perpetrators; culture; and other types of trauma experience all contribute to differing symptoms, dissimilar collages. In addition, specific symptoms may dominate at one point along the journey, while other effects may preside during a different phase. More recently, the attention to survivors' uniqueness has coincided with an increasing call to use a trauma-informed modular approach. This personalized treatment approach includes a flexible demeanor and tailoring interventions to clients depending on their unique symptoms, circumstances, culture, and readiness to grapple with specific concerns (Elsaesser et al., 2022).

Protection of privacy. Counseling, by its very nature, is a private profession. We typically sit with clients in rooms where no one else can hear what is said. However, when we write, we share stories to illuminate the darkness of others. Therefore, we have included narratives only when we have received permission, and in most cases where permission was granted, we do not use real names. Many stories are composites based on various experiences of multiple clients, designed to protect the brave souls who have shared their stories with us.

Pacing in reading. Readers will notice that chapter sections include pictures with dark hues and rough edges bereft of happily-ever-after shades. While we crave happy endings, many survivor stories involve getting back on the proverbial bandwagon repeatedly. These stories also need expression. Due to the darker hues, we do not intend this text to be a single-sitting textbook. Like athletes who engage in intense training, their bodies need recovery time. Overtraining can lead to poor performance and injuries. So, too, with clinicians. Overreading trauma material can lead to poor performance and injuries (body, mind, and soul). While we intend that this edition be imbued with hope, it is heavy too. For many clinicians, certain pages may mirror their own abuse experiences. Thus, it is essential for you to read at a tempo that supports both your personal and professional development.

Terminology. POWs, Holocaust survivors, and other groups of folks who have lived through evil experiences identify themselves in specific ways. There are varying opinions regarding the appropriate terminology to refer to individuals who have lived through CSA. The term *victim* connotes the truth of being sexually violated, raped, abused, molested, pawed, exploited, ravaged, powerless, and betrayed. This word allocates responsibility for the abuse to the perpetrator and underscores that abuse was something done *to* the person who was violated. However, some reject the usage of *victim* because people who have been abused are not only victims. They are also agents who make choices, not about the abuse but about ways to respond to the abuse. Others embrace the identification with the word *survivor* because it honors that while a person did not escape the evil of abuse, that person lived through it.

Neither word by itself fully captures the person who has been abused. No label does. People who have experienced CSA are so much more than their abuse. However, both terms suggest a portion of the picture. For some individuals, on a specific day, the term *victim* may more adequately express her feelings about the abuse and her experience; on another day, the designation of *survivor* is preferable. More descriptive. More appropriate.

Years ago, when I (Tammy) asked a group of students to gather in groups to discuss the most fitting term for individuals who have experienced abuse, the first person to speak was a woman whose husband had died in a war. She shared a story about filling out papers when she was asked to check off one of three boxes: single, married, or widowed. We felt her angst as she told our class that the years she was married to her husband and his death could never be captured by checking one little box on a piece of paper. Another student queried, "What do people who have been abused call themselves?" My students are so wise.

On the pages of *Freedom to Heal*, we use both *victim* and *survivor* when we speak of individuals who have experienced sexual violations. We realize, however, these terms will never capture the magnificence of image-bearers. Thus, we invite clinicians to ask individuals who have experienced sexual abuse what language is most fitting for them. We invite people who have experienced sexual abuse to select terminology that depicts their experience and identity most accurately at their present juncture of the healing journey. Yet, it is essential to understand that these words may change over time. Some clients may be liberated from identifying as a victim or even a survivor, and their experience of victimization may begin to feel like a portion of their narrative and not the entire story.

Over the years, we have found that the clinical pathway of healing for survivors is commonly a nonlinear journey marked by sharp turns, steep valleys, unexpected detours, and mountains beckoning onward. Many pages are raw and disturbing, bereft of the neat and tidy. Over the years, we have found that the wreckage of abuse in our own lives and the lives of survivors is not so easily pressed absent of wrinkles. Perhaps God does not want the mysteries of suffering so easily jettisoned. Thus, the theme that runs like a bright red thread through these pages is that clinicians need to invite survivors to speak about their suffering before they can sing the song of hope.

REFERENCES

Elsaesser, M., Herpertz, S., Piosczyk, H., Jenkner, C., Hautzinger, M., & Schramm, E. (2022). Modular-based psychotherapy (MoBa) versus cognitive-behavioural therapy (CBT) for patients with depression, comorbidities and a history of childhood maltreatment: Study protocol for a randomised controlled feasibility trial. *BMJ Open*, *12*(7). https://doi.org/10.1136/bmjopen-2021-057672

Putnam, F. W. (2003). Ten-year research update review: Child sexual abuse. *Journal of the American Academy of Child & Adolescent Psychiatry*, *42*(3), 269-78. https://doi.org/10.1097/00004583-200303000-00006

Rowland, G. E., Purcell, J. B., Lebois, L. A., Kaufman, M. L., & Harnett, N. G. (2024). Child sexual abuse versus adult sexual assault: A review of psychological and neurobiological sequelae. *Mental Health Science* 2(2). https://doi.org/10.1002/mhs2.51

1

TAMAR

A DESOLATE WOMAN

Someone was hurt before you . . . beaten before you; humiliated before you; raped before you; yet someone survived.

MAYA ANGELOU

Recovery can only take place within the context of relationships; it cannot occur in isolation.

JUDITH LEWIS HERMAN

In the sacred text of Scripture, there is a narrative tucked away between those familiar stories of David and Goliath and the one about the guy swallowed by a whale. It is a sordid story about deception, abuse of power, betrayal, and rape.

Few may have heard a sermon or Sunday school lesson based on Tamar (Van der Walt, 2012). But it is there, inspired by the Holy Spirit and recorded in the Word of God (2 Sam 13:1-22), imbued with depths of understanding regarding the dynamics and aftermath of sexual violence for clinicians *and* survivors.

Once upon a time, a long, long time ago, a beautiful girl lived in a royal palace. As many daughters of kings do, she waited for the day her Prince Charming would arrive, recognize her beauty, and fall in love with her. However, Prince Charming never came. She didn't live happily ever after. Something devastating happened instead. Her brother raped her. Her *brother.* David's firstborn, the crown prince, wielded power, prestige, and privilege (Karman, 2022).

"Amnon was so tormented that he made himself ill because of his sister Tamar, for she was a virgin, and it seemed impossible to Amnon to do anything to her" (2 Sam 13:2). She was a virgin. And she was his sister. So, she was closed off to him. He was not thinking of things he could do *with* her. Notice the word "to." It lacks any relational emphasis; "to" is about Amnon, not Tamar (Brouer, 2014).

In his frustration, he consulted a family member. Enter a man named Jonadab. Listen to Jonadab's words of wisdom. Jonadab: "Why are you so haggard morning after morning? Will you not tell me?" Amnon: "I love Tamar, my brother Absalom's sister" (2 Sam 13:4 ESV 2016).

Love.

The Hebrew word for "love" can hold myriad meanings (Hârlăoanu, 2009). Grasping the gist of a word in Scripture can also be gained by understanding the context. As later events in this story reveal, what Amnon was experiencing was the antithesis of love (Woodbridge & Joubert, 2018). Authentic love, in contrast, discussed in 1 Corinthians 13, is patient and kind; it is not proud, rude, self-seeking, easily angered, or delighting in evil; and it always protects. Amnon was in lust with Tamar.

"Jonadab said to him, 'Lie down on your bed and pretend to be ill, and when your father comes to see you, say to him, "Let my sister Tamar come and give me something to eat and prepare the food in my sight, so that I may see it and eat it from her hand"'" (2 Sam 13:5 ESV 2016).

Is it just us, or does it bother anyone else that Jonadab dispensed this advice without hesitation? We would have preferred to see: "Then Jonadab warned Amnon that Tamar was not property. He was not entitled to take her at will. His cousin was concerned that Amnon's feelings could lead to violation and violence. Then, having prayed about what Amnon had told him, he shared words of wisdom with him three days later." But the Bible does not say that.

It says that Jonadab shared his nefarious advice with unwavering bravado. In a condensed moment, Jonadab devised an entirely underhanded and violent scheme so the prince could possess what he wanted, underscoring awareness that sexual violence does not "just happen" (Winters & Jeglic, 2022).

Was Jonadab experienced in the ways of manipulation and evil seduction? Our knowledge is lean and spare, but one thing is evident: he connived, colluded, and conspired in the plot against Tamar, resulting in her being isolated and violated (Higgins, 2020).

Imagine that you were watching this incident take place on a stage. The mastermind of the upcoming act (Jonadab) has just exited stage right. Entering stage left is David, and somewhere in the distance, we see Tamar hard at work. The scene lacks any advanced warning, but the danger is advancing.

We notice that she is beautiful (2 Sam 13:1). On center stage, Amnon is feigning the groans one would make on their deathbed. He asked King David if he could have Tamar care for him in his bedridden condition. The king didn't hesitate. King David fell for it hook, line, and sinker—yet he was a wise king, one of the best (1 Sam 13:14). How did the king miss his son Amnon's predatory intentions?

Simply put, rapists are adept at lying about their motives and behaviors (Chopin et al., 2022). Perpetrators frequently use unwitting outsiders as pawns in their chess game, moving them one or two spaces simultaneously until a victim is trapped in a checkmate. Moreover, this is a like-father-like-son scene. Years earlier, David similarly pilfered what was not his (Woodbridge & Joubert, 2018).

Imagine when the king, her father, entreated Tamar to go to Amnon and take care of him. You saw the last scene; you know what is coming. She has no idea. It is tantamount to witnessing a horror movie where a woman is racing through a house to escape a nefarious villain. She enters a room and pauses to gulp for air. Meanwhile, the camera zooms in on the evildoer hiding behind the door. This is when you want to stand up and scream, "He's behind the door! Check behind you!" Unaware of the trap that awaited her, Tamar obeyed her father.

Tamar finished baking the cakes and walked to Amnon to feed him. He refused to eat what she had made him. Then the crown prince ordered everyone else in the room to leave to remove witnesses to his future deeds, and they complied. Perhaps Tamar began to feel uneasy, but we're not sure. Scripture doesn't specify. In response to his request, she followed him into the bedroom so that Amnon could "eat from [her] hand" (2 Sam 13:10 ESV 2016).

She drew near to feed him, care for him, and meet his needs. And when she began to feed him, he smelled her scent, heard her voice, and saw what she looked like up close. He saw that she was beautiful. Then he grabbed her, and she pleaded with Amnon to stop. Tamar was not silent. She was well acquainted with the law (Lev 20:13). She knew that this thing that Amnon was trying to do was disgraceful, this was wicked.

She said *no*.

Tamar's strong voice is particularly noteworthy as she is the only one in this biblical narrative who says no to the prince (Brouer, 2014). But her desperate pleas were spurned. In her own home, she was brutally violated by someone she knew. This is an all-too-common tale (Mondragon et al., 2022; Stoltenborgh et al., 2011). Tamar said no, but not every victim can voice that word (Katz & Nicolet, 2022).

Some are scared speechless, neurobiologically frozen.

Some do not realize that they can say no.

Some have a hand covering their mouth.

Others are too young even to speak an intelligible sound.

Somehow Tamar uttered something perhaps peculiar to our twenty-first century, North American cultural understanding: "As for me, where could I carry my shame? And as for you, you would be as one of the scoundrels in Israel. Now therefore, I beg you, speak to the king, for he will not withhold me from you" (2 Sam 13:13 ESV 2016).

What is Tamar saying here? Is she negotiating with her rapist? We do know that victims of sexual violence frequently fight back and oppose rapists with a variety of creative and complex resistance strategies that are often not recognized by even the survivors themselves. Negotiating with rapists can be one attempt to dissuade perpetrators from their crimes and a time-buying tactic (Karman, 2022; Randall, 2010).

As Tamar stares into her attacker's lust-filled eyes, she knows in her culture and time in history the cost of being raped. She would lose her marriageability, be blamed, and be cast aside as a soiled and sullied woman (Brouer, 2014).

Tamar stated accurately that Amnon would be seen as a wicked fool, and he would receive severe penalties, as the Old Testament viewed rape as a violent crime (Ex 22:16; Deut 22:25). Thus, Tamar provided a sort of counteroffer to Amnon's demand. She asked him to wait and then *she proposed marriage.*

Can you imagine committing your life to someone who looks at you as Amnon did at Tamar? She was a thing, an object, his playground. But Tamar knew that in her culture, there was nothing worse than being cast aside—a reputation beyond repair. She lived in a time and culture when a woman's worth was commonly gauged by her marital status and the number of sons she could bear. Who would want her if she was raped (Higgins, 2020)?

Tamar's petition was a bargaining tool with her brother and an acknowledgment of a cultural reality. There were no rape crisis hotlines for her to call. There were no shelters for her to turn to. If Amnon followed through with his plan, she would be empty. Alone. Desolate. Who would take her side, plead her case, or fight for her innocence?

Sadly, still today, in many countries around the world, rape is primarily viewed as a matter of dishonor toward the family (Amo-Adjei et al., 2022; Gorar, 2022; Shrivastava, 2022). The responsibility for tarnishing the family image often lies with the victim of the assault for being violated. Moreover, the central goal becomes the protection of the family's honor. Since the woman is no longer a virgin, a solution may involve marrying the rapist. Even when the marriage suitor *is* the rapist (Toniyo & Manoj, 2021).

In Tamar's mind, there was a possible way forward: "If he wants me this badly, then maybe he will marry me." But to her pleas, Amnon responded in the way he had been scheming all along: "But he would not listen to her, and being stronger than she, he violated her and lay with her" (2 Sam 13:14 ESV 2016).

Amnon wanted to own and possess Tamar. He wanted to envelop her, swallow her dignity, and spit out her innocence. He wanted to steal her beauty. So, he *ravaged* her. In vivid detail, this narrative draws attention to the fact that sexual violence is not sex gone too far. While there are varied factors underlying sexual violence (Seto, 2019), here sex was employed as a weapon.

"Then Amnon hated her with very great hatred, so that the hatred with which he hated her was greater than the love with which he had loved her. . . . Put this woman out of my presence and bolt the door after her" (2 Sam 13:15, 17 ESV 2016).

Wait a second. Amnon just captured and confined what he wanted, and now he . . . hates her? How could this be? We do not know for sure, but perhaps during the rape, the alarm, distress, and disgust on Tamar's face mirrored his malicious heart and the reflection was unsettling, too revealing. So, he smashed the mirror, and his servant swept up the royal pieces and dumped them in the trash.

"This woman" was disposable (2 Sam 13:17 ESV 2016).

This woman.

Amnon's brutalization and shaming amplify. He no longer used her name. She was barely human, scarcely a woman with mind and soul. She was not family. She was not "sister." She was *this woman*. Her entreaties before, during, and after the rape were loathed and dismissed.

Tamar, who had been wearing a distinctive royal robe that a virgin daughter of the king would wear, was banished from the place of the assault, and she did what Jews did when they were grieving: she put ashes on her head and tore her beautiful robes. She wept and wept. The robes symbolized that she was a virgin, but according to her culture, she could no longer make that claim. The Hebrew word for Tamar's loud cry reveals that she expressed anguish and a protest against injustice (Karman, 2022). With great courage, she made public what Amnon did surreptitiously. She begged for justice with each moan and wail until someone noticed. And someone did notice. Brother #2, Absalom.

Absalom's advice was pointed, clipped, and curt, masking the "vile" act done to Tamar (2 Sam 13:12). "Now hold your peace, my sister. He is your brother; do not take this to heart" (2 Sam 13:20 ESV 2016).

Do not take this matter to heart. In today's vernacular: "Don't let it get to you." "It could have been worse." "You should be grateful you are alive." "Protect the family image."

This is not the first time such censoring words have been spoken in this family. Not too far in the past, King David spoke similar silencing verbiage after he had Uriah eliminated. David said to the messenger, "Thus shall you say to Joab, 'Do not let this matter displease you, for the sword devours now one and now another'" (2 Sam 11:24-25 ESV 2016). The sins of the father are passed on to the next generation. David endeavored to cover up his sin, and Absalom, his son, did likewise.

Their father, King David, discovered what had happened, and Scripture tells us that "he was very angry" (2 Sam 13:21 ESV 2016). At this point, you might expect that the king meted out some harsh punishment. But the truth is that he did nothing. *Nothing.* King David failed to allow Amnon to bear the consequences demanded by Scripture and the law at that time in history (Lev 18:11, 29-30; Deut 22:28-29). David did not seek justice for his daughter. The silencing response of Tamar's brother and the inaction of her father illuminate an important fact: how families respond to abuse matters (Biss & Geist-Martin, 2022; Donagh et al., 2022). Belittling, dismissing, and passivity deepen the damage of sexual violence.

The plot thickens. Later in the story, we see Absalom scheming and carrying out lethal revenge against Amnon, the first in line for the throne (Woodbridge & Joubert, 2018). Sin begets sin. David was notified that Amnon was dead, and then he mourned. He tore his clothes and wept and wept. His servants and all his men wept and tore their clothes. Amnon's death elicited a widespread response—a group of men mourning (2 Sam 13:36).

But what about what happened to Tamar? Who mourned for her? Who wiped the tears from her eyes? "So Tamar lived, a desolate woman, in her brother Absalom's house" (2 Sam 13:20 ESV 2016).

Desolate. In Hebrew, this poignant word means to be deflowered, deserted, laid waste, devastated, or *ravaged* (Adelman, 2021; Vine, 1992). This word is frequently used in Scripture to refer to annihilated cities that are no longer inhabitable (e.g., Is 49:19) (Higgins, 2020). This is remarkably significant because Tamar means "palm tree," which signifies fruitfulness, the opposite of desolate (Strong, 2010). Tamar was designed to bear fruit. Perhaps she could have been a mom with several kids or a spiritual parent who led many to Yahweh. If she lived today, maybe she could have been a CEO calling leaders to empower employees and treat them with dignity because all individuals are made in the image of God. Instead, Tamar lived as a desolate woman.

Forsaken.

Abandoned.

Shamed.

Lonely.

Despondent.

Broken-hearted.

Grief-stricken.

Dejected.

Crushed.

This solitary evil act and the responses of those around her crushed her to the point that she no longer lived the life for which she was designed. In this biblical narrative, words of hope are in short supply. There is no happily ever after. Tamar lived a desolate life. Period.

This unsavory story raises an important question: *Why would God include this passage in Scripture?* We, the authors, have wrestled with this question and are deeply aware that there are no uncomplicated answers.

This vital question breaks into a kindergarten classroom, into the back seat of a Volkswagen Beetle, near a swing set at the local playground, into a bathtub where brightly colored toys are floating, or any other place where the ferocity of abuse happens. It raises another question: *Where was God when Tamar was being assaulted?* Tamar's life begs for there to be something more. Someone more.

Who wipes Tamar's tears? We emphatically believe God saw Tamar, her rape, and her life of desolation. He saw her weeping night after night. He heard the responses of others and knew the magnitude of her hurt. He walked all the way down to the deepest pit in her soul. He knew. He remembered. He has taken this matter to heart.

Yet again, we ask why God includes this unresolved, graphic, and disturbing story in Scripture. Perhaps this question is like other questions: Why would God include stories like this one in chapters of the lives of our clients, our loved ones, or ourselves?

Moreover, is God seeing and knowing enough? Why didn't he stop Amnon? Why does he not stop the individuals who perpetrate abuse daily worldwide? Does he care, or is he passive like David? We explore in this book these worthy queries and ways to bear witness to unanswerable questions. For now, we conclude this chapter with the emphatic statement that survivors of sexual violence were not designed to live a desolate life. They were made for something far greater. Survivors of abuse were made for what is beyond desolate. Way beyond.

We invite you, clinicians working alongside survivors of sexual violence, to dig deep into the complex concerns and questions Tamar's story brings to light. Many Tamars are living desolate lives, thirsting for a life beyond. Tamar was silenced. We are breaking the silence.

You have seen the wrong done to me, O Lord.

LAMENTATIONS 3:59

COUNSELING CONSIDERATIONS

- **Engagement with biblical trauma narratives.** Trauma narratives are a salient component throughout Scripture (e.g., rape [Gen 34], rape/murder [Judg 19], slavery [Ex 21], murder of infant boys [Mt 2], murder of John the Baptist [Mt 14], and the crucifixion of Jesus [Mt 27]). Some clients seeking spiritual meaning making may benefit from engagement with biblical trauma narratives (Ballaban, 2014; van der Walt, 2012; West & Zondi-Mabizela, 2004; Yaye, 2009). Qualitative accounts of survivor engagement with the Tamar narrative (2 Sam 13) indicated that this practice provided normalization of trauma experiences, awareness that sexual violence has not escaped God's awareness, the empowerment that silence has been broken in Scripture, and opportunities to discuss the Davids, Amnons, Jonadabs, servants, and Absaloms in the lives of survivors (van der Walt, 2012; West & Zondi-Mabizela, 2004; Yaye, 2009). Given that some individuals report that religious practices (e.g., reading Scripture) are a beneficial way of coping with trauma (Cetty et al., 2022; Dumulescu et al., 2022), and spiritually accommodated therapy can improve mental health outcomes and spiritual well-being (Captari et al., 2018), at wisely timed junctures clinicians can invite clients to read the Tamar narrative in a sexual abuse group or an individual session, followed by dialogue and processing, to enhance religious coping.
- **Developing coping skills.** Trauma exposure (e.g., reading/hearing Tamar's narrative) can potentially elicit sympathetic nervous system (SNS) activation (i.e., our stress response gas pedal), which cues the body for fight, flight, freeze behaviors. A key ingredient in many evidence-based approaches with trauma survivors is activating the parasympathetic nervous system (PNS) responses (i.e., our stress response brake pedal) to counter the SNS stimulation. Doing so increases oxygen to the brain, activates the vagus nerve, decreases amygdala

activation, and increases slow breathing. Specific imagery, meditative/mindfulness exercises, and slow deep breathing techniques can calm the body. Practicing these skills can help survivors carefully comprehend and reflect on the inherent wisdom in Tamar's story and other biblical trauma narratives.

- **Breaking the silence of child sexual abuse (CSA) in ministry settings.** Sexual abuse awareness and training in ministry settings, churches, and faith-based educational institutions are integral to preventing CSA and caring for survivors. Educating pastoral teams and speaking on CSA serves as a method of advocacy that clinicians can engage in to break the conspiracy of silence.

CHILDREN'S CORNER

- ***Tiny Finds His Whisper: A Little Mouse with a Big Secret About Childhood Sexual Abuse*** (Katz, 2021). This book is about a tiny mouse who holds a large secret that hurts him deeply, but his whisper is barely audible, so others cannot hear him. When a child is ready, this book invites children who have been sexually abused to express what happened, even when they can only whisper the details.
- ***God Made All of Me: A Book to Help Children Protect Their Bodies*** (Holcomb & Holcomb, 2015) is written to help children understand that their bodies are priceless. It also focuses on differentiating appropriate and inappropriate touch.

REFERENCES

Adelman, R. (2021). The rape of Tamar as a prefiguration for the fate of fair Zion. *Journal of Feminist Studies in Religion*, *37*(1), 87-102. https://doi.org/10.2979/jfemistudreli.37.1.06

Amo-Adjei, J., Deliege, A., Nurzhynska, A., Essuman, R., & Khan, M. R. (2022). A vignettes-based exploration of attitudes of parents toward reporting of child sexual abuse in Ghana. *Journal of Interpersonal Violence, 38*(7-8). https://doi.org/10.1177/08862605221127215

Ballaban, S. (2014). The use of traumatic biblical narratives in spiritual recovery from trauma: Theory and case study. *Journal of Pastoral Care & Counseling*, *68*(4), 1-11. https://doi.org/10.1177/154230501406800403

Biss, D. C., & Geist-Martin, P. (2022). "It's hard being strong for her, because sometimes I find myself weak": Reluctant confidants' sensemaking of survivors' sexual assault disclosures. *Women's Studies in Communication*, *45*(2), 210-31. https://doi.org/10.1080/07491409.2021.1959470

Brouer, D. (2014). Tamar's voice of wisdom and outrage in 2 Samuel 13. *Priscilla Papers*, *28*(4), 11.

Bryce, I., Horwood, N., Cantrell, K., & Gildersleeve, J. (2022). Pulling the trigger: A systematic literature review of trigger warnings as a strategy for reducing traumatization in higher education. *Trauma, Violence, & Abuse, 24*(4). https://doi.org/10.1177/15248380221118968

Captari, L. E., Hook, J. N., Hoyt, W., Davis, D. E., McElroy-Heltzel, S. E., & Worthington, E. L., Jr. (2018). Integrating clients' religion and spirituality within psychotherapy: A comprehensive meta-analysis. *Journal of Clinical Psychology, 74*(11), 1938-51. https://doi.org/10.1002/jclp.22681

Cetty, L., Jeyagurunathan, A., Roystonn, K., Devi, F., Abdin, E., Tang, C., . . . & Subramaniam, M. (2022). Religiosity, religious coping and distress among outpatients with psychosis in Singapore. *Journal of Religion and Health*, *61*(5), 3677-97. https://doi.org/10.1007/s10943-022-01596-4

Chopin, J., Paquette, S., & Fortin, F. (2022). Geeks and newbies: Investigating the criminal expertise of online sex offenders. *Deviant Behavior 44*(4), 493-509. https://doi.org/10.1080/01639625.2022.2059417

Donagh, B., Taylor, J., al Mushaikhi, M., & Bradbury-Jones, C. (2022). Sibling experiences of adverse childhood experiences: A scoping review. *medRxiv*. https://doi.org/10.1101/2022.02.04.22270452

Dumulescu, D., Nečula, C. V., Sarca, D. M., & Cristea, G. W. (2022). Spiritual practices in psychological counseling: The return to the self. *Journal for the Study of Religions and Ideologies, 21*(62), 20-36.

Gorar, M. (2022). Honour suicide and forced suicide in the UK. *The Journal of Criminal Law*, *86*(5), 308-26. https://doi.org/10.1177/00220183221115294

Hârlăoanu, C. P. (2009). The main Hebrew words for love: Ahab and hesed. *Analele Ştiinţifice ale Universităţii» Alexandru Ioan Cuza «din Iaşi. Teologie Ortodoxă*, 51-66.

Higgins, R. S. (2020). He would not hear her voice: From skilled speech to silence in 2 Samuel 13:1-22. *Journal of Feminist Studies in Religion*, *36*(2), 25-42.

Holcomb, J. S., & Holcomb, L. A. (2015). *God made all of me: A book to help children protect their bodies.* New Growth Press.

Karman, Y. (2022). A tale of two Tamars: Domestic violence in the Hebrew Bible. *Verbum et Ecclesia*, *43*(1), 1-5.

Katz, C., & Nicolet, R. (2022). "If only I could have stopped it": Reflections of adult child sexual abuse survivors on their responses during the abuse. *Journal of Interpersonal Violence*, *37*(3-4), NP2076-NP2100. https://doi.org/10.1177/0886260520935485

Katz, M. (2021). *Tiny finds his whisper: A little mouse with a big secret about childhood sexual abuse.* Amazon Digital Services.

Mondragon, N. I., Munities, A. E., & Txertudi, M. B. (2022). The breaking of secrecy: Analysis of the hashtag# MeTooInceste regarding testimonies of sexual incest abuse in childhood. *Child Abuse & Neglect, 123*. https://doi.org/10.1016/j.chiabu.2021.105412

Randall, M. (2010). Sexual assault law, credibility, and "ideal victims": Consent, resistance, and victim blaming. *Canadian Journal of Women and the Law*, 22(2), 397-433. https://doi.org/10.3138/cjwl.22.2.397

Seto, M. C. (2019). The motivation-facilitation model of sexual offending. *Sexual Abuse*, *31*(1), 3-24. https://doi.org/10.1177/1079063217720919

Shrivastava, N. (2022). India-rape and the prevalent culture of silence in Indian cinema and television. In M. S. Schotanus (Ed.), *Gender violence, the law, and society* (pp. 131-41). Emerald Publishing.

Stoltenborgh, M., Van Ijzendoorn, M. H., Euser, E. M., & Bakermans-Kranenburg, M. J. (2011). A global perspective on child sexual abuse: Meta-analysis of prevalence around the world. *Child Maltreatment*, *16*(2), 79-101. https://doi.org/10.1177/1077559511403920

Strong, J. (2010). *The new Strong's expanded exhaustive concordance of the Bible* (Red letter ed.). Thomas Nelson.

Toniyo, R. J., & Manoj, C. M. (2021). Marry-Your-Rapist law: An exquisite solution to rape. *Supremo Amicus*, *27*, 395.

Van der Walt, C. (2012). Hearing Tamar's voice: Contextual readings of 2 Samuel 13:1-22. *Old Testament Essays*, 25(1), 182-206.

Vine, W. E. (1992). Desolate. In *Vine's expository dictionary of New Testament words*. Nelson. https://www.blueletterbible.org/search/Dictionary/viewTopic.cfm?topic=VT0000722

West, G., & Zondi-Mabizela, P. (2004). The Bible story that became a campaign: The Tamar Campaign in South Africa (and beyond). *Ministerial Formation*, *103*.

Winters, G. M., & Jeglic, E. L. (2022). *Sexual grooming: Integrating research, practice, prevention, and policy*. Springer.

Woodbridge, N., & Joubert, C. (2018). Biblical, psychological and moral analysis of the rape of Tamar in 2 Samuel 13: A pastoral response. *Conspectus: The Journal of the South African Theological Seminary*, 25(1), 106-23.

Yaye, C. O. (2009, May 25). *Taming the tide of gender-based violence and HIV & AIDS in Kenya: The TAMAR approach* [Conference session]. Technologies and Health: A Faith Based Perspective, Buckeystown, Maryland. https://elibrary.pu.ac.ke/handle/123456789/561

2

ANGUISH UNVOICED

Sometimes when we believe we are keeping a secret,
that secret is actually keeping us.

FRANK WARREN

Of course I deny it,
can hardly believe it,
dismiss or demean it
'Cause I know I can't speak it
but when I began to tell
it became the hardest thing I ever said out loud
The words got locked in my throat;
man, I choked
And this is what it feels like to be free
even though it follows back down,
stares into the dark with me.

MARCUS MUMFORD, "CANNIBAL"

Wherever sexual abuse resides, secrets flourish. Scores of survivors haul around narratives that are seemingly impossible to voice. Individuals who sexually violate others count on their victims to keep these stories muted. A man who molested more than a thousand boys explained:

> For me, secrecy was the glue that held my fantasies together. Secrecy was the element that added a feeling of excitement, heightening the overall thrill I

> got from offending. It represented a twisted sense of personal power and personal worth, and ultimately it was my critical weapon both to entice and ensnare my young victims. (Hammel-Zabin, 2003, p. 8)

Psychiatrist Rolland Summit (1983, p. 5) explained that some survivors are reluctant to disclose the abuse for varied reasons. Fearing that they will be disbelieved, despised, disposed of, sent away, the cause of their family disintegration, and the reason a family member is sent to jail. A survivor may be too young, lacking a vocabulary to describe what happened. The fear of telling may be complicated by the fact that the one who ravaged her body may also be the one who taught her to drive; he may be the one who inspired the survivor to dream, who fed him food, who taught her Bible stories at Sunday school. Giving voice to the abuse risks erasing all the memories on the chalkboard—the bad and the good. Moreover, talking about the abuse means admitting at a deeper level that it really did happen.

A novel pathway of abuse disclosures began years after activist Tarana Burke began the #MeToo movement when Alyssa Milano used the Twitter hashtag to respond to Hollywood producer Harvey Weinstein's sexual violence against women. Milano encouraged survivors to reveal the extent of sexual violence, culminating in the hashtag #MeToo being used twelve million times in the first twenty-four hours (CBS, 2017; Mondragon et al., 2022). Since then, social media platforms have transformed into venues for survivors to break the silence and discuss the pain stemming from sexual violence. These venues for disclosing abuse foster spaces for developing a collective identity and support, effective communication among survivors and supporters, and a way to mobilize action against sexual violence (Mondragon et al., 2022).

Still, despite this groundswell movement of disclosing CSA online, some survivors may never disclose (Ettinger, 2022), while others do not speak about the abuse until adulthood (McElvaney, 2015). Alaggia and colleagues' (2019) examination of fifteen adult studies revealed that the mean age of disclosure was between 40 and 50. Others may tell tentatively, as though a bomb was strapped to their very being. Often, the weight of the hurt is immense, yet the descriptions of the anguish are lean and spare, as language can be limited and inadequate to convey the complexities and the weight of trauma. Some experiences are *ineffable*—that is, the trauma defies expression or description. For example, a client shared that as a young girl, she would spend the summers at the home of her aunt and uncle. A ritual began where her uncle would haul her to the back shed, lock the door, and molest her. On one occasion, her uncle hushed her cries when he said, "God wanted me to do this." *God wanted her uncle to do this?* How could words adequately depict her confusion, her helplessness, her savage experience, and her narrative?

In this chapter, we will examine informal and formal ways of disclosing abuse; cultural considerations concerning the sharing of secrets; the use of expressive arts therapy in assisting survivors to "tell"; a picture of ways clinicians can use an evidenced-based trauma approach to aid in a survivor disclosure; the benefits of telling abuse secrets to God; and clinical considerations that provide various ways clinicians can assist clients in the disclosure journey.

TYPES OF DISCLOSURES

In my (Tammy's) family, there were a lot of secrets. My mom developed a bipolar illness after giving birth to me. Her sad times were punctuated by times of elevated energy: singing hymns in the wee hours of the morning and shopping for peculiar gifts for people with money we did not have. Her illness began in the 1960s when many did not understand mental illness. When my mom was depressed, I told people at church she was "sick." When she was experiencing mania, well, she was "sick" again. The thought of anybody knowing our family secret was frightening for a little girl who believed she needed to protect her dad's job as a pastor, strengthen her mom's dignity, and stave off her own feelings of helplessness. So, by the time a janitor from my elementary school sexually abused me at nine years of age, I was already a seasoned veteran at stashing secrets in our family vault.

The prospect of speaking the unspeakable may prompt some survivors to freeze when it comes to the prospect of telling. The fervent passion for disclosing is simultaneously fused with feeling incapable of doing so. The prospect of releasing the secret feels like death.

Some survivors come to the point where they can bear the silence no more, and the stories rush out like a midnight-black Labrador Retriever yanking on the leash, yearning to run. With a friend or in a caregiver's office, the tale of trauma is disclosed at break-neck speed. The secret is no longer tolerable. Sometimes, there comes a point when it is more painful *not* to speak. All in all, the reasons people tell and do not tell are just about as numerous as there are survivors.

Telling someone about sexual abuse can be an onerous process, and it is frequently impacted by a multiplicity of factors. Disclosure is often an ongoing, interactive, relational venture (Ettinger, 2022; McGill & McElvaney, 2022). The therapeutic connection in revealing and receiving secrets is pivotal in healing. Survivors are continually assessing how their secrets are received. Thus, responses by professionals, family members, and friends hold the capacity to aid in both healing and harming.

When a survivor unveils her narrative and is greeted with comfort, belief, and support, frequently there is a desire to reveal more chapters, more stories, and more of one's soul. In this section, we discuss two types of disclosures: informal and formal disclosures.

Informal disclosures. Clinicians have the privilege of being on the receiving end of formal disclosures, but they do well to learn from the literature on and lived experience of survivors' informal disclosures. Often, survivors experience *insult-to-injury* stories: moments of disclosure that did not go well, resulting in added traumatic experiences (Watkins-Kagebein et al., 2019). Not simply tuning in to stories of CSA but eliciting stories of harmful disclosures, stories of not being believed, and stories of being blamed becomes essential work for clinicians.

Peers are the most common recipients of CSA disclosures by adolescents, highlighting a need to equip young people with education on CSA and support for the hearers of harrowing stories (Manay et al., 2022). A study of 487 adult male survivors found that many reported that the first person they talked to about the abuse was a spouse or partner (27%) or a close friend (18%) (Easton, 2013). Some of the themes that emerge around the hesitation among youth disclosing to their peers included the lack of certainty around whether their experience was abusive and how their peers might respond. In one study, adolescents who disclosed also felt responsible for the intense emotional reaction of their peers on hearing the disclosure, reporting that they were effectively burdening their peers and needed to offer them support (Manay et al., 2022). While many young people (and adults) may not be trained in hearing disclosures of abuse, clinicians can offer a space where individuals, young and old, do not have to take care of the person receiving the information.

One study highlighted that many young people wanted to tell *and* simultaneously did not want to tell (McElvaney et al., 2014). At the top of the list of critical factors related to being able to disclose is being *believed*. Another key factor was the experience of being *asked*. However, those not open to believing are not the ones who should be asking.

Circling back to Tamar, we see that she told her story both in words *and* in action within an informal setting (her brother). Scripture tells us that after the rape, "And Tamar put ashes on her head and tore the long robe that she wore; And she laid her hand on her head and went away, crying aloud as she went" (2 Sam 13:19). In response to her cries and disclosure, Absalom responded by telling Tamar: "Do not take this to heart" (2 Sam 13:20).

His harsh response to her raw and vulnerable disclosure reverberated in distancing and silencing Tamar. Learning from Absalom's mistake, clinicians, family members, and friends need to savor each word as monumental; stand in awe that a person has chosen life and chosen to speak; be curious about what has kept that person alive; listen to their earthly stories and, over time, help them to see the bigger story, the eternal story; and ferret out the portraits of hope and underscore God's fingerprints amid the pain.

Formal disclosures. Children who disclose abuse in forensic contexts do so with professionals trained to conduct child-centered and nonleading conversations to assess the safety of a child or adolescent and collect information about the circumstances the minor may have experienced or witnessed (Larner, 2022). This section focuses on disclosures by survivors in nonforensic therapeutic contexts and what clinicians can do to assist the disclosure process in this setting.

While some survivors enter therapy having talked about the abuse with supportive family or friends and have a more developed and coherent sense of what they endured, others initiate therapy with an absence of words, bereft of labels that define what happened to them as abuse, carrying fragmented and incomplete narratives. Some survivors may drop hints about the abuse versus explicitly disclosing details (Larner, 2022), all the while waiting to see whether the clinician is following the breadcrumbs dropped thus far. When clients offer words such as, "Something happened with my dad," we can respond with a close-ended question: "Would you be comfortable telling me a *little bit* more about what happened?" The word choices of "little" and "bit" can minimize expectations that entire narratives must be shared immediately, and they provide an acknowledgment that the details may be difficult to voice (Larner, 2022, p. 289).

Using nonleading questions in an unrushed manner can diminish confusion and provide ample space for survivors to share at an unhurried pace. As the therapeutic alliance is developed and deepened, a survivor may learn that a godly therapist, while imperfect, can be a tried-and-true recipient of his stories. Over time, a survivor can begin to understand that the caregiver will wait until they are ready to convey what happened.

Many male survivors have delayed disclosing abuse for over twenty years, frequently due to heightened shame (Easton, 2013). The hesitation to tell was particularly true for Antwone Fisher, whose abuse began at about the age of three and lasted for many years. Willenda, a neighbor who "helped out" by babysitting, would lug Antwone to the basement like an overstuffed bag of unwanted belongings en route to the garbage dump. What went on downstairs should never have happened to a little boy. There the shame intensified. Antwone explained:

> Then she's finished. Her voice lays empty as she says, "Where your clothes at? Put some clothes on." She sounds like it's my fault I don't have clothes on. She dresses, tosses my clothes at me, and says, "Go on outside in the shade and play. I think they makin' mud pies out there." For a second Willenda smiles. But then her face flashes a warning. She doesn't even need to tell me in words. I know what it says—never, never, never tell, or something more horrible than you can ever imagine will happen to you.
>
> It wasn't really the fear of her punishing me that kept me from telling anyone all those years. It was the unspeakable shame I felt about what went on with her in the basement, and *my unspeakable shame* that maybe it was my fault. [emphasis added] (Fisher & Rivas, 2001, p. 44)

Years after the abuse ended, when Antwone was in the United States Navy, he began therapy with a psychiatrist. For the first time, he talked about the abuse in this context.

> Before that meeting with Commander Williams, I had never told anyone my story. I had never been given the chance to connect the dots of my existence,

> to see the shape and the course of my life, to observe for myself how everything that had happened had its reason, its lesson. To talk was liberation from the prison of silence, from the burden of my own secrets. But by the end of the hour, I had only begun. (Fisher & Rivas, 2001, p. 283)

Antwone's daring disclosure with his military-appointed psychiatrist engendered freedom and a desire to speak further. Because so many survivors have a sort of autobiographical laryngitis, the clinician's task is to help the survivor reclaim his voice. Sometimes it is prudent for therapists to make the first move—not pushing our clients but simply being willing to hear and enter their stories in whatever language they speak.

CULTURE, CONCEALMENT, AND CANDID ACCOUNTS

What cannot be said will get wept.

SAPPHO

The challenge of disclosing abuse may be exacerbated by cultural values related to shame and honor, legal system inadequacies and impediments, the stigma attached to mental health concerns, fears that sexual abuse claims will be dismissed, and fears of being blamed or harmed for telling (Fontes, 2005; Haboush & Alyan, 2013; Güven et al., 2022; Mathews, 2022; Shafe & Hutchinson, 2014). Western cultures tend to attach high value to articulating thoughts and feelings, while for other cultures, the practice of breaking secrets may not be highly regarded. Instead, telling secrets might cast aspersions on family members or someone highly respected in the community. In contrast, muting certain information may be perceived as exhibiting greater respect. Survivors in communities who hold an understandable distrust of law enforcement and other authority figures come to therapeutic settings with magnified concerns (Ettinger, 2022).

A missionary working with Muslim women in another part of the world contacted me (Tammy). This compassionate woman had gained the trust of many dear women in her community after years of involvement. Over time, she received many invitations for tea with women in her community, which frequently segued into disclosures of abuse. There were countless tales about an uncle, father, brother, or cousin robbing young girls' bodies. Prying open these cans of words could merely serve to brand these women as adulterers, and having lost their virginity, they would be considered fair game for other men to seduce or assault because they were trash anyway (Güven et al., 2022). Obtaining legal intervention is a complex consideration only intensified in contexts where honor, respect, modesty, and shame and embarrassment require protection of the family or community (Gilligan & Akhtar, 2006). An attempt to ignore these cultural values can result in being disowned, banished, or shunned. In some societies, life-threatening danger may be lurking for those considering telling.

Danger must always be assessed. Disclosing abuse with certain individuals in specific cultural contexts may be unwise. When adult abuse victims remain in dangerous settings, disclosures of abuse must be done with trusted individuals familiar with the context and setting. Fontes (2005) underscored the importance of clinicians consulting with professionals from the survivor's culture to provide a unique understanding that can aid in developing culturally prudent interventions related to abuse disclosure. Moreover, clinicians are advised to learn about the cultural factors and dynamic changes in a specific culture and grow in awareness of their own biases and perspectives that may require modifications (Fontes & Plummer, 2010). Clinicians can support the development of child abuse prevention programs on a systemic level. However, the development of these needed programs is impacted by (a) the availability of professionals who possess training and knowledge, (b) institutions supportive, willing, and able to train professionals, and (c) funding to support prevention programs (Mikton et al., 2013).

Giving voice to secrets of sexual abuse looks different around the world. Countless survivors are waiting for clinicians to listen to tales no one wants to hear. Generalized assumptions about culture are as unhelpful as being blind to culture. Recognizing the consequences of disclosures in various cultures and faith traditions can help survivors overcome the barriers to speaking the unspeakable.

EXPRESSIVE ARTS THERAPIES

I found I could say things with color and shapes that I couldn't say any other way . . . things I had no words for.

GEORGIA O'KEEFFE

When survivors garner the courage to tell, there are many ways beyond traditional talk therapy to reveal long-kept secrets. For some survivors, speaking or writing about the abuse may not yet be possible. Expressive arts therapies (also called creative arts therapies) use mediums such as paintings, sketches, images in clay, play, sand trays, dance, and drama as avenues to help some utter their angst (Malchiodi, 2003; Rouse et al., 2022; Sesar et al., 2022). While clinicians may not be registered/credentialed expressive art therapists, they can learn with some training to use different forms of creative arts that can benefit survivors as a means of self-expression and communication.

In one systematic qualitative review of the therapeutic impact of arts-based activities on the healing journey of adults sexually abused in childhood (Rouse et al., 2022), the researchers highlighted that these activities often provided a safe space to find one's voice and provided an option for deeper self-exploration, reflection, discovery, and to have fellow witnesses to their journeys.

Creative art therapies such as Solution-Focused Brief Art Therapy (SFBAT) and Person-Centered Expressive Arts Therapy (PCEAT) may be beneficial when working with adolescents (Sesar et al., 2022). SFBAT is a time-limited, less confrontational approach that is more likely to align with the developmental requirements of adolescents and provides an increased sense of autonomy. PCEAT involves a therapist serving as an "empathic witness," not interpreting or directing the artistic intervention but listening to and encouraging the self-exploration taking place for the client through the act of drawing, painting, writing, sculpting, music, or movement.

With increasing attention to the mind-body connection, therapeutic dance can be powerful for some in healing sexual trauma (Lee et al., 2022). Music can embody the mood of one's soul, while lyrics furnish words to experiences, impressions, and feelings. The secretiveness surrounding abuse engenders isolation and feelings of difference and separation from others. Lines from a poignant song can link the lyricist and the listener, signaling their relatedness (Hammel-Zabin, 2003).

The psalms are teeming with songs of anguish. Approximately half of the psalms are laments (Card, 2005). The Lord kindly designed music to express the innermost self. Thus, a valuable therapeutic endeavor can involve inviting the survivor to select and share a song that expresses his present experience, mood, and secrets not yet ready to be directly disclosed.

Painting, sketches, or clay can also provide helpful mediums for telling trauma stories. Jenny Murphy explained, "Art therapy can be seen to offer a transitional space which is experienced as safer and less intense than a verbal therapy relationship. . . . These art materials or images provide a means of expressing, holding, and recognizing the feelings" (Murphy, 2005, p. 3). While art therapy can only be practiced by therapists who have obtained the required training, certification, or licensure, with some training, clinicians can incorporate art into therapy.

Like a prisoner set free after a twenty-year sentence, long-kept secrets can be unshackled through writing. Poetry, short stories, a memoir—the writing possibilities are profuse. For example, Virginia Woolf, hailed as one of the twentieth century's most innovative writers, applied the literary approaches of stream of consciousness, indirect narration, and poetic impressionism to chronicle of her experience of incest (Teacher & Powell, 1994). Virginia declared she was abused as a child and adolescent, and she made these previously kept secrets known in a passel of ways. As a child, she endeavored to tell her parents about the abuse by compiling stories in the family newspaper to "tell" indirectly; however, no one seemed to get the drift of her plight (DeSalvo, 1989). As an adult, she unpacked her epic tragedy with her trusted friends in detail. She divulged her childhood horror through her fictional characters, who wore sundry symptoms that Virginia personally exhibited throughout her life.

Virginia penned an autobiographical essay four months before her suicide. *A Sketch of the Past* details a sexual violation by her sixteen- or seventeen-year-old half-brother, Gerald Duckworth, when Virginia was only five or six years old.

> There was a slab outside the dining room door for standing dishes upon. Once when I was very small Gerald Duckworth lifted me onto this, and as I sat there he began to explore my body. I can remember the feel of his hand going under my clothes; going firmly and steadily, going lower and lower. I remember how I hoped he would stop; how I stiffened and wiggled as his hand approached my private parts. But it did not stop. His hand explored my private parts too. I remember resenting it, disliking it—what is the word

> for so dumb and mixed of feeling? It must have been strong, since I still recall it. (Schulkind, 1985, p. 69)

Virginia also disclosed that her second half-brother, George Duckworth, sexually abused her and her sister for several years during their teenage years.

I (Hannah) had the privilege of witnessing a disclosure inspired by another survivor's artistry. In our drop-in center, women sit around a large table in the kitchen to eat together. But it's not a typical table. The table has been refurbished from old doors that used to sit in the abandoned building that stood on this now sacred ground. The table was decorated by dozens of survivors—pieces of their stories, inspirational statements, sobriety and freedom dates, and sunflowers. One older woman sat at the table to eat and began reading the table. Moments passed, and she told me she was being trafficked and wanted to talk to someone about it. For several hours that day, she got to tell her story. The woman returned weeks later to let us know that she was doing well, and she highlighted, "I got the courage to tell when I saw all those quotes and messages from other survivors; I knew I too could survive." An artistic table declaring the stories of dozens of survivors inspired one woman's disclosure. She sat down for a meal and rose up with courage.

It was not until I (Tammy) graduated from a counseling program, began counseling, and subsequently sat in an abuse seminar that I told a counselor the specifics of the abuse that happened to me. I had always remembered my abuse, but it took a decade and a half for me to tell my counselor about the two individuals who abused me during my formative years and a senior manager who sexually assaulted me after high school. It was during the abuse seminar, that I realized that God wanted to work *in* me so that he could work *through* me and that I was a limited vessel for his plans until I allowed him access to the secrets of my soul. During this disclosure process, I thought about abuse when I woke up in the morning and before I went to sleep. Memories hounded me throughout the day. Over time, I realized that the Lord wanted to free me up in so many areas of my life (e.g., avoidance, secret-keeping, unforgiveness), and his intent was always to heal, not hurt, his girl.

Over the years, as I have traveled to various countries and shared my story of sexual abuse, I have individuals tell me, sometimes through translators, sometimes on a sheet of paper, and sometimes in their own words for the very first time, "It happened to me too." And then, another one of God's kids begins their journey of speaking the truth so that she might be set free.

COUNSELING APPLICATION

> *The soul is like a wild animal—tough, resilient, savvy, self-sufficient and yet exceedingly shy. If we want to see a wild animal, the last thing we should do is to go crashing through the woods, shouting for the creature to come out. But if we are willing to walk quietly into the woods and sit silently for an hour or two at the base of a tree, the creature we are waiting for may well emerge, and out of the corner of an eye we will catch a glimpse of the precious wildness we seek.*
>
> PARKER PALMER

Angelica was single (never married), biracial, natal sex female who identified as nonbinary (utilizing the pronouns they/them) and bisexual. They sought therapy for the first time at the age of thirty-four with me (Adam) primarily to address "anger issues" about recent sexual harassment in the workplace and long-term anger associated with intimate partners and authority figures. We talked openly/candidly about working with a white, male, heterosexual psychologist. They later remarked, "That shocked me that you went right there—but I knew then you could *see* me and were *for* me." During the initial therapy session, Angelica disclosed that they experienced "evil" in their relationship with their biological father but did not wish to elaborate. They also reported intense anger and self-hatred beginning in childhood (at approximately age 5-6) and symptoms consistent with childhood trauma (e.g., nightmares, re-experiencing, hypervigilance, externalizing behaviors, mood swings).

Over the subsequent sessions, Angelica established increased trust and rapport with me and increasingly hinted at childhood sexual abuse with their father. Eventually, Angelica remarked, "I think I'm ready to talk about what happened with my dad." We were standing on shaky ground, never before traversed. They never said the story out loud. I normalized the daunting process of sharing a trauma story with another person and offered empathy and support. Having helped many others on their own distinct yet similarly arduous journey, I often reference those previous experiences to add credibility and compassion to the moment. I talked about several forms of therapy that can aid in sharing these stories and highlighted the strengths and limitations of each. I emphasized that many individuals (but not all) benefited from each approach presented and that these therapies are rigorously studied and proven effective before dissemination. Together, we watched videos online from The National Center for PTSD to compare various therapies (prolonged exposure, Cognitive Processing Therapy, EMDR, SSRI/medication, etc.). Angelica and I viewed two- to three-minute videos about each approach to therapy from the website to learn about each approach. This allowed Angelica and me to compare/contrast therapy approaches and see how disclosure and treatment progress with each form of therapy. This appealed to Angelica's agency to make an informed decision about what and how to share their trauma history while also adding credibility to various forms of therapy. Together, Angelica and I selected EMDR and began the protocol with education about trauma and developing resources.

TELLING SECRETS TO GOD

Human speech is like a cracked kettle on which we tap crude rhythms . . . while we long to make music that will melt the stars.

GUSTAVE FLAUBERT

Growing empirical research suggests that religiously or culturally accommodated interventions increase client usage of skills gained, contribute to a reduction of symptoms, and result in more sustained benefits from therapeutic interventions relative to nonaccommodated interventions (Dixon et al., 2017). This effectiveness increase may be due to religiously or culturally accommodated interventions being value- and belief-congruent. Moreover, a recent meta-analysis (Captari et al., 2018) revealed that religiously accommodated interventions have mental health outcomes that are at least as effective as carefully matched secular interventions and better outcomes than less well-matched interventions or no treatment at all.

For some faith-based survivors, it is helpful to disclose secrets in informal and formal settings and with God (Pertek, 2022). For some, religious coping involving prayer can be an essential part of the healing journey at the outset. For other survivors, wrestling through conversations with God comes later during the healing journey. Catherine Foote wrote *Survivor Prayers,* a wise and vulnerable book of poems and prayers to God about abuse:

> As wounded children we learned to conceal the levels of pain and loss from family and friends because we were told to, or because we feared the truth would not be believed, or because it seemed too overwhelming. Many of us have learned also to "hide" from God. Talking to God about our childhood sexual abuse means placing before God all the fears, the rage, and the confusion of the hurting child. Breaking silence with God may mean standing before God and asking why. It may mean ending a pattern of "taking care" of God, trying to put a nice face on the raw pain, or ending every prayer with a "happily ever after" to keep God happy. We may have tended to say, "Well, yes, it was hard, but everything's OK now, so please don't leave me." Breaking silence with God means telling God the truth. (Foote, 1994, p. 31)

There is much more to say about tuning into prayer as a religious coping resource for some survivors, which we will look at more in-depth in the "Attached to God" chapter. But for now, we understand that sometimes it feels like the most significant risk for survivors involves disclosing the abuse narratives (ironic as this is) and telling our story to the omniscient One.

COUNSELING CONSIDERATIONS

As a junior clinician working in a clinic with clients experiencing PTSD, I (Adam) was inexpressibly appreciative of structured processes to educate, prepare, and facilitate various trauma disclosure forms during sessions. I was overwhelmed as the hearer of trauma stories and unsure how to proceed. Overreliance on treatment manuals can be potentially problematic. However, as a young clinician, I felt protected and empowered in learning and using treatment manuals to guide such meaningful, heavy work. In learning more than one approach, clinicians can review different approaches to disclosure (as illustrated with Angelica). Manualized forms of PTSD treatment outline specific characteristics about disclosure because exposure to trauma memories and creating a narrative is a core/common element of therapy. In each of the below therapies, the clinician provides education about why disclosure is an important form of exposure in the therapy process. See also the appendix.

Disclosure via writing.

- *Narrative Exposure Therapy (NET).* In this approach, trauma survivors compose their life stories chronologically, emphasizing trauma events. This chronological approach aids in fostering a sense of personal identity and draws insight/connections to interrelated aspects of life. Careful attention is paid to fragmented and distressing memories from traumatic events to ensure they have a coherent narrative within the context of the life story.
- *Written Exposure Therapy (WET).* In this approach, the therapist reviews a script in each session before a 30-minute writing session to provide instructions about writing in detail about an identified traumatic event. At the end of the writing session, the therapist reviews the written material and provides a conclusion script.

Written and spoken disclosure combinations.

- *Cognitive Processing Therapy (CPT).* In this approach, the client writes an impact statement about an identified traumatic event. This is typically done early in treatment and outside of the therapy room. This written account is referenced throughout therapy, and a concluding therapy component involves rewriting the impact statement.

Verbal and nonverbal disclosure.

- *EMDR.* One of the unique aspects of EMDR is that reflection on trauma memories is often nonverbal as a client engages in bilateral stimulation (e.g., eye movements, tapping, buzzers in left and right hands). Verbal prompts are made to the client throughout the processing session to assess the degree of distress, maladaptive thoughts, adaptive thoughts, and some content. Thus, detailed disclosure of trauma events is sometimes not linear or 100 percent verbalized compared to several other therapies in this section.
- *Person-Centered Expressive Arts Therapy.* This approach involves a therapist serving as an "empathic witness," listening to and encouraging the self-exploration taking place for the client through the act of drawing, painting, writing, sculpting, music, or movement. Expressive arts therapy invites clients toward disclosure aligned with signature

strengths in ways that words may not fully convey. This type of approach may be particularly salient to bolster agency for survivors.

Disclosure via verbal processing.

- *Prolonged exposure (PE).* In this approach, the therapist provides background/justification for verbalizing disclosure. Here, disclosure occurs verbally in the session with a therapist, and portions of the disclosure are reviewed by the client between sessions.
- *Acceptance & Commitment Therapy (ACT).* This transdiagnostic approach utilizes aspects of psychological flexibility, such as mindful acceptance, and classic exercises, such as "Saying Yes," to allow clients to hold memories, thoughts, emotions, and bodily sensations versus patterns of avoidance. Steven Hayes's book *A Liberated Mind* (2020) includes numerous acceptance-oriented exercises that can be useful for trauma survivors who have developed patterns of avoidance.
- *Sensorimotor Psychotherapy (SP).* Although cognitive-oriented therapies (top-down) are potent and effective, there are times when a somatic approach (bottom-up) can be beneficial. Somatic therapy focuses on the multifaceted language of the body as the starting place to assist in becoming "unstuck" from the fight, flight, or freeze responses. Here, we can help survivors pay attention to the arousal in their bodies, facial expressions, and posture, and to develop somatic resources. Inviting a client to "find or notice a place in your body that feels calm or neutral" can be helpful. Alternatively, inquire: "Could we check if we can enhance your breathing? Can we notice what happens when you sit up in your chair and we practice breathing for a couple of minutes?" See *Sensorimotor Psychotherapy* (2015) by Pat Ogden and Janina Fisher.

Exercises to help during the disclosure journey.

- *Containment exercise.* An imaginal experience (i.e., visualization exercise) frequently used in EMDR at the end of a session involves inviting clients to place their distressing thoughts, images, or feelings in a container that is strong enough to hold until they can return to the disclosure/processing work. The purpose is not to avoid problems. Instead, imaginal containers hold concerns that cannot be resolved in the present moment. Clients are invited to close their eyes, imagine their container's size, shape, and color, and develop a lid to hold their concerns securely. Others may need a more concrete example of a container that the clinician might have in their office.

- *Connecting with God during disclosure.* During some of the most challenging moments, as survivors face pain-filled memories and enter the crucible of their enormous sorrows, lifelines are needed. A prayer journal can be a particularly meaningful repository to God in which survivors express their deepest concerns: "I pour out my complaint before him; I reveal my trouble before him" (Ps 142:2). To assist in this journey, a couple of books might be beneficial: *Every moment holy: Death, grief, and hope* (Kaine, 2021) is a treasure trove of liturgies and prayers for seasons of dying and grieving. I (Tammy) have been enormously comforted by its pages. Also, *Prayer in the night: For those who work or watch or weep* (Warren, 2021) offers authentic prose without palliating fears or sorrows. Her tender reflections about the dark night of our souls offer another option, beyond our countless ways of numbing the pain. She offers connecting through authentic prayer with God who sees our suffering.

CHILDREN'S CORNER

- ***The Rabbit Listened*** (Doerrfeld, 2018). When individuals have been hurt, oftentimes, many try to fix the ache. This book details the offers of advice by the chicken, the bear, and others when Taylor is hurt, all of which fail to provide comfort. Instead, the rabbit listens. A book to be read to children and adults alike on the gift of truly listening to people's pain.

REFERENCES

Alaggia, R., Collin-Vézina, D., & Lateef, R. (2019). Facilitators and barriers to child sexual abuse (CSA) disclosures: A research update (2000–2016). *Trauma, Violence, & Abuse, 20*(2), 260-83. https://doi.org/10.1177/1524838017697312

Anderson, L. & Gold, K. (1998). Creative connections. *Women and Therapy, 21*(4), 15-36. https://doi.org/10.1300/J015v21n04_02

Captari, L. E., Hook, J. N., Hoyt, W. T., Davis, D. E., McElroy, S. E., & Worthington, E. L., Jr. (2018). Integrating clients' religion and spirituality within psychotherapy: A comprehensive meta-analysis. *Journal of Clinical Psychology, 74*(11), 1938-51. https://doi.org/10.1002/jclp.22681

Card, M. (2005). *A sacred sorrow*. NavPress.

CBS News. (2017, October 17). More than 12M "Me Too" Facebook posts, comments, reactions in 24 hours. CBS News. https://www.cbsnews.com/news/metoo-more-than-12-million-facebook-posts-comments-reactions-24-hours.

DeSalvo, L. A. (1989). *Virginia Woolf: The impact of childhood sexual abuse on her life and work*. Beacon Press.

Dixon, L. E., Ahles, E., & Marques, L. (2017). Treating posttraumatic stress disorder in diverse settings: Recent advances and challenges for the future. *Current Psychiatry Reports, 18*(108), 1-16. https://doi.org/10.1007/s11920-016-0748-4

Doerrfeld, C. (2018). *The rabbit listened.* Penguin Young Readers Group.

Easton, S. D. (2013). Disclosure of child sexual abuse among adult male survivors. *Clinical Social Work Journal, 41*(4), 344-55. https://doi.org/10.1007/s10615-012-0420-3

Ettinger, T. R. (2022). Children's needs during disclosures of abuse. *SN Social Sciences,* 2(7), 1-25. https://doi.org/10.1007/s43545-022-00397-6

Fisher, A. Q., & Rivas, M. E. (2001). *Finding fish: A memoir*. Morrow.

Fontes, L. A. (2005). *Child abuse and culture: Working with diverse families*. Guilford.

Fontes, L. A., & Plummer, C. (2010). Cultural issues in disclosures of child sexual abuse. *Journal of Child Sexual Abuse, 19*(5), 491-518. https://doi.org/10.1080/10538712.2010.512520

Foote, C. J. (1994). *Survivor prayers: Talking with God about childhood sexual abuse*. Westminster/John Knox Press.

Gilligan, P. A., & Akhtar, S. (2006). Cultural barriers to the disclosure of child sexual abuse in Asian communities: Listening to what women say. *British Journal of Social Work, 36*(8), 1361-77. https://doi.org/10.1093/bjsw/bch309

Güven, T., Kalfoglou, S., & Kalfoğlu, E. (2022). Sexual assault crisis center: The first interdisciplinary effort in Turkey. In E. Kalfoğlu & S. Kalfoglou (Eds.), *Sexual abuse—An interdisciplinary approach.* IntechOpen. https://doi.org/10.5772/intechopen.90974

Haboush, K. L., & Alyan, H. (2013). "Who can you tell?" Features of Arab culture that influence conceptualization and treatment of childhood sexual abuse. *Journal of Child Sexual Abuse,* 22(5), 499-518. https://doi.org/10.1080/10538712.2013.800935

Hammel-Zabin, A. (2003). *Conversations with a pedophile*. Barricade Books.

Hayes, S. C. (2020). *A liberated mind: How to pivot toward what matters.* Avery.

Kaine, D. (2021). *Every moment holy: Death, grief, and hope* (Vol. 2). Rabbit Press.

Kardam, F. (2005). *The dynamics of honor killing in Turkey*. United Nations Development Program.

Kettlewell, C. (1999). *Skin game.* St. Martin's Press.

Larner, S. (2022). Facilitating children's informal disclosures of sexual abuse: The role of online counsellors at a national children's helpline. *Journal of Child Sexual Abuse, 31*(3), 276-96. https://doi.org/10.1080/10538712.2022.2047854

Lee, J., Dhauna, J., Silvers, J., Houston, M., & Barnert, E. (2022). Therapeutic dance for the healing of sexual trauma: A systematic review. *Trauma, Violence, & Abuse, 24*(4), 1-22. https://doi.org/10.1177/15248380221086898

Leseho, J., & Maxwell, L. R. (2010). Coming alive: Creative movement as a personal coping strategy on the path to healing and growth. *British Journal of Guidance & Counselling, 38*(1), 17-30. https://doi.org/10.1080/03069880903411301

Malchiodi, C. A. (2003). *Handbook of art therapy*. Guilford.

Manay, N., Collin-Vézina, D., Alaggia, R., & McElvaney, R. (2022). "It's complicated because we're only sixteen": A framework for understanding childhood sexual abuse disclosures to peers. *Journal of Interpersonal Violence, 37*(3-4), 1704-32. https://doi.org/10.1177/0886260520933052

Mathews, B. (2022). Developing countries and the potential of mandatory reporting laws to identify severe child abuse and neglect. In S. Deb (Ed.), *Child safety, welfare and well-being* (pp. 485-521). Springer.

McElvaney, R. (2015). Disclosure of child sexual abuse: Delays, non-disclosure and partial disclosure: What the research tells us and implications for practice. *Child Abuse Review, 24*(3), 159-69. https://doi.org/10.1002/car.2280

McElvaney, R., Greene, S., & Hogan, D. (2014). To tell or not to tell? Factors influencing young people's informal disclosures of child sexual abuse. *Journal of Interpersonal Violence, 29*(5), 928-47. https://doi.org/10.1177/0886260513506281

McGill, L., & McElvaney, R. (2022). Adult and adolescent disclosures of child sexual abuse: A comparative analysis. *Journal of Interpersonal Violence, 38*(1-2). https://doi.org/10.1177/08862605221088278

Mikton, C., Power, M., Raleva, M., Makoae, M., Al Eissa, M., Cheah, I., Cardia, N., Choo, C., & Almuneef, M. (2013). The assessment of the readiness of five countries to implement child maltreatment prevention programs on a large scale. *Child Abuse & Neglect, 37*, 1237-51. https://doi.org/10.1016/j.chiabu.2013.07.009

Mondragon, N. I., Munitis, A. E., & Txertudi, M. B. (2022). The breaking of secrecy: Analysis of the hashtag# MeTooInceste regarding testimonies of sexual incest abuse in childhood. *Child Abuse & Neglect, 123*, 105412. https://doi.org/10.1016/j.chiabu.2021.105412

Murphy, J. (Ed.). (2005). *Art therapy with young survivors of sexual abuse: Lost for words*. Taylor & Francis.

Ogden, P., & Fisher, J. (2015). *Sensorimotor psychotherapy: Interventions for trauma and attachment.* W. W. Norton.

Pertek, S. I. (2022). "God helped us": Resilience, religion and experiences of gender-based violence and trafficking among African forced migrant women. *Social Sciences, 11*(5), 201. https://doi.org/10.3390/socsci11050201

Rouse, A., Jenkinson, E., & Warner, C. (2022). The use of "art" as a resource in recovery from the impact of sexual abuse in childhood: A qualitative systematic review. *Arts & Health, 15*(1), 86-109. https://doi.org/10.1080/17533015.2022.2034900

Schulkind, J. (Ed.). (1985). *Moments of being* (2nd ed.). Harcourt Brace.

Sesar, K., Dodaj, A., Vasilj, V., Sesar, D., Smoljan, I., & Mikulic, M. (2022). The creative art therapies in work with children and adolescents with traumatic experiences. *Paediatric Psychology, 18*(1). https:doi.org/10.5457/p2005-114.319

Shafe, S., & Hutchinson, G. (2014). Child sexual abuse and continuous influence of cultural practices: A review. *The West Indian Medical Journal, 63*(6), 634. https://doi.org/10.7727/wimj.2013.246

Summit, R. (1983). Child sexual abuse accommodation syndrome. *Child Abuse and Neglect, 7*(2), 177-93. https://doi.org/10.1016/0145-2134(83)90070-4

Teacher, J. B. (Ed.), & Powell, J. (Ill.). (1994). *Women of words: A personal introduction to thirty-five important writers*. Courage Books.

Terr, L. C. (1990). Who's afraid of Virginia Woolf? Clues to early sexual abuse in literature. *The Psychoanalytic Study of the Child, 45*, 533-46. https://doi.org/10.1080/00797308.1990.11823533

Warren, T. H. (2021). *Prayer in the night: For those who work or watch or weep*. InterVarsity Press.

Watkins-Kagebein, J., Barnett, T. M., Collier-Tenison, S., & Blakey, J. (2019). They don't listen: A qualitative interpretive meta-synthesis of children's sexual abuse. *Child & Adolescent Social Work Journal, 36*(4), 337-49. https://doi.org/10.1007/s10560-019-00615-w

3

CESSPOOLS OF SHAME

For me, vulnerability led to anxiety, which led to shame, which led to disconnection, which led to Bud Light.

BRENÉ BROWN

Quia amastime, fecistime amabilem.
In loving me, you made me lovable.

SAINT AUGUSTINE

In the movie *Good Will Hunting*, there is a poignant scene where Will (Matt Damon), a young man who raced ahead of the pack in perspicacity, converses with Shaun (Robin Williams), his trusted therapist (Sant, 1997). Shaun cradles Will's counseling file, jammed with gruesome pictures of injuries that Will experienced at the hands of his alcoholic dad. Shaun gently declares to Will that the pages he is looking at—the pictures of bruises from beatings—were *not* his fault. Will brushes off the statement by responding that he knew this already, but Shaun is unconvinced. So, Shaun continues telling Will repeatedly that the abuse was not his fault, and Will erupts in rage, taking steps back as Shaun continues to echo his words. Finally, Will allows Shaun's words to come near and touch his soul, and he begins to weep as Shaun embraces him. Will's response is different this time. This time Will says, I'm so sorry.

But why was Will sorry? Tracing back to Tamar, we see that she begged her half-brother not to rape her, and then she says, "As for me, where could I carry my shame?" (2 Sam 13:13). These all-too-common shame-fused abuse experiences prompt the question: why are survivors who are manhandled, mishandled, and molested so sorry about what was done *to* them? A scoping review of twenty-eight empirical studies on adult survivors' experiences following child sexual abuse revealed that shame is a common symptom and appears to aggravate other outcome effects, relationships, disclosure, core identity, and the recovery of survivors (MacGinley et al., 2019). Thus, wrapping our minds around shame is central to understanding the aftermath experiences of survivors of abuse.

In this chapter, we provide therapists with an understanding of the strain of shame shackled to sexual abuse. We consider what underlies personal blame for the abuse done *to* a survivor. We grapple with the question that frequently looms large with traumatic experiences: *What is it about me that caused the abuse?* In the second half of the chapter, we focus on several evidence-based strategies and faith-based practices to help clients counteract shame.

THE GIST OF SHAME

I am gall, I am heartburn God's most deep decree.
Bitter would have me taste and my taste was me.

GERARD MANLY HOPKINS

Obtaining a solid grasp of shame can be an onerous task as it is often hidden, masquerading as other feelings and behaviors, and many feel ashamed for feeling shame (Taylor, 2015). Psychiatrist Curt Thompson (2015, p. 23) explains that "elusiveness is a key element of [shame's] power." Brené Brown (2006, p. 45) defined shame as "an intensely painful feeling or experience of believing we are flawed and therefore unworthy of acceptance and belonging." There are differing views on shame, with some saying that all shame is pejorative (Brown, 2006), while others argue that emotions are dualistic and that some forms of shame can be purposeful and signal individuals regarding certain behaviors that do not align with specific values (Cibich et al., 2016; Mayer & Vanderheiden, 2019).

There is a continuum of shame responses ranging from mild embarrassment to intense humiliation (Wilson et al., 2006). There are also several facets of shame, including biological, emotional, cognitive, and relational. One of the hallmarks of shame is the neurobiological experience of becoming increasingly visible through blushing (for fair-skinned individuals), while simultaneously desiring to hide, a slumped and sagging posture, averting one's gaze, bowing the head, and covering one's face with the hands. Speech and ideas are often obscured, giving way to a "relatively wordless state" (Herman, 2011, p. 263). Shame is also a common and painful self-conscious emotional experience that is frequently felt as intense and overwhelming, and it is often associated with feelings of helplessness and betrayal (Dearing & Tangney, 2011; MacGinley et al., 2019; Platt & Freyd, 2015). Cognitively, toxic shame emanates from a condemning core view about who I am (e.g., "I am a vile woman") (Luoma & Platt, 2015). Internalized core beliefs about one's sense of self frequently culminate in the sense of being stained, soiled, flawed, damaged, defective, defiled, disgusting.

Shame is the deep-seated belief that when I was a ten-year-old child, if only I hadn't gone to my elementary school on that Saturday, then the janitor wouldn't have touched me. It shouts that if my sister uses me for sex, I must only be good for that. It is the I-should-have-known-better kind of mortification. It screams the lie, *You're not good enough.* If shame is doing the math, then something about me doesn't add up. It's believing I'll never amount to anything.

Shame surfaces relationally in the desire to cover oneself from being exposed (MacIntosh et al., 2016). Individuals frequently seek safety through disconnection and separation to avoid the perceived scornful looks in the eyes of others (Herman, 2011).

PTSD AND SHAME

Sometimes I wonder if I'm *a mistake.*

DANIEL TIGER,
MISTER ROGERS' NEIGHBORHOOD

A sizeable shift occurred in the *Diagnostic and Statistical Manual-5* (*DSM-5*; American Psychiatric Association, 2013), resulting in the removal of PTSD from the anxiety disorders category due to the burgeoning research revealing that other emotions such as shame are related to the development and maintenance of PTSD (Andrews et al., 2000; Bannister et al., 2019; Dorahy et al., 2017; Saraiya & Lopez-Castro, 2016; Taylor, 2015). Since shame following trauma often prompts withdrawal and avoidant behaviors similar to other anxiety experiences, PTSD was previously viewed as being primarily a fear response. For many, fear plays a central role in posttraumatic symptoms. However, among survivors of interpersonal trauma where dominance and control occur, shame is a primary affect (Gnaulati, 2019; La Bash & Papa, 2014). In the "Trust and Treachery" chapter, we will explain further that high-betrayal traumas predict increases in shame compared to low-betrayal traumas (Platt & Freyd, 2015). Interestingly, Judith Herman, a renowned Harvard professor, researcher, author, and psychiatrist, referred to PTSD as a shame disorder (Herman, 2011).

Moreover, although extensive empirical evidence has accrued concerning the "gold-standard therapies" for PTSD (e.g., Cognitive Processing Therapy [CPT], Prolonged exposure [PE]), many survivors remain symptomatic following treatment (Saraiya & Lopez-Castro, 2016), and a substantial number of individuals drop out of therapy (Gnaulati, 2019). This has urged researchers and clinicians to understand the role of shame related to the development and maintenance of PTSD (Cunningham et al., 2018), as well as wise ways to counsel survivors of abuse experiencing shame.

PTSD, GUILT, AND SHAME

Shame, boatloads of shame. Day after day, more of the same.
Blame, please lift it off. Please take it off, please make it stop.

THE AVETT BROTHERS, "SHAME"

Distinguishing shame and guilt can be challenging. Many agree that guilt seems to say, "I regret doing a specific behavior," whereas shame comments, "I regret being the type of person I am" (Saraiya & Lopez-Catro, 2016). While the overlap between definitions of shame and guilt makes distinguishing between the two difficult, one thing is clear: *both* shame and guilt are important to understand trauma-related symptomatology.

There is a mountain of combat-related trauma research, and more recently, there is a growing number of studies on shame and guilt related to combat trauma. While complex trauma (i.e., interpersonal trauma) differs from combat trauma, there may be some things we can learn. For example, Cunningham and colleagues (2018) examined a military population to understand the unique ways that guilt and shame influence the severity of PTSD. Interestingly, trauma-related shame and guilt played a larger role than any other variable related to the severity of PTSD. Additionally, shame predicted the severity of PTSD more than guilt in this study. Bannister, Colvonen, Angkaw, and Norman (2019) similarly examined guilt and shame related to PTSD severity among 144 veterans in therapy, and they found both shame and guilt were related to PTSD severity. However, shame was more strongly associated with PTSD than guilt. Interestingly, Bannister and colleagues also found that guilt was accompanied by shame in 100 percent of the participants. Thus, while more research about the relationship between shame and guilt and survivors of child sexual abuse is needed, it appears that shame and guilt experiences are not so easily disentangled, which has implications for trauma therapists regarding the need to assess both guilt and shame.

SHAME SAVAGES

Are they ashamed of their detestable conduct? No, they have no shame at all; they do not even know how to blush.

JEREMIAH 6:15 NIV

Circling back to the question of why Will and so many survivors of abuse experience a sense of being fundamentally flawed for the abuse done *to* them, one of the reasons is that perpetrators of abuse are adept at flicking shame on their victims by using deceptive techniques (Lorenzo-Dus & Kinzel, 2019). Consequently, survivors often internalize the noxious labels doled out by offenders (Finkelhor, 1979). Researcher Anna Salter (1995, p. 185) explained, "Survivors often internalize the sex offender's version of the abuse, partly because he is the only person who knows about it at the time, and therefore is in a unique position to define her reality."

I (Tammy) learned much about shame from my work with perpetrators who molest children. A common ploy by perpetrators is to dispense self-disclosing experiences and emotions to engender trust, create closeness, and elicit sympathy from their victims (Chiu et al., 2018). One father I worked with, who frequently sexually abused his ten-year-old daughter, unloaded his loneliness and loss on her so that she became his surrogate wife. On one occasion, he recited an onslaught of personal woes to seek sympathy from his daughter. Her sadness over her father's plight prompted her to hug her dad. Then, he proceeded to molest her. As her body froze and fear became etched on her face, he attempted to assuage her agitation with words: "You're my special helper." He added, "Please don't tell. Others wouldn't understand our relationship."

Eventually, she did tell her school counselor, and his actions landed him in jail. I asked this father what he thought his daughter might struggle with due to what he did *to* her. With certainty, he said *she would think it was her fault*. He further elaborated, telling me that he had quizzed her several times if she minded his touch and if she was all right with what he was doing. His specious fondness fused with fondling left his daughter in knots, and she ultimately felt complicit concerning the abuse. Added to the mix, her mom was missing in action, and this ten-year-old daughter was thirsty for love. A perfect mix for people who prey.

Perpetrators deploy other tactics that sully survivor identities as well. They may dispense accolades over their victim's developing body. They may "gently" caress their victim, providing the appearance of care and relationship. Each ruse leaves victims languishing in a confusing, shameful state. Lisa Fontes (2005, p. 139) throws light on the matter: "Most children seek affection. If they receive sexual abuse instead, they may come to believe it was their desire for closeness that brought about the sexual acts."

To add to the complexity, a child who is sexually violated frequently feels shame for the abuse due to what trauma expert John Briere (1996, p. 56) calls the "abuse dichotomy." This is the dilemma of determining who is to blame for the abuse: my brother, uncle, neighbor, youth pastor, or grandmother was sexual with me because she or he is bad, or I am being hurt because *I am bad*. Commonly, the only tenable solution to this quandary is *I am bad.* As painful as this option is, at least the abuse can be decoded. Shame short circuits that out-of-control feeling. The abuse is my fault. And since it is my fault, I can do something about it. I can become a better kid, a better woman, or a better man.

If the abuse is my fault, I can annihilate my masculinity because being male is what got me in trouble in the first place. Or I will spend the rest of my days proving there was nothing about my maleness that made him do that to me. I will never let myself need again because needing is what got me into this mess. *I* climbed up on my daddy's lap. *I* nestled my head on his chest. It was *my* entreaty that brought his rapt attention.

The sense of shame is pronounced, especially if she enjoys the attention. If her body responds, that further confirms her badness and adds to the shame. Christiane Sanderson (2006, p. 325) explained,

> If the child's body responds to the sexual contact with pleasure, sexual arousal, or orgasm, he may feel doubly ashamed that his body responded and "betrayed" him. This is particularly true for the older child, who may know that child sexual abuse is wrong and yet derive some pleasure from the sexual acts.

This was certainly true for a woman named Jennifer, who described herself as a lonely child who felt a lot of shame for enjoying her perpetrator's attention. Jennifer grew up with a father diagnosed with bipolar illness, a neglectful mother and abusive stepfather, and substance abuse galore in her family. So, at age fourteen, when a married man in his thirties living next door began paying attention to her, she recalled that she "enjoyed" it. As she told me (Hannah), she described that she eventually "had sex" with him and "fell for him." Weeks into this "relationship," she began calling his house, despite his pleas to her not to do so. It wasn't long before this teenager was charged with her first of many criminal charges—telephone harassment—placed on probation, and labeled as a "bad girl." Despite being a superior student-athlete (and being offered a full-ride scholarship to play college basketball), her life ended up taking a sad turn. This victim of childhood abuse, neglect, and rape by the older neighbor was blamed on her "bad choices." And you better believe she blamed herself. It wasn't long before she used hard drugs and was recruited into prostitution. As she shared her story, she said she cried the whole time as she turned her first trick. She assured the john that it wasn't his fault. She poignantly stated, "shame had a hold on me."

Pettersen's (2013) study of shame related to incestuous sexual abuse further reveals how difficult it is for survivors to rightly assign blame to perpetrators. In this study, daughters who were sexually abused by their fathers rarely attributed guilt to their fathers. Instead, they were more inclined to assign guilt and feel shame toward their mothers and themselves. Shame padlocks Pandora's box of helplessness. It gives us the mistaken impression that we have some level of control.

SHAME STRATEGIES

Therapist shame.

> *You're not what happened. You're more than the shame*
> *you were recklessly given.*
>
> COMMON HYMNAL, "HE HAS TIME"

As we have mentioned, the burgeoning PTSD and CPTSD literature demonstrates that shame is central to and not merely a secondary symptom of PTSD. Thus, we as trauma therapists need to attend to our client's shame, as unacknowledged shame stands as a barrier to not only therapy engagement but also therapy completion (Taylor, 2015). However, shame frequently begets shame. Consequently, many therapists with unresolved shame who bear witness to clients experiencing raw, toxic shame may attempt to rescue and reassure clients, minimize their agony, dispense cerebral explanations, and/or switch to safer topics (Teyber & Teyber, 2017).

In contrast, therapists who are well practiced at noticing their own shame-proneness; who are increasingly inclined to face instead of flee the presence of events that trigger personal shame experiences; who are committed to being seen, known, and enjoyed in committed communities and by our good God; who are frequent dispensers of grace to the others in their lives are more likely to attune to the shame in their clients' lives and demonstrate compassion (Cibich et al., 2016; Thompson, 2015). Thus, effectively working with our clients' shame begins first and foremost with working on our shame as therapists.

Shame assessment.

If we can share our story with someone who responds with empathy and understanding, shame can't survive.

BRENÉ BROWN, *DARING GREATLY*

Given that a significant portion of therapy involves discussions concerning painful feelings and experiences, Gilbert (2011, p. 331) explains that "psychotherapy is an inherently shame managing process." Thus, therapists need to become attuned to the layers of shame that survivors wear (Saraiya & Lopez-Castro, 2016). However, drawing near the multifaceted nuances of shame within our clients' lives is best done carefully and empathically, as many survivors have spent much of their lives covering their shame, fearing they will be exposed, rejected, and abandoned once again. Moreover, Herman (2011) explained that traumatized individuals can be stuck in a "feelings trap" whereby survivors feel profound shame for feeling shame. Much like an individual stricken with a panic disorder who, after experiencing a panic attack, develops a fear of future panic, so too shame-prone survivors experience future shame because of their present and past shame. Paradoxically, however, the less survivors talk about their shame, the more power it has over them.

Using reliable and validated shame measures is one way to identify shame severity and track shame reduction during therapy. Notably, Lear et al. (2022) reviewed nineteen scales assessing trait- and state-shame and concluded that much work remains to enhance the reliability and validity of generalized shame measures. There seems to be no doubt that given the pervasiveness of shame related to trauma, accurate assessment tools would be useful in therapy. However, existing measures suffer less-than-optimal methodological quality. DeCou and colleagues (2019) recommended assessing shame using the twenty-four-item, self-report Trauma Related Shame Inventory (TRSI) (Øktedalen et al., 2014), in which clients use a four-point Likert scale to rate trauma-related shame experiences over the past seven days. Alternatively, Rizvi's (2010) Shame Inventory is a fifty-three-item self-report measure that assesses potential shame situations. Informal shame assessment involves the therapist being attuned to the variants of shame vocabulary such as *stupid, ugly, worthless,* and *humiliated,* as well as linguistic cues such as stammering, silences, barely audible speech, confusion, and derisive laughter (Herman, 2011).

Clients can also become increasingly aware of the breadth and width of shame in their lives by developing a shame inventory based on the common mental health adage "we need to name it to tame it." Psychiatrist Curt Thompson (2015) invites clients to use 3 x 5 cards throughout the day to list shame encounters that include physical sensations, feelings, thoughts, and behaviors. As he explains to his clients, the purpose of the exercise is not to initially analyze the experiences. Rather, the purpose is to incite client awareness of their shame.

It was during her Human Trafficking Assessment that Jennifer (mentioned earlier) described her "head-to-heart moment" of realizing that, like Will, *it wasn't her fault*. She explained:

> When I told my experiences to the person who assessed me, I had what I can only describe as an out-of-body experience where I looked down at the fifteen-year-old [Jennifer]. I somehow realized so many mixed messages were dumped on me as a kid. And some of the ideas I was learning in therapy came to mind. I realized that day that I was groomed for the abuse, used, and trafficked. And I remember the person assessing me said: "the justice system failed you." I felt angry at the justice system. I was angry with my parents. I was angry that no one had protected me, and I thought to myself, *I'm not going to let people keep using me.* That day was a watershed moment in my life.

Not often are assessments the impetus to substantial life change. But an empathic listener who gives words to abuse and misuse can sometimes help a survivor to come one step closer to bravely shifting the blame from herself to giving the responsibility of the abuse to the ones who perpetrated it, failed to protect, and enabled the abuse to continue, which of course, can also be painful.

Shame repair through an integrative approach.

Shame derives its power from being unspeakable.

BRENÉ BROWN, *DARING GREATLY*

So, what does overcoming shame related to abuse look like? While there are several gold-standard interventions for individuals with PTSD, with the inclusion of complex PTSD (CPTSD) in the International Classification of Diseases (ICD-11), the official diagnostic system used globally (World Health Organization, 2019), we are only beginning to learn what specific clinical interventions are most effective for survivors of interpersonal trauma with CPTSD (Cloitre, 2015; Karatzias et al., 2019). Moreover, there are few empirically validated shame-focused therapies, and more outcome research is necessary to reveal optimal interventions for toxic shame (Tangney & Dearing, 2011). Based on the information we do have currently, the key to effective approaches regarding toxic shame involves providing a range of therapeutic approaches tailored to the specific client. Thus, we offer an integrative approach that highlights some principles regarding shame repair in which we draw from Emotion Focused Therapy (EFT), Interpersonal Process Approach, Acceptance and Commitment Therapy (ACT), Cognitive Processing Therapy (CPT), and our own clinical experiences to enhance and integrate your approaches, to provide personalized care for clients, and to maximize therapy outcomes (Greenberg, 2015; Luoma & Platt, 2015; Teyber & Teyber, 2017).

First and foremost, since shame stemming from abuse is ignited and the flames fanned in a relational context, it is important that undergirding all remedies for "shame spirals" are therapists whose demeanors are characterized by empathy and acceptance (Brown et al., 2011). Jennifer told Hannah what she would want most for therapists working with survivors of sexual trauma is to "make a safe place. I never had that safe place. For one reason or another, I always thought if I talked, I was going to get in trouble. I didn't feel safe to share." Brené Brown (2006, p. 32) reinforces this idea: "If you put shame in a Petri dish, it needs three things to grow exponentially: secrecy, silence and judgment. If you put the same amount of shame in a Petri dish and douse it with empathy, it can't survive."

Using a phase-based approach to trauma therapy (Cloitre et al., 2011), it is also important to determine client readiness to process shame in the present moment based on the degree of client social support, stabilization and safety, and their ability to regulate painful affect and destructive impulses (Greenberg & Iwakabe, 2011). Some clients with extensive abuse histories may need to spend more time practicing regulating shame and other overwhelming emotions before processing shame in the present moment. As clients are ready to process shame in manageable doses, therapists can draw near to their client's shame by using previously mentioned formal or informal shame assessments (Øktedalen et al., 2014; Rizvi, 2010; Thompson, 2015).

At the outset, it is also important to note that at each intervention phase, clients are ever-prone to flee from their shame for fear of having another person hear their humiliating heartaches and be exposed as foolish, weak, and unlovable. Moreover, as clients name their shame stories, it is difficult not only to voice their anguish but to acknowledge their shame to themselves at a deeper level. Thus, providing a rationale for experiencing and discussing shame can be beneficial (e.g., "I realize that talking about shameful experiences may seem counter-intuitive, but paradoxically, the more we avoid shame, the more it expands. Like a snowball rolling downhill, growing larger and larger, picking up speed.")

Drawing from EFT and Interpersonal Process approaches, and providing ample space to clients to discuss shame experiences in the present moment, the clinician can provide opportunities for clients to begin to overcome their shame avoidance and to identify the sensations and beliefs attached to their shame (e.g., "It takes a lot of courage for you to allow yourself to feel these feelings with me. How about if we sit with this for a moment?") (Greenberg, 2015; Greenberg & Iwakabe, 2011; Teyber & Teyber, 2017). As clients give voice to their shame experiences in the presence of a compassionate clinician, they can learn that it is possible to not be judged or seen as dirty, damaged, and different for the abuse, and instead, it is possible to be delighted in and enjoyed (e.g., "You are so brave to share this with me," or "I hear your deep desire to be seen and enjoyed. It is stunning"). Since clients may alternatively talk about shameful experiences yet avoid emotional connection with the experience or dissociate, stopping and noticing the client's feelings is also important (e.g., "As you are talking about this, I notice that you seem far away. How are you feeling about talking about such a vulnerable part of yourself?")

As clients begin to face their shameful experiences, probing comments can highlight the painful wounds underlying the shame using an EFT approach (e.g., "I am deeply saddened to hear that when you wanted your dad to hug you, instead he violated you") (Greenberg & Iwakabe, 2011). It is equally important to listen for and speak to the desire of clients (i.e., the longing to be loved, enjoyed, admired, cherished, welcomed, to belong; e.g., "I wonder what you would have wanted from your mom instead of her look of reproach?" or "I wonder what a little boy would have hoped for from his uncle instead of being abused?" or "What would have been the most loving words your dad could have said to you at the time?" and "Notice what you feel when you say this"). As a therapist stands as a witness and ally with clients and probes places of heartache, shame, and desire, it is also important to give room to grieve unmet needs.

From a faith-based practice perspective, at wise junctures therapists can inquire about the longing for God with Christian clients, which can foster sacred moments in therapy (e.g., "I wonder when the abuse was happening, what you might have wanted from God?" or "I wonder what a little girl would have wanted from the Lord when her brother was coming in her room at night?"). Since discussing desire can provoke significant emotions, it is important to provide an opportunity to process these experiences (e.g., "What is it like to talk about these experiences for you?" "How are you feeling now?").

For many survivors of abuse, learning to regulate shame (and other emotions) is a primary goal in therapy so that clients can come to understand and accept their emotions and reduce emotional volatility (Greenberg & Iwakabe, 2011). Since survivors tend to "over-utilize relatively ineffective emotion regulation strategies such as expressive suppression" (Boden et al., 2013, p. 297), there are an abundance of useful self-regulation interventions that therapists can employ with survivors (e.g., deep breathing exercises).

More recently, the emerging compassion-oriented therapy literature has shown promising support for increasing self-compassion as a mechanism of change among individuals experiencing shame-based PTSD (Hoffart, et al., 2015; Kearney et al., 2013; Zeller et al., 2015). Self-compassion involves relating to the self in a caring way similar to how one would relate to a trusted friend or beloved child (Luoma & Platt, 2015). With this in mind, therapists can exhibit compassionate curiosity as they use probing questions to inquire about relationships in which clients felt a sense of connection and kindness (e.g., "Who treated you with warmth when you were a young boy?" or "Can you tell me about any faith experiences that you may have had in which you experienced God as compassionate?") (ACT With Compassion, n.d.). In addition, as clients discuss shameful experiences and are inclined to disconnect in session, therapists can center on shame by cultivating caretaking actions through processing (e.g., "What is the most compassionate thing you can do for yourself at this moment?" or "What would it look like for you to be gracious with yourself right here and now?") (ACT With Compassion, n.d.). It is important to note, however, that engaging in self-compassion during shame spirals is a complex cognitive endeavor that "requires the person to be able to observe their own behavior and respond to it in a manner that evokes these evolved caregiving repertoires" (Luoma & Platt, 2015, p. 97).

Helping survivors relinquish the lie *It was my fault* is a journey. Part of the work involves embracing the truth that just because the perpetrator said his victim wanted it doesn't make it true. Just because she was "kind" does not mean the sex signified a relationship or an affair. And just because the survivor may have loved or does love the perpetrator does not mean he had the right to violate someone more vulnerable and less powerful. Embracing these truths is a step of monumental proportions. While we want to avoid oversimplifying a complicated process, from a Cognitive Processing Therapy (CPT) framework, therapists can use a variety of Socratic questions to identify automatic shame-related thoughts (e.g., "What do you mean when you say . . ." or "Can you give me an example of . . .") and modify those stuck points that may sustain and/or exacerbate PTSD symptomatology ("What alternative ways of looking at this are there?" or "What do you think might happen if you gave up this belief?").

The journey of shame repair also means that survivors need others beyond their therapists (i.e., social support). Counteracting shame involves survivors entering into communities with individuals who delight in them outside of the therapeutic dyad. These include places where they can be exposed and share the parts of themselves that are most hidden. This can encompass communities of faith where they can be known, embraced, and prayed over.

Stretching toward freedom.

Why not go out on a limb? That's where the fruit is.
MARK TWAIN

Finally, over the years we have found that counteracting shame is one of the most challenging aspects of therapy. Like performing brain surgery during your first semester of medical school, it can feel like work that is just too challenging. We have discovered that there are limitations to the strategies we have named so far. While they are important interventions that can provide healing, it might also be the case that certain types of shame tumors can only be remedied via a radical encounter with God. When clients cannot seem to grasp the truth about who is responsible for the abuse, or our care and compassion are insufficient, another option may be available. If a client consents to the inclusion of faith-based interventions, there might be an opportunity to invite God to share where God was when the event happened and how he feels about your client as they process an abuse memory or as they are discussing shame experiences. One practice I (Hannah) have gleaned from also being trained as a spiritual director is the practice of "sitting in the loving gaze of God." This practice is inspired by the work of Saint Ignatius of Loyola, who suggested this practice at the start of prayer. The idea is to "place yourself in the Lord's presence, considering God's care for you" (McKoy, n.d.). As Ignatian spiritualist John Eagan expresses, "How do you, Lord, look at me? What do you feel in your heart for me?" There is something remarkably orienting about the loving gaze of God, and it seems that we can choose God's view of us (and our abuse) over our limited view (as cited in Harter, 2005).

There's no doubt that Jennifer's years in therapy brought a lot of healing to her, but on the day that she graduated from a restorative justice program, she credited God with work that was beyond the best of therapy. Having been involved in the criminal justice system for nearly thirty years, she spoke of the Good Shepherd who left the ninety-nine to go looking for the one lost sheep. After being viewed as a criminal since the age of fifteen, she told the story of a kind judge who crossed the street from one courthouse to another, walked down to the holding cell where incarcerated defendants were held before their court appearances, and introduced himself to her. She said a judge had never done anything like that before, and it gave her a picture of a God who runs after his children who are lost. It's difficult for shame to survive the joyful gaze of the Good Shepherd, who is delighted to have his sheep placed rightfully on his shoulders.

COUNSELING CONSIDERATIONS

- **ACT psychoeducation handouts and exercises.** There are some excellent shame psychoeducation tools for clients, including exercises that describe the gist of shame, ways shame affects our thoughts, the impact of shame on the body, and how shame affects our relationships. See the ACT with Compassion website, which offers extensive resources for therapists, including shame handouts, audio and video recordings, and shame assessment information. See also the appendix.
- **Somatically based approaches.** Somatic comes from the Greek word *soma* (body), referring to something related to the body. Somatic therapy holds that traumatic experiences leave lasting impressions on the body, so body-based therapies (or "bottom-up" approaches in contrast to "top-down" cognitive-oriented approaches) are used to promote holistic healing. Therapists can invite clients to describe their "felt-sense" of bodily sensations and inquire about their experience (e.g., "Is that sensation pleasant, unpleasant, or neutral?") (Grabbe & Miller-Karas, 2018, p. 80).
- **Shame assessment measures.** See the Trauma Related Shame Inventory (TRSI) (Øktedalen et al., 2014) and Rizvi's (2010) Shame Inventory as ways to identify shame severity and a means to track reductions in shame during therapy.
- **CPT and shame.** Working with beliefs underlying shame is an important part of the work we do with clients. In CPT there are two general types of "stuck points" that become a primary focus of therapy. The first is labeled assimilation. For example, if a thirteen-year-old was sexually abused by a trusted teacher, the abuse might merge with previous beliefs she had she had about the world (i.e., bad things happen to bad people and good things happen to good people), which eventually leads her to the conclusion, *I must be a bad person.* The second stuck point is labeled over-accommodation and occurs when a person significantly evolves her belief system due to trauma-related

information. An example of over-accommodation is when a thirteen-year-old female is sexually abused by a trusted teacher and forms the underlying belief that all male teachers are abusers. From a CPT approach, the therapist provides education on automatic thoughts and stuck points, and gives handouts to appropriately assess and challenge stuck points.

- **DBT and shame.** In Marsha Linehan's (2015) manual, stage two of treatment allows therapists to specifically address shame, guilt, and sensitivity to criticism and to develop distress-tolerance skills (i.e., Radical Acceptance). Linehan outlines specific clinical interventions to assist clients in acknowledging and accepting life in truth and reality. She also allows for tailoring the content of the skills training to diverse worldviews/religious backgrounds regarding meaning and freedom.
- **Written Exposure Therapy (WET).** Championed by research from Denise Sloan and Brian Marx, WET is now identified by the National Center for PTSD as an evidence-based treatment. In this brief, five-session, 30-minutes-per-session treatment, clients are provided psychoeducation about PTSD and are guided in writing about their index trauma and the meanings associated with that trauma in each session. Therapists are provided with scripts to guide each session and assist clients in identifying their experiences (rather than solely focusing on the trauma itself). The therapist utilizes Socratic questioning to assist the client in identifying and modifying unhelpful thinking patterns. This approach may be useful for survivors as they write and process their shameful experiences.
- **Faith intervention considerations.** For faith-based clients who consent to faith integration practices, explicit integration could include discussions regarding certain men and women in Scripture from a shame lens. For example, therapists can wonder aloud how the infamous sinful woman who interrupted a dinner party, wept, and poured perfume on Jesus' feet could have dared to invite herself to the meal when no one wanted her there but Jesus (Lk 7:36-50). What compelled this woman with such a sinful past to want to be near the Lord? And how did Jesus respond to her? What can we learn from this narrative about what broken people long for and what heals shame?

Another example could include a discussion about the impact of 430 years of slavery on the people of Israel. What forms of abuse did they experience (e.g., beatings by slave drivers, Ex 2:11), and what types of trauma sequelae did they exhibit (Ex 2:23; 3:7)? Further discussions could revolve around what helped the Israelites to march out of Egypt with their "heads held high" (as shame often prompts us to bow our heads), and who was the One who brought them out of slavery (Lev 26:13 NIV)?

CHILDREN'S CORNER

- ***The Boy, the Mole, the Fox, and the Horse*** (Mackesy, 2019) is a powerful book for children and adults that traces the journey of a curious boy, a greedy mole, a wary fox, and a wise horse. Over time, they learn to share their fears and shame and discover the gifts of vulnerability, compassion, intimacy, and love.

REFERENCES

ACT with Compassion resources for therapists. (n.d.). www.actwithcompassion.com

American Psychiatric Association. (2013). *Diagnostic and statistical manual of mental disorders* (5th ed.). https://doi.org/10.1176/appi.books.9780890425596

Andrews, B., Brewin, C. R., Rose, S., & Kirk, M. (2000). Predicting PTSD symptoms in victims of violent crime: The role of shame, anger, and childhood abuse. *Journal of Abnormal Psychology*, *109*, 69-73. https://doi.org/10.1037/0021-843X.109.1.69

Bannister, J. A., Colvonen, P. J., Angkaw, A. C., & Norman, S. B. (2019). Differential relationships of guilt and shame on posttraumatic stress disorder among veterans. *Psychological Trauma: Theory, Research, Practice, and Policy*, *11*, 35-42. https://doi.org/10.1037/tra0000392

Boden, M. T., Westermann, S., McRae, K., Kuo, J., Alvarez, J., Kulkarni, M. R., Gross, J. J., & Bonn-Miller, M. O. (2013). Emotion regulation and posttraumatic stress disorder: A prospective investigation. *Journal of Social and Clinical Psychology*, *32*(3), 296-314. https://doi.org/10.1521/jscp.2013.32.3.296

Briere, J. (1996). *Therapy for adults molested as children: Beyond survival* (2nd ed., rev. and expanded ed). Springer.

Brown, B. (2006). Shame resilience theory: A grounded theory study on women and shame. *Families in Society*, *87*(1), 43-52. https://doi.org/10.1606/1044-3894.3483

Brown, B., Hernandez, V. R., & Villarreal, Y. (2011). Connections: A 12-session psychoeducational shame resilience curriculum. In R. L. Dearing & J. P. Tangney (Eds.), *Shame in the therapy hour* (pp. 355-71). American Psychological Association. https://doi.org/10.1037/12326-015

Chiu, M. M., Seigfried-Spellar, K. C., & Ringenberg, T. R. (2018). Exploring detection of contact vs. fantasy online sexual offenders in chats with minors: Statistical discourse analysis of self-disclosure and emotion words. *Child Abuse & Neglect, 81*, 128-38. https://doi.org/10.1016/j.chiabu.2018.04.004

Cibich, M., Woodyatt, L., & Wenzel, M. (2016). Moving beyond "shame is bad": How a functional emotion *can* become problematic. *Social and Personality Psychology Compass, 10*, 471-83. https://doi.org/10.1111/spc3.12263

Cloitre, M. (2015). The "one size fits all" approach to trauma treatment: Should we be satisfied? *European Journal of Psychotraumatology*, 6, 27344. https://doi.org/10.3402/ejpt.v6.27344

Cloitre, M., Courtois, C. A., Charuvastra, A., Carapezza, R., Stolbach, B. C., & Green, B. L. (2011). Treatment of complex PTSD: Results of the ISTSS expert clinician survey on best practices. *Journal of Traumatic Stress, 24*, 615-27. https://doi.org/10.1002/jts.20697

Cunningham, K. C., Davis, J. L., Wilson, S. M., & Resick, P. A. (2018). A relative weights comparison of trauma-related shame and guilt as predictors of DSM-5 posttraumatic stress disorder symptom severity among US veterans and military members. *British Journal of Clinical Psychology, 57*, 163-76. https://doi.org/10.1111/bjc.12163

Dearing, R. L., & Tangney, J. P. (2011). Introduction: Putting shame in context. In R. L. Dearing & J. P. Tangney (Eds.), *Shame in the therapy hour* (pp. 355-71). American Psychological Association.

DeCou, C. R., Mahoney, C. T., Kaplan, S. P., & Lynch, S. M. (2019). Coping self-efficacy and trauma-related shame mediate the association between negative social reactions to sexual assault and PTSD symptoms. *Psychological Trauma: Theory, Research, Practice, and Policy, 11*(1), 51-54. https://doi.org/10.1037/tra0000379

Dorahy, M. J., Corry, M., Black, R., Matheson, L., Coles, H., Curran, D., Seager, L., Middleton, W., & Dyer, K. F. W. (2017). Shame, dissociation, and complex PTSD symptoms in traumatized psychiatric and control groups: Direct and indirect associations with relationship distress. *Journal of Clinical Psychology, 73*, 439-48. https://doi.org/10.1002/jclp.22339

Finkelhor, D. (1979). *Sexually victimized children*. Free Press.

Fontes, L. A. (2005). *Child abuse and culture: Working with diverse families*. Guilford.

Gilbert, P. (2011). Shame in psychotherapy and the role of compassion focused therapy. In R. L. Dearing & J. P. Tangney (Eds.), *Shame in the therapy hour* (pp. 325-54). American Psychological Association.

Gnaulati, E. (2019). Potential ethical pitfalls and dilemmas in the promotion and use of American Psychological Association–recommended treatments for posttraumatic stress disorder. *Psychotherapy, 56*, 374-82. https://doi.org/10.1037/pst0000235

Grabbe, L., & Miller-Karas, E. (2018). The trauma resiliency model: A "bottom-up" intervention for trauma psychotherapy. *Journal of the American Psychiatric Nurses Association, 24*, 76-84. https://doi.org/10.1177/1078390317745133

Greenberg, L. S. (2015). *Emotion-focused therapy: Coaching clients to work through their feelings*. American Psychological Association. https://doi.org/10.1037/14692-000

Greenberg, L. S., & Iwakabe, S. (2011). Emotion-focused therapy and shame. In R. L. Dearing & J. P. Tangney (Eds.), *Shame in the therapy hour* (pp. 69-90). American Psychological Association.

Harter, M. J. (2005). *Hearts on fire: Praying with Jesuits*. Loyola Press.

Herman, J. L. (2011). Posttraumatic stress disorder as a shame disorder. In R. L. Dearing, & J. P. Tangney (Eds.), *Shame in the therapy hour* (pp. 261-75). American Psychological Association.

Hoffart, A., Øktedalen, T., & Langkaas, T. F. (2015). Self-compassion influences PTSD symptoms in the process of change in trauma-focused cognitive-behavioral therapies: A study of within-person processes. *Frontiers in Psychology*, *6*, 1273. https://doi.org/10.3389/fpsyg.2015.01273

Karatzias, T., Hyland, P., Bradley, A., Cloitre, M., Roberts, N. P., Bisson, J. I., & Shevlin, M. (2019). Risk factors and comorbidity of ICD-11 PTSD and complex PTSD: Findings from a trauma-exposed population based sample of adults in the United Kingdom. *Depression and Anxiety, 36*(9), 887-94. https://doi.org/10.1002/da.22934

Kearney, D. J., Malte, C. A., McManus, C., Martinez, M. E., Felleman, B., & Simpson, T. L. (2013). Loving-kindness meditation for posttraumatic stress disorder: A pilot study. *Journal of Traumatic Stress, 26*, 426-34. https://doi.org/10.1002/jts.21832

La Bash, H., & Papa, A. (2014). Shame and PTSD symptoms. *Psychological Trauma: Theory, Research, Practice, and Policy*, *6*, 159-66. https://doi.org/10.1037/a0032637

Lear, M. K., Lee, E. B., Smith, S. M., & Luoma, J. B. (2022). A systematic review of self-report measures of generalized shame. *Journal of Clinical Psychology*, *78*(7), 1288-1330. https://doi.org/10.1002/jclp.23311

Linehan, M. M. (2015). *DBT skills training manual* (2nd ed.). Guilford.

Lorenzo-Dus, N., & Kinzel, A. (2019). "So is your mom as cute as you?": Examining patterns of language use in online sexual grooming of children. *Journal of Corpora and Discourse Studies*, *2*, 15-39. https://doi.org/10.18573/jcads.31

Luoma, J. B., & Platt, M. G. (2015). Shame, self-criticism, self-stigma, and compassion in Acceptance and Commitment Therapy. *Current Opinion in Psychology*, *2*, 97-101. https://doi.org/10.1016/j.copsyc.2014.12.016

MacGinley, M., Breckenridge, J., & Mowll, J. (2019). A scoping review of adult survivors' experiences of shame following sexual abuse in childhood. *Health & Social Care in the Community*, *27*, 1135-46. https://doi.org/10.1111/hsc.12771

MacIntosh, H., Fletcher, K., & Collin-Vézina, D. (2016). "I was like damaged, used goods": Thematic analysis of disclosures of childhood sexual abuse to romantic partners. *Marriage & Family Review*, *52*, 598-611. https://doi.org/10.1080/01494929.2016.1157117

Mackesy, C. (2019). *The boy, the mole, the fox and the horse*. HarperCollins.

Mayer, C. H., & Vanderheiden, E. (Eds.). (2019). *The bright side of shame: Transforming and growing through practical applications in cultural contexts*. Springer.

McKoy, M. (n.d.). Resting in the Lord's gaze. *Ignatian Spirituality.* www.ignatianspirituality.com/resting-lords-gaze

Øktedalen, T., Hagtvet, K. A., Hoffart, A., Langkaas, T. F., & Smucker, M. (2014). The Trauma Related Shame Inventory: Measuring trauma-related shame among patients with PTSD. *Journal of Psychopathology and Behavioral Assessment, 36,* 600-615. https://doi.org/10.1007/s10862-014-9422-5

Pettersen, K. T. (2013). A study of shame from sexual abuse within the context of a Norwegian incest center. *Journal of Child Sexual Abuse*, *22*, 677-94. https://doi.org/10.1080/10538712.2013.811139

Platt, M. G., & Freyd, J. J. (2015). Betray my trust, shame on me: Shame, dissociation, fear, and betrayal trauma. *Psychological Trauma: Theory, Research, Practice, and Policy*, *7*(4), 398. https://doi.org/10.1037/tra0000022

Rizvi, S. L. (2010). Development and preliminary validation of a new measure to assess shame: The Shame Inventory. *Journal of Psychopathology and Behavioral Assessment*, *32*, 438-47. https://doi.org/10.1007/s10862-009-9172-y

Salter, A. C. (1995). *Transforming trauma: A guide to understanding and treating adult survivors of child sexual abuse*. Sage Publications.

Sanderson, C. (2006). *Counselling adult survivors of child sexual abuse* (3rd ed.). Jessica Kingsley Publishers.

Sant, G. V. (Dir.). (1997). *Good will hunting* [Film]. A Band Apart and Lawrence Bender Productions.

Saraiya, T., & Lopez-Castro, T. (2016). Ashamed and afraid: A scoping review of the role of shame in post-traumatic stress disorder (PTSD). *Journal of Clinical Medicine*, *5*(11), 94. https://doi.org/10.3390/jcm5110094

Tangney, J. P., & Dearing, R. L. (2011). Working with shame in the therapy hour: Summary and integration. In R. L. Dearing, & J. P. Tangney (Eds.), *Shame in the therapy hour* (pp. 375-404). American Psychological Association.

Taylor, T. F. (2015). The influence of shame on posttrauma disorders: Have we failed to see the obvious? *European Journal of Psychotraumatology*, *6*(1). https://doi.org/10.3402/ejpt.v6.28847

Teyber, E., & Teyber, F. (2017). *Interpersonal process in therapy: An integrative model* (6th ed). Cengage Learning.

Thompson, C. (2015). *The soul of shame: Retelling the stories we believe about ourselves.* InterVarsity Press.

Wilson, J. P., Droždek, B., & Turkovic, S. (2006). Posttraumatic shame and guilt. *Trauma, Violence, & Abuse*, *7*, 122-41. https://doi.org/10.1177/1524838005285914

World Health Organization (2019). *International statistical classification of diseases and related health problems* (11th ed.). https://icd.who.int/

Zeller, M., Yuval, K., Nitzan-Assayag, Y., & Bernstein, A. (2015). Self-compassion in recovery following potentially traumatic stress: Longitudinal study of at-risk youth. *Journal of Abnormal Child Psychology*, *43*, 645-53. https://doi.org/10.1007/s10802-014-9937-y

4

TRUST AND TREACHERY

Et tu, Brute?

WILLIAM SHAKESPEARE, *JULIUS CAESAR*

This isn't the neighborhood bully mocking me—I could take that.
This isn't a foreign devil spitting invective—I could tune that out.
It's you! *We grew up together!* You! *My best friend!*
Those long hours of leisure as we walked
arm in arm, God a third party to our conversation.

PSALM 55:12-14, *THE MESSAGE*

Paper, crayons, vanilla wafers and juice, toys, toys, and more toys, brightly colored flannel-graph Adam and Eve figures hiding behind the bushes . . . these are essential ingredients in a children's ministry room.

Banners hanging on the walls say things like, "Scars of love: He bore your pain," or "Jesus loves the little children." Stained-glass windows show Jesus on the cross, Jesus in the garden, Jesus with his disciples, and Jesus' nativity. A towering cross is positioned center stage. A man wearing a robe, holding his Bible, speaks with passionate and persuasive words. There is an aroma of lit candles, musical crescendos, quiet prayers, bread and wine, offering plates. Kneeling. Standing. Sitting. Reciting Scripture. Hands raised. Talks of revival. Cleansing.

These religious items and experiences may convey pleasing and comforting thoughts for many individuals. But for others, these haunting sights, sounds, and smells are indelibly wedded to being molested. The repetition of the music can later provide a parroting soundtrack to memories that won't be hushed. A sexual abuse perpetrator shows up as the conductor of soul-crushing cadences to come. Churches are not the sole vicinity of serial predations, however. Sadly, there are countless women, men, girls, and boys who have been bullied, abused, and betrayed by pastors, police officers, politicians, Boy Scout leaders, football coaches, Olympic gymnastics physicians, teachers, military commanders, film directors, celebrities. Over the past few years, the news has been chock-full of stories chronicling how perpetrators of sexual violence frequently prey on less-powerful people they know *and* their families. Like an unannounced tornado that touches down before unsuspecting residents have a chance to take cover, betrayal blindsides survivors in its wake.

Because betrayal exists where trust has been established, perpetrators use trust as their foot-in-the-door maneuver, which often leaves victims enraged at themselves for "opening the door." According to the National Children's Alliance (2015), 90% of children who have been abused knew their perpetrator. In 39% of the cases, children were abused by a parent or caregiver, 51% were abused by family members, and 10% by individuals they knew with no familial ties. Similarly, the United States' largest anti-sexual violence organization, Rape, Abuse and Incest National Network (RAINN, 2017), revealed that 93% of minor-aged survivors of sexual abuse/assault knew their perpetrators. Among adults who experienced sexual assault, 80% knew their perpetrator. Thus, when it comes to sexual violence, betrayal is more the norm than the exception.

In this chapter, we discuss how trust is trampled underfoot in the aftermath of sexual abuse. Various studies highlight how high-betrayal traumas exacerbate suffering and prolong posttraumatic stress (Gobin & Freyd, 2014; Wolf & Pruitt, 2019). We begin with an understanding of the role of grooming associated with sexual abuse, and we conclude this chapter with mental health and theological insights regarding the remedy for betrayal with recommendations regarding client education and specific treatment interventions.

GROOMING

Things are not always what they seem.

PLATO, *PHAEDRUS*

All adverse events are harmful, but some forms seem to rupture trust and foster betrayal more extensively than others (Freyd et al., 2005). Sexual violations committed by trusted leaders or caregivers are arguably more likely to result in heightened distress versus harm incurred from exposure to low-betrayal traumas (Edwards et al., 2012). The intimate, bodily, and interpersonal nature of sexual trauma, paired with the high percentage of survivors who are violated by individuals with whom they had trusting relationships, yields sizeable aftereffects (RAINN, 2017). We begin this chapter by examining the construct of grooming to highlight the unique way sexual trauma tortures trust and beckons betrayal.

A central tactic that perpetrators use to access, abuse, and ultimately betray their targeted victims either online or in person is called grooming. Perpetrators carefully orchestrate these grooming tactics to normalize abusive behavior through desensitization, lessen the likelihood victims will tell, and gain the trust of the child/adolescent *and* the surrounding guardians to sexually abuse without detection (Canadian Centre for Child Protection Inc., 2019; Pollack & MacIver, 2015). Not only do grooming maneuvers lure victims in, but Wolf and Pruitt (2019) also found that the degree of coercive grooming behaviors used relates to the extent of harm experienced. Their findings revealed that among three types of perpetrators' grooming behaviors (i.e., verbal coercion grooming, grooming that used drugs/alcohol, and threatening/violent grooming) the victims who endured the most coercive and violent form of grooming (i.e., threatening/violent grooming) also experienced the most severe trauma symptoms.

Individuals who abuse understand the desires of young people. Sexual abuse doesn't "just happen," despite the claims of many who molest. There tends to be a pattern of abuse. Perpetrators frequently prepare their victims and work to establish a relationship and trust. They do this by being helpful, offering a "special relationship," giving gifts or toys, providing pornography/illegal substances, extending tenderness, spending time, and invitations to participate in rough-and-tumble play.

These "gifts" or involvements entice children deeper into the web to acquire access, cultivate compliance, and sustain secrecy (Plummer, 2018). What seems like an act of kindness to many onlookers is miles apart from something good-hearted. These acts pull kids into the perpetrator's malicious magnetic field.

With adolescent survivors, this same "special relationship" takes place, but it is simply a more grown-up version. A perpetrator may seek to treat the adolescent as an adult (which most adolescents hunger after), dole out extra responsibility (e.g., being a coach's or teacher's assistant), expose personal information never designed for a young person (e.g., "I can talk to you so much better than to my wife"), and provide a listening ear to a street-hardened teen in need of a sheltering sanctuary.

These calculated acts of kindness serve to form a relationship with someone less powerful to lure the victim. This carefully stage-managed, premeditated grooming strategy may take weeks or even months to construct. At some point, the perpetrator may include seemingly innocuous tickling, wrestling, and hugging. All are forms of the indispensable ingredient of life: touch.

The trap may also include creating an atmosphere where swearing, telling dirty jokes, and viewing pornography are acceptable yet part of the special relationship that needs to be kept under wraps. This component further serves to normalize a sexual element in the relationship, distance the child from loved ones, and entrap the child in the sense that he is a willing accomplice. Step by step, boundary violations escalate, culminating in sexual violence and an erosion of trust.

In the "Tamar: A Desolate Woman" chapter, we discussed in extensive detail the sexual violence perpetrated against Tamar by her half-brother Amnon. We noted that while specific grooming terminology was not included on the pages of Scripture, grooming existed. Second Samuel 13 chronicles the elaborate ruse designed to set up Princess Tamar for sexual violence. We see a trap carefully positioned (with the aid of Jonadab), the scent of human deception (involving the authority King David), the trigger set (Amon pretending to be ill), and the obedient victim caught (Tamar betrayed):

> Jonadab said to him, "Lie down on your bed and pretend to be ill, and when your father comes to see you, say to him, 'Let my sister Tamar come and give me something to eat and prepare the food in my sight, so that I may see it and eat it from her hand.'" So Amnon lay down and pretended to be ill, and when the king came to see him, Amnon said to the king, "Please let my sister Tamar come and make a couple of cakes in my sight, so that I may eat from her hand."
>
> Then David sent home to Tamar, saying, "Go to your brother Amnon's house and prepare food for him."

> So Tamar went. . . .
> And being stronger than she, he forced her and lay with her. (2 Sam 13:5-8, 14)

Tamar's story reveals the often-braided threads of betrayal: interpersonal, institutional, and divine.

INTERPERSONAL BETRAYAL

To betray, you must first belong.

HAROLD PHILBY

Over the past several decades, researcher Jennifer Freyd has examined the fundamental impact of betrayal stemming from interpersonal violations (Gobin & Freyd, 2014; Schultz et al., 2003). Betrayal trauma theory (Freyd, 1996) shares attachment theory's framework that the caregiver-child relationship has a significant impact on child development and that breaches in these formative relationships can cause significant distress. Building on attachment theory, the betrayal trauma framework suggests that the more significant one's relationship with the perpetrator, the greater the degree of betrayal (Berstein & Freyd, 2014).

There is also ample empirical evidence that betrayal stemming from interpersonal traumas may play a role in the development of trauma symptom effects. For example, high betrayal stemming from abuse perpetrated by trusted or dependent individuals may be associated with increased dissociation, posttraumatic distress, and shame compared with individuals who have experienced low-betrayal traumas (Freyd & Birrell, 2013; Gnaulati, 2019; Platt & Freyd, 2015).

According to betrayal trauma theory (Freyd, 1996), individuals may cope with significant relational ruptures (e.g., child sexual abuse) by blocking awareness of the betrayal, often referred to as "betrayal blindness" (Gobin & Freyd, 2014). This "blindness" allows a child to remain attached to a person critical in their development, someone on whom they rely for their survival. It may also be the key ingredient for future victimization, as the ability to discern trustworthiness in the future is negatively impacted.

Thus, while substantial betrayal frequently prompts survivors to develop high levels of distrust, others struggle with trusting too soon, resulting in an "inaccuracy in trust" (Gobin & Freyd, 2014, p. 505). I (Hannah) think about the women I've worked with who have exited the sex trade. I recall one woman who experienced CSA and who eventually developed significant attachments to men she met on the streets. I was grieved as she told me the story of how she entered prostitution—a man with whom she had fallen in love coerced her into smoking heroin. The high on heroin was unlike anything she had ever experienced, and she was hooked. Only a few days earlier this man had required her to "walk the block" to fund their drug use. She was not allowed to handle the money. He gave her strict directions, which she followed. When he accused her of disobeying, he would make her strip naked and beat her. Eventually, neighbors called the police, and he went to prison for domestic violence. Even years later, as she told me this story, she stated that she had not wanted him to go to prison because "he took care of me." He provided her with drugs and made her feel at times "like a princess." Her cracked rib would beg to differ.

The same woman went on to describe the abhorrent treatment by another man she had been with for years. He would pour boiling hot water on her, beat her, and keep other women around to make her jealous. She acknowledged that, at times, she wanted out, yet she couldn't go because he was taking care of her kids, providing her shelter, and so on. This woman spent literal decades "trusting" individuals despite significant exploitation and violence. This is the mark of betrayal.

For many who have been sexually violated, trusting others becomes characterized by an either-or perspective. Individuals are trusted to excess or not at all (Resick et al., 2017). Some survivors who have experienced significant betrayal come to view individuals as unavailable or undependable and consequently avoid intimacy so that the trapdoor of betrayal will never be unlocked again (Hocking et al., 2016). This aversion to trusting (i.e., never trust again) may also prevent survivors from seeking the social and professional support needed for healing. Alternatively, some survivors develop pervasive fears of abandonment, which can foster attempts to increase intimacy and the maintenance of unhealthy relationships despite destructive dynamics, leading to continued revictimization (i.e., betrayal blindness).

The betrayal of trust due to sexual abuse can also prompt survivors to develop a profound mistrust of their perceptions, reasoning, and feelings. They may question whether the abuse occurred or whether they were simply being overly sensitive, leading to an erosion of personal value and a questioning of their ability to judge character and situations (Resick et al., 2017).

Betrayal for some survivors surfaces in relation to their bodies. During the abuse, they may have experienced the physiological effects of sexual stimulation and/or an orgasm, which can prompt conflicted feelings of arousal and revulsion. Consequently, some may experience a profound disconnect with their bodies, others are at war with their bodies, and some may feel "internally trapped" (Mischke-Reeds, 2018, p. 251).

We do not know what Tamar's relationship with her body was like after being raped, and we are unsure if she was ever revictimized or if she ever enjoyed a trusting relationship after the assault. What we do know is that she was betrayed both by her brother, who violated her, and by the justice system and the institutional authority around her, as her father (the king) failed to respond to the violation that occurred.

INSTITUTIONAL BETRAYAL

No snowflake in an avalanche ever feels responsible.

VOLTAIRE

Betrayal comes in a variety pack of characters. There is the betrayal by the perpetrator, but what can be equally damaging is the betrayal committed by the bystander, the nonoffending parent, or the neighbor who hears the violent blows but does nothing. There is the betrayal of those in the movie industry who for years sought to silence survivors; the betrayal of those who distance themselves from the survivor because of the abuse; the betrayal of people in power who permit perpetrators to continue their violations without consequence; and the apparent betrayal of God who seemingly doesn't care.

Father James Porter's victims were legion. He began his unrestrained bout of molesting children in the 1960s, on the heels of best wishes and tassels turned at his seminary graduation. But soon after his arrival at his new parish, Porter preyed on little girls and little boys (Fraga, 2013). Eventually, complaints were made by several parishioners that resulted in his transfer to another parish. More complaints ensued, and in the wake of ongoing allegations, he was referred for medical and psychological treatment multiple times, and more reassignments to additional parishes. His molesting spree continued unabated for decades. Eventually, after further complaints, Porter was advised to petition to leave the priesthood, and his request was granted by the pope in 1974. The former priest was ultimately arrested in September 1992, after far too much time. During a recorded interview, Porter admitted that he abused fifty to one hundred children and was eventually convicted of molesting twenty-eight children during the 1960s. His molesting spree left a trail of victims (Fraga, 2013).

Indeed, the interpersonal betrayal experienced by countless survivors was enormous. However, what is also striking is the protracted and pernicious institutional betrayal that was marked by a pattern of coverups that allowed the abuse to continue:

Molestation allegation.

Relocation to another parish.

Molestation allegation.

Relocation to another parish . . .

Over the past several decades, the violations of thousands of children by Catholic priests have revealed CSA on a seismic, global scale (Terry, 2015). However, abuse is not exclusive to any religious denomination. Since the Catholic Church is more centralized and many Protestant congregations are independent, the trail of breadcrumbs leading to abuse has been easier to bury in Protestant circles until more recently (Rashid & Barron, 2019). A series of investigative articles, high-profile lawsuits, and the #MeToo and #ChurchToo movements have revealed serial predation, coverups, and the blaming of victims in Protestant churches as well (Demuth, 2019).

One of the most devastating details of abuse narratives involving people in places of power is the added betrayal of institutions that failed to protect the victims. While the stories of high betrayal by individual perpetrators are horrific, institutions have the power to bring further harm to survivors, effectively bringing insult to injury (Smith & Freyd, 2013). For example, substantial institutional betrayal can occur when institutions establish environments that set the stage for sexual assaults to occur, then fail to respond supportively when assaults do occur (Smith & Freyd, 2013, p. 119), and blame the victims when the abuse is uncovered. Because there is often an additional systemic layer of betrayal, it is important for therapists to address this double betrayal by both the perpetrator *and* the surrounding systems.

An example of this double betrayal also occurs with adult sexual assault. For instance, in the US military, certain environmental variables enhance the likelihood of abuses of power and exploitation of minority groups. According to a 2018 Department of Defense Sexual Assault report, sexual assaults increased 38% between 2016–2018. Despite this sizeable increase, it is estimated that less than half of assaults are ever reported, and data suggests the main barrier to reporting sexual assault is the fear of reprisal or institutional betrayal (Kintzle et al., 2015). Among those females who did report sexual assault between 2016–2018, the overwhelming majority were junior enlisted members with low rank, experience, and authority. As an active-duty military psychologist, I (Adam) sat with numerous female service members who experienced military sexual assault, and in 100 percent of my clinical cases, alcohol was utilized to impair and victimize my clients.

Thus, while processing interpersonal betrayal is important in therapy, therapists must also be mindful of broadening their gaze beyond the individual perpetrator. This shift from the perpetrator's behaviors to systemic corruption and those in power who enable abuse is not intended to absolve responsibility for the perpetrator's choices. Simply put, attention to institutional betrayal provides increased awareness that one bad apple corrupts the batch *and* the barrel itself is tainted.

DIVINE BETRAYAL

Jesus cried with a loud voice . . .
"My God, my God, why have you forsaken me?"

MATTHEW 27:46

While a close relationship with God can serve as a safe refuge during abuse, perceptions of divine betrayal can alternatively rupture a relationship with God (Leo et al., 2019). From an attachment perspective, just as parents are supposed to protect their children, survivors may have difficulty reconciling the idea of trusting God with the fact that he did not prevent the abuse (Van Deusen & Courtois, 2015). Thus, for many, the question "Why didn't you stop the abuse, God?" stands like a towering billboard on a desert highway, unable to be ignored. Also, some survivors may transfer their perceptions of and feelings toward their perpetrator onto God. One survivor wrote, "If Heavenly 'Father' is anything like my earthly father, I don't even want to meet him" (Pritt, 1998, p. 137). Despite God being the sole true trustworthy relationship, abuse can prompt survivors to perceive God as nonresponsive, inattentive, and uncaring, which is related to negative religious coping and negative mental health adjustment (Kirkpatrick & Shaver, 1992; Parenteau et al., 2019).

Pastor and teacher A. W. Tozer (2021) once said, "What comes into our minds when we think about God is the most important thing about us." If Tozer's statement is true, exploring the impact of abuse on one's view of God is essential. When I (Hannah) was in a survivors' group, the counselor passed around a sheet of paper that listed (front and back) all the different names/titles of God and asked us to respond to the question, "How would you describe, from this list, who God was at the time of your abuse?"

It felt like a trick question.

You see, the list had only positive biblical names. Nowhere on this list were names like "the God Who Abandons," "the God Who Is Not There," or "the Passive God." And the sad reality is that some survivors struggle to have a positive image of God, especially when their abuser claimed to be a representative of him.

When sexual abuse has an added overlay of spiritual abuse, as in the story of Renee Altson, the healing journey is often lengthy, and the seeds of confusion, doubt, and betrayal are buried deep. Her abuse story begins with this chilling fact: "My father raped me while reciting the Lord's Prayer . . . my father molested me while singing Christian hymns" (Altson, 2004, p. 14). Consequently, Renee struggled with frequent references to God as "Father":

> My father sometimes forced my eyes open, made me look at him as he raped me. I live with the visions of his face still. Sometimes from the depths of the middle of the night I wake up screaming. Sometimes I pray, and my father's face is the face of God I see in my mind. God has my father's hands. . . . I feel an ongoing fury at the comparison of God with father. I swallow tears every time, every single time, someone prays to our "heavenly Father," "Father in heaven," or any variation thereof. . . . How can you dare to compare yourself to a father, God? Who are you to think that I can ever trust you with that perception? Who are you to give me that image that went so badly? Why did you insist on a relationship that was so wrong? (Altson, 2004, pp. 52-53, 65-66)

The Bible uses a variety of metaphors to describe our relationship with God, which is so wise of him because here on earth, many experience a myriad of human relationships in evil ways. Thus, if a survivor is having a difficult time relating to God as a father because her earthly example was neglectful, absent, emotionally distant, addicted, demeaning, or sexually abusive, there are many other pictures God has given us of himself—for example, king, shepherd, mother hen. Each of these God images may be troublesome, difficult to relate to, and fear-provoking. But he is in no rush. An imposter has lied, cheated, and violated. He realizes that identity theft takes time to resolve, and he will wait. He lingers with anticipation that his kids will someday realize that he is not at all like their abuser. In the meantime, he longs for the day his kids might realize that he adores, esteems, values, and cradles them. He always did and always will have their best interests in mind, even when experiences may suggest a different reality.

FROM DISCONNECTION TO RECONNECTION

And the day came when the risk to remain tight in a bud
was more painful than the risk it took to blossom.

ANAÏS NIN

Due to the high betrayal associated with the interpersonal nature of child sexual abuse, attention to the value of a close therapeutic relationship is particularly important. Wampold (2015) explains that an indispensable aspect of effective therapy involves a focus on common factors and that establishing rapport between therapists and clients is one of the most essential "common factors." From an attachment perspective, Ducharme (2017) explains that helping survivors form and sustain satisfying relationships in the therapeutic context provides the opportunity for relationship skill building to be explored and repaired.

Still, for many survivors, relationships have meant trickery, violation, and *danger*. Thus, the journey to bonding, connection, and trust in therapy is often arduous. Yet, effective trauma processing occurs in the therapeutic context of trust and connection (Briere, 2019; Hocking et al., 2016). As Gomez and colleagues (2016, p. 173) explain, "If authentic connection and the reparation of disconnections through mutual empathy are the source of healing and growth, and chronic disconnections are the primary source of suffering, then every moment in therapy becomes an important moment of connection."

Therapeutic relationships that emphasize mutuality and authentic connection can inspire survivors to develop trustworthy and supportive relationships outside of therapy and become individuals who are increasingly trustworthy and supportive themselves. Over time, survivors can learn to avoid or disentangle from relationships that are unhealthy and toxic (Aten et al., 2015). Given that trust falls on a spectrum and is multifaceted, trust is developed slowly, taking one step at a time, and titrating trust levels depending on the relationship (Resick et al., 2017). Thus, it can be helpful for therapists to discuss varying types of trust so that survivors can avoid free-falls into trust on one end of the continuum and step out from being cocooned away from relationships at the other end of the spectrum.

When it comes to healing stuck points related to trust, while evidence-based practices are essential, it is also the case that a singular focus on symptom reduction and manualized treatments without being attuned to the relational impact of interventions on clients can increase the isolation, disconnection, and betrayal that survivors experience (Birrell & Freyd, 2006). Therapists who rigidly wed themselves to protocols and impose techniques on survivors fail to be client-centered and instead mirror unhealthy power dynamics and objectify clients versus creating safe environments (Gomez et al., 2016).

I (Hannah) have worked with hundreds of survivors of sex trafficking, and they have taught me that trust begins to be built from the moment they see my face. These are women who have been scanning the faces of men (buyers) for decades, trying to discern if they are safe and trustworthy. And they made these decisions in a split second. If I am authentic and compassionate in my face, they are more likely to open up a little. If they risk sharing, and my face communicates that I am present and listening and "in it" with them, they often will open up a little bit more. It has been one of the most wonderful privileges of my life to be trusted with the stories of survivors. It's been an honor to earn that trust, one facial expression at a time.

RECONNECTION TO GOD

I searched for my soul; but my soul I could not see. I searched for my God, but he eluded me. I searched for my brother and I found all three.

MARTIN LUTHER KING JR.

When a sheep does not merely wander into the woods on its own but is essentially maimed and kicked out of the flock, it becomes difficult to trust other sheep, and it can be even more difficult to trust a shepherd. Thus, when the concept of a loving and just God has been obstructed through abuse, explicit forms of spiritual interventions may be initially contraindicated (Aten et al., 2015). Alternatively, some survivors may seek a relationship with God in order to develop an adult attachment substitute, a secure base, and as a way to make meaning of the abuse (Gall et al., 2007). Some may pose questions such as "Why did God allow this to happen?" and "Did it matter to God that I was abused?" Others may experience conflicted feelings of betrayal by God, while simultaneously longing for him. It is important that therapists foster environments where clients have the space to explore such God queries and ambivalent feelings (Brown, 2008). In contrast, due to extensive betrayal in human relationships, some survivors may come to believe that God is *all* they need, leaving little room for personal reflection and relationships with others (Van Deusen & Courtois, 2015). As mentioned, since avoidance is one of the hallmarks of posttraumatic stress, therapists who provide a secure base can help survivors explore an alternative God image and try out new ways of responding to God.

Since the Old Testament is replete with authentic explorations of thoughts and feelings with God, the psalms of lament may provide helpful illustrations concerning ways to process distressing feelings toward God (Lewis Hall, 2016) and ways to give voice to suffering (Wolterstorff, 2001). Snow, McMinn, Bufford, and Brendlinger (2011) explain that some psalms commence with cries of dissatisfaction yet ultimately culminate with expressions of praise, while other psalms alternate from discouragement to hope back to cries of despair. Thus, when complaint is encouraged to be part of an authentic discourse in a relationship with God, it can allow individuals to address spiritual ruptures as well as explore and work through their spectrum of thoughts and feelings (Snow et al., 2011).

God's response to his sheep is one full of compassion. God steps into our fields and seeks out all of us who are scattered, as he did in Renee Altson's life, finding her in her most lost place.

> I chose to believe that I was better off alone, protected from the ninety-nine, isolated and untouchable. I chose to sit in the wilderness, believing it was my home, struggling to make it comfortable, trying to convince myself that I belonged there. And I did belong there. I belonged in my desperate aloneness. I belonged in my lack of belonging. My hurt was raw, the damage

> done to me was real and tangible; a trail of blood showed the woundedness was not just in my imagination. . . .
>
> I heard the shepherd coming a long way off. He was whistling. "Hey," he said to me. "I have missed you. I am so glad I have found you." He extended a hand to wipe my tear-stained, dusty cheeks. "Come back with me," he said. "Come back to the others." I shook my head and pulled away. "No," I said. He looked surprised, but it did not change the immense compassion on his face. "No," I said again. "I can't go back. I don't want to. I don't trust the other ninety-nine. I don't want to be hurt again." The shepherd sat down on the ground next to me. "Okay," he said quietly, "I'll just stay here with you then." (Altson, 2004, pp. 127, 145)

The Good Shepherd promises he will find us, rescue us, and stay with us as long as it takes. God himself highlights these promises through his prophet in Ezekiel 34:10-16:

I will rescue my flock (v. 10).
I myself will search for my sheep (v. 11).
I will bring them out and gather them (v. 13).
I will bring them into their own land (v. 13).
I will tend them (v. 14).
They will lie down (v. 14).
I will bind up the injured (v. 16).
I will strengthen the weak (v. 16).

May we as Christian therapists divinely deployed commit to ethical and effective practice grounded in awareness of contemporary research and persistent reliance on the Good Shepherd, and may our clinical hospitality echo the third-century prayer of Saint Augustine:

> God of our life, there are days when the burdens we carry chafe our shoulders and weigh us down; when the skies are gray and threatening; when our lives have no music in them, and our souls have lost courage. On such days, flood the path with light, we beseech Thee; turn our eyes to where the skies are full of promise; tune our hearts to brave music; give us the sense of comradeship with heroes and saints of every age; and so quicken our spirits that we may be able to encourage the souls of all who journey with us on the road of life, to Thy honor and glory, we pray. Amen.

COUNSELING CONSIDERATIONS

- **Assessment.** The Adult Attachment Interview (AAI) can help provide the opportunity to discuss the extent and ways traumatic losses/ betrayals have been experienced (Bakermans-Kranenburg & Van IJzendoorn, 1993; Steele et al., 2009).
- **Psychoeducation.** Survivors of sexual abuse can benefit from receiving information about grooming, betrayal trauma theory, and the continuum of relationships that are marked by high levels of distrust to betrayal blindness.
- **Process comments.** Based on Teyber and Teyber's (2017) interpersonal process approach, clients re-create relational themes within the therapeutic relationship that mirror problematic patterns (e.g., high distrust, betrayal blindness). In a curious and compassionate way, therapists can use a here-and-now, present-focused intervention such as exploring what is happening currently in the therapeutic relationship to invite clients to explore and rework their attachment styles.
- **Dialectical Behavior Theory (DBT) and detaching.** Learning how to identify, tolerate, and express emotions through affect regulation and distress tolerance interventions can be considered for survivors desiring to detach from unhealthy relationships despite destructive dynamics (e.g., betrayal blindness) (Grefe et al., 2020). See also the appendix.
- **Cognitive Processing Therapy (CPT) and healthy trust.** Session nine in Resick, Monson, and Chard's (2017) CPT comprehensive treatment manual is specifically devoted to ruptures in trust following trauma. This session may be helpful in engaging in Socratic dialogue with clients concerning how and whom to trust. It includes relatable examples, worksheets, metaphors for illuminating the complexity of trust following trauma, and instructions for treatment.
- **Prolonged Exposure (PE) and growth-fostering relationships.** Therapists can encourage clients to develop growth-fostering relationships with individuals outside of the therapeutic relationships. (i.e., social support). Using in-vivo exposure based on the PE approach, the therapist and the client identify ways in which the client can revive aspects of his or her life to include social engagement (Foa, 2011).

- **EMDR and positive beliefs.** Francine Shapiro's (2014) eight phases of treatment involve inviting clients to identify negative beliefs related to the trauma (e.g., I cannot trust myself, I cannot trust others). During the fifth phase, installation, an EMDR therapist can work with a client to strengthen positive beliefs (e.g., I can choose to trust) with bilateral stimulation.
- **Somatic interventions.** As betrayal ruptures affect the mind, soul, *and* body, therapists have the opportunity to use somatic resources (e.g., body scan, diaphragmatic breathing) to help clients recognize and tolerate strong emotions and physical sensations related to abuse (Shilson, 2019). With this approach, therapists can model curiosity and interest in body sensations by introducing somatic resources as an experiment (e.g., "Notice what happens when you . . ." or "How do you know that you are feeling scared? What in your body tells you that you feel scared?")
- **Betraying others.** As we help survivors sift through the rubble of being betrayed at multiple levels, it is equally important, at wise junctures, to invite clients (and ourselves) to consider ways they have betrayed the trust of others so they can be forgiven and free.

CHILDREN'S CORNER

- *Hope Rising* (Meeder, 2003). A ranch where mistreated horses and mistreated children meet is the place where the impossible can occur. This book is brimming with chapters on growing the tiny seeds of trust after so much hurt has happened, a trust that only God can fully understand. I (Tammy) particularly love the chapter "Angels in Horsehairs" and read it to my graduate students.

REFERENCES

Altson, R. (2004). *Stumbling toward faith*. Zondervan.

Aten, J. D., Courtois, C. A., & Walker, D. F. (2015). *Spiritually oriented psychotherapy for trauma*. American Psychological Association.

Bakermans-Kranenburg, M. J., & Van IJzendoorn, M. H. (1993). A psychometric study of the Adult Attachment Interview: Reliability and discriminant validity. *Developmental Psychology*, 29(5), 870-79. https://doi.org/10.1037/0012-1649.29.5.870

Bernstein, R. E., & Freyd, J. J. (2014). Trauma at home: How betrayal trauma and attachment theories understand the human response to abuse by an attachment figure. *Attachment: New Directions in Psychotherapy and Relational Psychoanalysis, 8*, 18-41. https://doi.org/10.1002/jclp.22616

Birrell, P. J., & Freyd, J. J. (2006). Betrayal trauma: Relational models of harm and healing. *Journal of Trauma Practice, 5*, 49-63. https://doi.org/10.1300/J189v05n01_04

Briere, J. (2019). *Treating risky and compulsive behavior in trauma survivors*. Guilford.

Brown, L. S. (2008). *Cultural competence in trauma therapy: Beyond the flashback*. American Psychological Association.

Canadian Centre for Child Protection Inc. (2019). The prevalence of sexual abuse by K-12 school personnel in Canada, 1997–2017. *Journal of Child Sexual Abuse, 28*, 46-66. https://doi.org/10.1080/10538712.2018.1477218

Demuth, M. (2019). *We Too: How the church can respond redemptively to the sexual abuse crisis*. Harvest House Publishers.

Ducharme, E. L. (2017). Best practices in working with complex trauma and dissociative identity disorder. *Practice Innovations, 2*, 150-61. https://doi.org/10.1037/pri0000050

Edwards, V. J., Freyd, J. J., Dube, S. R., Anda, R. F., & Felitti, V. J. (2012). Health outcomes by closeness of sexual abuse perpetrator: A test of betrayal trauma theory. *Journal of Aggression, Maltreatment & Trauma, 21*, 133-48. https://doi.org/10.1080/10926771.2012.648100

Foa, E. B. (2011). Prolonged exposure therapy: Past, present, and future. *Depression and Anxiety, 28*, 1043-47. https://doi.org/10.1002/da.20907

Fraga, (2013, June). Fall River predator-priest Father James Porter: A timeline. BishopAccountability.org. www.bishop-accountability.org/news2013/05_06/2013_06_25_Fraga_FallRiver.htm

Freyd, J. J. (1996). *Betrayal trauma: The logic of forgetting childhood abuse*. Harvard University Press.

Freyd, J., & Birrell, P. (2013). *Blind to betrayal: Why we fool ourselves we aren't being fooled*. Turner.

Freyd, J. J., Klest, B., & Allard, C. B. (2005). Betrayal trauma: Relationship to physical health, psychological distress, and a written disclosure intervention. *Journal of Trauma & Dissociation, 6*, 83-104. https://doi.org/10.1300/J229v06n03_04

Gall, T. L., Basque, V., Damasceno-Scott, M., & Vardy, G. (2007). Spirituality and the current adjustment of adult survivors of childhood sexual abuse. *Journal for the Scientific Study of Religion, 46*(1), 101-17. https://doi.org/10.1111/j.1468-5906.2007.00343.x

Gnaulati, E. (2019). Potential ethical pitfalls and dilemmas in the promotion and use of American Psychological Association–recommended treatments for posttraumatic stress disorder. *Psychotherapy, 56*, 374-82. https://doi.org/10.1037/pst0000235

Gobin, R. L., & Freyd, J. J. (2014). The impact of betrayal trauma on the tendency to trust. *Psychological Trauma: Theory, Research, Practice, and Policy, 6*, 505-11. https://doi.org/10.1037/a0032452

Gómez, J. M., Lewis, J. K., Noll, L. K., Smidt, A. M., & Birrell, P. J. (2016). Shifting the focus: Nonpathologizing approaches to healing from betrayal trauma through an emphasis on relational care. *Journal of Trauma & Dissociation, 17*, 165-85. https://doi.org/10.1080/15299732.2016.1103104

Grefe, C. N., Brown, E. J., Lang, C., & Sharma-Patel, K. (2020). Implementation of a trauma-specific, evidence-informed treatment for adolescents: Two cases highlighting how to and how not to integrate. *Cognitive and Behavioral Practice, 27*(2), 149-68. https://doi.org/10.1016/j.cbpra.2019.07.009

Hocking, E. C., Simons, R. M., & Surette, R. J. (2016). Attachment style as a mediator between childhood maltreatment and the experience of betrayal trauma as an adult. *Child Abuse & Neglect, 52*, 94-101. https://doi.org/10.1016/j.chiabu.2016.01.001

Kintzle, S., Schuyler, A. C., Ray-Letourneau, D., Ozuna, S. M., Munch, C., Xintarianos, E., . . . Castro, C. A. (2015). Sexual trauma in the military: Exploring PTSD and mental health care utilization in female veterans. *Psychological Services, 12*, 394-401. https://doi.org/10.1037/ser0000054

Kirkpatrick, L. A., & Shaver, P. R. (1992). An attachment-theoretical approach to romantic love and religious belief. *Personality and Social Psychology Bulletin,18*, 266-75. https://doi.org/10.1177/0146167292183002

Leo, D., Izadikhah, Z., Fein, E. C., & Forooshani, S. A. (2019). The effect of trauma on religious beliefs: A structured literature review and meta-analysis. *Trauma, Violence, & Abuse, 22*(1), 161-75. https://doi.org/10.1177/1524838019834076

Lewis Hall, M. E. (2016). Suffering in God's presence: The role of lament in transformation. *Journal of Spiritual Formation and Soul Care*, 9(2), 219-32. https://doi.org/10.1177/193979091600900207

Meeder, K. (2009). *Hope rising: Stories from the ranch of rescued dreams*. Random House.

Mischke-Reeds, M. (2018). *Somatic psychotherapy toolbox: 125 worksheets and exercises to treat trauma and stress.* PESI.

National Children's Alliance. (2016). *2015 Children's Advocacy Center (CAC) Statistics.* www.nationalchildrensalliance.org/2015-cac-statistics

Parenteau, S. C., Hurd, K., Wu, H., & Feck, C. (2019). Attachment to God and psychological adjustment: God's responses and our coping strategies. *Journal of Religion and Health, 58*, 1286-1306. https://doi.org/10.1007/s10943-019-00765-2

Platt, M. G., & Freyd, J. J. (2015). Betray my trust, shame on me: Shame, dissociation, fear, and betrayal trauma. *Psychological Trauma: Theory, Research, Practice and Policy, 7*(4), 398-404. https://doi.org/10.1037/tra0000022

Plummer, M. (2018). Lived experiences of grooming among Australian male survivors of child sexual abuse. *Journal of Interpersonal Violence, 33*(1), 37-63. https://doi.org/10.1177/0886260517732539

Pollack, D., & MacIver, A. (2015). Understanding sexual grooming in child abuse cases. *Child Law Practice, 34*, 161-68.

Pritt, A. F. (1998). Spiritual correlates of reported sexual abuse among Mormon women. *Journal for the Scientific Study of Religion, 37*, 273-85.

Rape, Abuse, & Incest National Network (RAINN). (2017). Perpetrators of sexual violence: statistics. www.rainn.org/statistics/perpetrators-sexual-violence

Rashid, F., & Barron, I. (2019). Why the focus of clerical child sexual abuse has largely remained on the Catholic Church amongst other non-Catholic Christian denominations and religions. *Journal of Child Sexual Abuse, 28*, 564-85. https://doi.org/10.1080/10538712.2018.1563261

Resick, P. A., Monson, C. M., & Chard, K. M. (2017). *Cognitive processing therapy for PTSD: A comprehensive manual*. Guilford.

Schultz, T., Passmore, J. L., & Yoder, C. Y. (2003). Emotional closeness with perpetrators and amnesia for child sexual abuse. *Journal of Child Sexual Abuse*, *12*, 67-88. https://doi.org/10.1300/J070v12n01_04

Shapiro, F. (2014). The role of eye movement desensitization and reprocessing (EMDR) therapy in medicine: Addressing the psychological and physical symptoms stemming from adverse life experiences. *The Permanente Journal*, *18*, 71. https://doi.org/10.7812/TPP/13-098

Shilson, K. L. (2019). *Somatic methods for affect regulation: A clinician's guide to healing traumatized youth*. Routledge.

Smith, C. P., & Freyd, J. J. (2013). Dangerous safe havens: Institutional betrayal exacerbates sexual trauma. *Journal of Traumatic Stress*, *26*, 119-24. https://doi.org/10.1002/jts.21778

Snow, K. N., McMinn, M. R., Bufford, R. K., & Brendlinger, I. A. (2011). Resolving anger toward God: Lament as an avenue toward attachment. *Journal of Psychology and Theology*, *39*, 130-42. https://doi.org/10.1177/009164711103900204

Steele, H., Steele, M., & Murphy, A. (2009). Use of the Adult Attachment Interview to measure process and change in psychotherapy. *Psychotherapy Research*, *19*, 633-43. https://doi.org/10.1080/10503300802609698

Terry, K. J. (2015). Child sexual abuse within the Catholic Church: A review of global perspectives. *International Journal of Comparative and Applied Criminal Justice, 39*, 139-54. https://doi.org/10.1080/01924036.2015.1012703

Teyber, E., & Teyber, F. (2017). *Interpersonal process in therapy: An integrative model*. Cengage Learning.

Tozer, A. W. (2023). *The knowledge of the holy*. Good Press.

Van Deusen, S., & Courtois, C. A. (2015). Spirituality, religion, and complex developmental trauma. In. D. F. Walker, C. A. Courtois, & J. D. Aten (Eds.), *Spiritually oriented psychotherapy for trauma* (pp. 29-54). American Psychological Association.

Wampold, B. E. (2015). How important are the common factors in psychotherapy? An update. *World Psychiatry*, *14*, 270-77. https://doi.org/10.1002/wps.20238

Wolf, M. R., & Pruitt, D. K. (2019). Grooming hurts too: The effects of types of perpetrator grooming on trauma symptoms in adult survivors of child sexual abuse. *Journal of Child Sexual Abuse*, *28*, 345-59. https://doi.org/10.1080/10538712.2019.1579292

Wolterstorff, N. (2001). If God is good and sovereign, why lament? *Calvin Theological Journal, 36*, 42-52.

5

ADDICTION

AN ENSLAVING SOLUTION

What is addiction, really? It is a sign, a signal, a symptom of distress. It is a language that tells us about a plight that must be understood.

ALICE MILLER

The difference between passion and addiction is that between a divine spark and a flame that incinerates.

GABOR MATÉ

"My name is Vicki, and I'm an alcoholic and an addict."

"Hey, Vicki."

This refrain is the familiar sound of countless twelve-step meetings across the globe. Vicki's story is also far too common. Vicki grew up in a rural Midwest town and is always good for a townie joke when she begins her story. Her dad was not around, and her stepdad "came into my room and did things that no child should have done to them." She didn't use the term "child sexual abuse," but in a room full of twelve-steppers, she did not have to say those words. People knew.

Vicki talked about the culture in the family—lots of drinking and drugs and a commitment to *never* call the police. Vicki described her first sip of alcohol at age ten. Her "solution," she called it. It was a powerful solution to the problem of her pain. It worked. For a time. Eventually, she added marijuana, cocaine, and synthetic opiates into the mix, and shortly after her eighteenth birthday, she fled to the closest urban city where the drugs were "better and cheaper."

While the increased amount of and escalating intensity of drugs she used continued to provide a solution, her problems also increased dramatically. She became homeless. She was assaulted many times before and after becoming a sex worker. She was trafficked. She began picking up legal charges.

And . . . she lived to talk about it.

MODELS OF ADDICTION

It is impossible to understand addiction without asking what relief the addict finds, or hopes to find, in the drug or the addictive behaviour.

GABOR MATÉ

The word *addiction* is derived from the Latin roots for enslavement, depicting the encaged experience of individuals addicted to substances or a panoply of behavioral addictions (e.g., eating, spending, sex, self-harm, and overworking) (Najavits, 2019). A substance use disorder (SUD; a term frequently used interchangeably with *addiction*) is defined as a "treatable mental disorder that affects a person's brain and behavior, leading to their inability to control their use of substances like legal or illegal drugs, alcohol, or medications" (National Institute of Mental Health, 2024). No single factor explains why some individuals use substances or engage in certain behaviors without developing an addiction while others use and engage and develop a dependency. Thus, numerous models of addiction reflect sophisticated comprehension of the interaction between (a) neurobiological factors (e.g., dopamine), (b) environmental and cultural factors (social and cultural systems, trauma exposure), and (c) protective factors (e.g., supportive families/communities, religious coping) that impact an individual's vulnerability (Foote et al., 2014).

Substantive advances in neuroscience have deepened our understanding regarding the impact of SUDs and repeated engagement in certain behaviors and changes in the brain. A well-known neurotransmitter, dopamine, has received ample attention regarding addictive behaviors (Blum et al., 2022; Toates, 2022). While there are other neurotransmitters involved in the brain's pleasure and reward system, one of the notable functions of dopamine is the "want" or "desire" for more of an experience (Giordano, 2022, p. 21). Dopamine is naturally fostered through pleasurable activities such as eating, connecting, and exercising. Substances and repeated engagement in rewarding behaviors can open the floodgates of dopamine in the brain, eliciting elation. Problematically, dopamine derived in artificial ways disrupts the pleasure and reward systems, which can result in tolerance (i.e., more frequent use is required to achieve the same effects). Hence, individuals need more to feel "normal." When this occurs, the brain compensates for the surge of dopamine by decreasing the production of dopamine, resulting in the brain's desensitization to dopamine (Foote et al., 2014). Thus, when individuals stop using an illicit substance, the lack of dopamine incites irritability, a loss of pleasure and interest, and the absence of rewards from naturally occurring events that previously elicited pleasure (e.g., a blue sky, pleasant music, and significant relationships) (Foote et al., 2014; Giordano, 2022).

Moreover, decreased dopamine levels, along with the yearning for dopamine's feel-good experience (i.e., cravings), can prompt individuals to keep using drugs (e.g., heroin) despite the painful consequences and the urge to change (Volkow & Boyle, 2018). Continual engagement in specific behaviors (e.g., gambling, gaming, sexual activity) can also "overstimulate neurotransmitter release and lead to changes in the brain" (Giordano, 2022, p. 19). The encouraging news is that the dopamine system in the body can recover, leading to pathways of possibility when it ceases to be flooded. However, this process takes time. Consequently, during withdrawal, individuals often feel much worse before they feel better, as their bodies bellow that something is profoundly missing, which can propel individuals to relapse. Understanding what is happening neurobiologically can help individuals continue their recovery and restore their dopamine balance (Foote et al., 2014).

From an environmental and cultural framework, not all individuals bear the same degree of susceptibility to addictions. The availability of specific SUD and attitudes toward addictions have revealed differences in rates of SUDs and behavioral addictions with certain minority groups.

Increased risk factors, including poverty, discrimination, microaggressions, environments in which products are provided, commercial tactics that promote consumption (e.g., gambling), and protective factors (e.g., availability of spiritually based programs) play a role (Galanter et al., 2023; Johnson et al., 2023).

Another key variable at play in increasing the risk for addictions is trauma. Gabor Maté, one of the world's most revered thinkers on addiction and trauma, asserted that the origin of addictions is not found in our genes; instead, it is a "forlorn attempt to solve the problem of human pain" (Maté, 2020, p. xxiii). An extensive body of research based on the seminal adverse childhood experiences (ACEs) study by Felitti and colleagues (1998) reveals a dose-related relationship (Guarino et al., 2017; LeTendre & Reed, 2017) between the number of ACEs (e.g., parental divorce, physical or sexual abuse, family violence, etc.) and the risk of multiple adult harmful outcomes (e.g., heart disease, diabetes, and obesity) (Felitti et al., 1998), alcohol use (Dube et al., 2002), and illicit drug use (Dube et al., 2003). Early trauma can disrupt the body's stress response system, leading to chronic activation of the amygdala in the brain and continual release of stress hormones. This dysregulated stress response, stemming from trauma, elicits an increased vulnerability for some individuals to attempt to regulate disturbing emotions through substances and addictive behaviors (Giordano, 2022).

From a spiritual lens, addictions may be viewed as a *disordered attachment* to ideas, work, substances, behaviors, power, or people. Christian psychiatrist Gerald May (2007, p. 13) explains that when we become fastened or enslaved to objects or individuals, this "displaces and supplants God's love as the source and object of our deepest true desire." The book of Isaiah speaks of these counterfeit connections using terminology such as "make an alliance" and "rely on" something other than God (Is 30:1; 31:1; 36:6-7). Ultimately, these disordered attachments become our idols. This idea is also found in John Calvin's *Institutes of the Christian Religion.* He states that people's hearts are "a perpetual factory of idols" (Calvin, 1536, as cited in McNeill, 1960, p. 108). Franciscan priest Richard Rohr (2011, p. xxviii) argued that we are all addicts and what the Bible calls sin, medieval Christians called "passions" or "attachments." SUDs are more noticeable addictions; however, the more *acceptable* enslavements are "often hardest to heal because they do not look like addictions" (Rohr, 2011, p. xxi). People can become addicted to people, things, and experiences to feel more of something (e.g., calm, peace) or less of something (e.g., rage, fear, shame). Whatever it is we can't live without—more trophies on the mantle, the bottle of Dewars in the cupboard, endless scrolling through dating apps, late-night cybersex, the Snickers bar hiding in the glove compartment, just one more laser treatment to rid the signs of aging, repeated yesses to work side hustles, his seductive glance from across the room, chasing the next big hit of likes on social media, the incessant pursuit of exceptionalism, or admiring faces from the people staring up in the pulpit—*addictions work for a season.*

Ultimately, survivors run *from* the personal hell they have experienced through CSA or another type of pain. But the real desire beneath all these addictive behaviors is, in fact, heaven. Not having been made for an imperfect home, our hearts grow weary from existing in this world of endless imperfections. Having been made for heaven, we continually grapple with dissatisfaction and groan for a place that is too magnificent for our imaginations to handle.

Multifaceted frameworks for understanding addiction are intricate and nuanced. Moreover, while the relationship between trauma, especially CSA, and SUD and other behavioral addictions has resulted in a burgeoning body of literature, historically when individuals present with both PTSD and SUD clinicians have not addressed them simultaneously (Maté, 2020; McLean et al., 2015; Najavits, 2015). Instead, survivors with addictions have frequently been given the message by clinicians that once abstinence has been achieved, then trauma-focused therapy can begin (i.e., a sequential approach) (Najavits, 2015; Roberts et al., 2022). This perspective makes sense at first glance. Many clinicians have feared that the intensity of processing trauma will worsen the addictions and lead to a relapse. Alternatively, survivors are told that they need to first deal with the trauma before SUD treatment to resolve the reasons they are using.

Unfortunately, many clinicians have not received training in integrative approaches for working with survivors who have addictions, thereby not perceiving SUD and trauma as *intricately related* since many individuals are self-medicating for the trauma and individuals with SUD are more likely to experience or re-experience traumatic events. Without a doubt, journeying with survivors who have experienced extensive trauma and are carrying numerous addictions is complicated, and it takes much training to understand and attend to both. However, the false treatment dichotomy that many of us as clinicians have held frequently leaves survivors trying "to integrate what our field has not" (Najavits, 2015, p. 318).

In this chapter, we focus on a model of addictions that encompasses how neurobiological, cultural, environmental, and protective factors influence how a person engages with SUD and other behavioral addictions, with a specific focus on the connection between CSA and addictions. While there are myriad SUDs and behavioral addictions that survivors carry, we will examine three well-researched addictions that many CSA survivors wrestle with, including (1) SUDs, (2) disordered eating patterns, and (3) nonsuicidal self-injury. These have also been prominent concerns with survivors we have walked alongside in our clinical practices. Integrated therapeutic approaches for both CSA and addictions will follow.

STILL TAKING SHOTS: SUDS

Recovery is . . . about dealing with that hole in the soul.

WILLIAM C. MOYERS

Trauma can trigger a cascade of mental health concerns, including SUDs (Parisi et al., 2022; Tripp et al., 2019). The comorbidity between PTSD and SUD is so prevalent that therapists are wise to do a thorough assessment early in the therapy process. Epidemiological data have suggested that there is nearly a 50 percent likelihood that a trauma survivor with PTSD also meets the criteria for SUD. For example, a United States epidemiological study revealed that greater than 46 percent of trauma survivors who met the diagnostic criteria for PTSD in their lifetime also met the criteria for a SUD (Pietrzak et al., 2011). Najavits (2009) explains that trauma can precede or follow SUD, and both can contribute to the development of each other. Substances are easily "hired" by survivors to accomplish various avoidance or coping roles (Najavits et al., 2020). As previous chapters illuminated, traumatic memories are often associated with intense effects culminating in avoidance. Substances provide a seemingly controllable pathway whereby survivors avoid distress via altered mental status and reduce or eliminate distress.

When world mental health surveys were given in twenty-two countries (N= 65,165 adults), researchers found that the most common traumatic events consistently related to the development of SUDs were sexual (20.3%) and interpersonal violence (26.6%) (Degenhardt et al., 2022). Moreover, they found that sexual and interpersonal violence were associated with the most elevated likelihood of developing PTSD. Their findings underscore that certain types of trauma exposure might increase the risk of adverse outcomes, including SUDs and behavioral addictions.

Substances can be utilized to extinguish unwanted memories, emotions, and bodily sensations, and anesthetize distress as a survivor confronts challenging circumstances that elicit anxiety. In this way, substances are used as a survival/coping strategy as CSA survivors endeavor to engage with life challenges. However, this insufficient salve frequently leads to additional suffering. Paradoxically, substances used to cope with sexual violence increase the vulnerability to more sexual victimization (Braun et al., 2023). SUD is a contaminated cure that calcifies healing and keeps CSA survivors cemented in the self-amplifying misery of avoiding misery.

Interestingly, what begins as a pursuit of the next buzz or rush to stave off sorrows can eventually resemble a relationship with a "lover." Carolyn Knapp (1996, p. 104) described the path of obsession with her lover:

> It's not at all unusual in AA to hear people refer to alcohol as a best friend, and to mean that on the most visceral level: when you're drinking, liquor occupies the role of a lover or constant companion. It sits there on its refrigerator shelves or on the counter or in the cabinet like a real person, as present and reliable as a best friend. At the end, when I started hiding bottles of Scotch around the house, and tucking nips of brandy into my bathrobe pockets, I did so in the manner of a child who's afraid to be without a favorite blanket or a teddy bear. Protect me. Shield me from being alone in my own head.

It might be difficult to imagine how a substance could replace relationships until you understand that many substance users describe their drug of choice in a way that hearkens back to a time when they felt safe in a relationship. Gabor Maté tells the story of a female heroin addict who describes her first hit as a "warm, soft hug" and the story of a man who had been injected with morphine at the age of eleven and then sexually exploited. Looking back, this man describes that first hit as "like a warm, wet blanket . . . a place of safety—the safety that came before pain and danger, before the enormity of being born, pushed and dragged, kicking and screaming, into this world" (Maté, 2020, p. 247). Maté highlights this relational quality with a substance, but concludes, "Addiction is always a poor substitute for love" (Maté, 2020, p. 259).

Using can also hinder a survivor from recognizing that the sexual violations were, in fact, abuse. Because SUD and other behavioral addictions merely *cover* rather than *cure* the angst, the problem mushrooms. It becomes a vicious cycle. The added irony for the survivor entering recovery for SUD is that survivors must come face to face with the pain—that "hole in the soul"—that they are trying to avoid with substances. This was true for Vicki (see above narrative). Vicki had attempted to get sober multiple times, but something always drew her back in. Vicki knew she had a problem, but she had never been given a chance to name it, share it, or process it. Every time she had any period of sobriety, she ended up desperate for her "solution," even when she realized that her solution was killing her.

Vicki and many others have attempted to get sober and relapsed multiple times. Embodying a stages of change perspective (transtheoretical model of change, Prochaska & DiClemente, 1983) that acknowledges change frequently occurs gradually and through a cyclical process can be helpful. In addition, because of the high risk associated with many kinds of illicit substances, a harm reduction approach (Marlatt, 1996) can serve as a stepping stone toward later stages of change and additional treatment while keeping individuals alive. Harm reduction psychotherapy is defined as "psychological interventions that seek to reduce the harm associated with active substance use without having abstinence as the initial goal" (as cited in Tatarsky & Marlatt, 2010, p. 119). The Substance Abuse and Mental Health Services Administration (SAMHSA; 2023) further explains:

> Harm reduction is an approach that emphasizes engaging directly with people who use drugs to prevent overdose and infectious disease transmission, improve the physical, mental, and social wellbeing of those served, and offer low-threshold options for accessing substance use disorder treatment and other health care services.

One of the critical principles worth highlighting from the harm reduction approach is that "substances are used for adaptive reasons" (Tatarsky & Marlatt, 2010, p. 120). This speaks to Vicki's story, and many like it—survivors who found a solution (albeit a toxic one) using drugs or alcohol. Another principle is "starting where the patient is" (Tatarsky & Marlatt, 2010, p. 120). Survivors with persistent SUD are often also dealing with other significant stressors (legal issues, physical health problems, homelessness, etc.), and therapists will need to collaborate with a coordinated and comprehensive range of services in the health and social service space (Beaulieu et al., 2022).

It can be challenging for therapists to watch clients suffer greatly from SUD who are not ready, willing, or capable of making changes. However, in Vicki's case, compassionate front-line professionals using a stages of change and harm reduction approach provide the necessary health care, support, and compassion to help her stay alive long enough for her to consider a different kind of future. Today, Vicki is fourteen years sober—fourteen years of abstinence from drugs and alcohol. We can anticipate the years of abstinence while simultaneously working with those still using drugs and alcohol in a way that nurtures the conditions of change, primarily through hope and connection.

Thus, trauma, and frequently CSA, increases the risk of SUD among survivors. In addition, there is also a connection between CSA and eating disorders (EDs) and the cooccurrence of SUD and EDs (Robinson et al., 2021; Wiss et al., 2022). Let's look.

STUFFED AND FAMISHED: BROKEN FORMS OF EATING

Courage does not always roar. Sometimes courage is the quiet voice at the end of the day saying, "I will try again tomorrow."

MARY ANNE RADMACHER

Recent research has revealed that there is a significant relationship between CSA and EDs (e.g., failed attempts at weight suppression, binge eating, obesity, and other EDs) (Hailes et al., 2019; Malet-Karas et al., 2022; Mitchell et al., 2012; Trickett et al., 2011; Wiss et al., 2022). Brewerton and colleagues (2015) found a relationship between CSA, obesity, and class III obesity. Based on the protective measure theory, following CSA, survivors may come to believe (often unconsciously) that obesity insulates them from unwanted sexual attention and minimizes sexual attractiveness, even though sexual perpetrators do not necessarily choose victims based on perceived norms of attractiveness (Wiss et al., 2022). Sadly, this conclusion may prompt survivors to believe their beauty, attractiveness, or sexuality *caused* the CSA.

While gambling disorder is the only behavioral addiction identified in the *DSM-5-TR*, some point out the overlap between EDs and addiction (Colaianni, 2021). Binge eating can provide a sense of numbness, a way to evade traumatic memories, and decrease anxiety and hyperarousal related to trauma (Robinson et al., 2021). Malet-Karas and colleagues (2022) contend that given the relationship between disordered eating and sexual violence, EDs should be viewed as emotional regulation coping strategies. Growing empirical research related to CSA and EDs also centers on biological embedding, the process whereby early life experiences impact biological processes that affect adult health outcomes (e.g., inflammation, increased hypothalamic-pituitary-adrenal [HPA] axis activity over extended time, resulting in high concentrations of cortisol; insulin resistance) (Wiss et al., 2022).

From an addiction perspective, there are neurobiological similarities between eating disorders and substance use (Colaianni, 2021; Leigh & Morris, 2018; Wise, 2013). For example, individuals can "self-stimulate dopamine release" by eating specific foods (e.g., particularly highly processed foods high in sugar and carbohydrates) (Giordano, 2022, p. 190). Leigh and Morris (2018, p. 38) explain, "food addiction may be understood as a disorder involving a dysregulated stress response where compulsive overeating functions as a coping mechanism." There are distinctions between food addiction and EDs, and the concept of food addiction is not without controversy. As with most mental health concerns, a consensus regarding the connection between CSA, food addiction, and EDs is lacking (Wiss et al., 2021).

One survivor explained her relationship between abuse and food in this way:

> No, I wasn't going to allow anyone to "feel me up" anymore. I didn't want that. But I was also going to dress very carefully, fold my collar just so, and walk with my heel touching first, my knees very rigid, and my posture erect. I was going to run between the two piers on the beach every day and do my series of floor exercises. I could only eat once a day, and only after postponing it (mainly with exercise) as long as I could. In fact, eating was not allowed unless I had completed my exercise rituals and organized certain of my belongings in special ways. I carefully selected and measured portions of the same ("healthy") food day after day, chewing each bite a certain number of times and putting my fork and knife down between bites. I changed my writing style by printing very neatly and extremely small.
>
> I also changed my tempo of speech and I chose when and to whom I spoke. I started withdrawing from people and feelings because I felt that I could maintain my path better without these interferences. I became extremely controlled in all areas of my life, especially those related to eating and exercising. With this new lifestyle, I started losing weight and defying

> puberty. . . . Indeed, these obsessions were my *salvation.* [emphasis added] (As cited in Vanderlinden & Vandereycken, 1996, p. 16)

Her *salvation.* When we think our lovers will save us, that is addiction. This piece of cake will save me from feeling this pain. If I run eight miles, it will save me from taking up too much space. If I purge, it will save me from being noticed, from being ugly. If I starve, I will save myself from my own desires.

High rates of EDs are also challenging for survivors with comorbid SUD. Rapid weight gain is common as survivors recover from SUD (Wiss et al., 2022). However, when survivors carry weight and body image concerns, significant weight gain can trigger ED behaviors and disengagement from SUD recovery (Robinson et al., 2021). Robinson and colleagues (2021) further explain that abstinence from substances can also result in a return of appetite and consuming high-sugar foods. Thus, clinicians need to identify SUD, EDs, and food addiction comorbidly among CSA survivors using a trauma-informed approach. Specifically, clinicians can assess food intake as a means of coping and emotional regulation (Giordano, 2022) (e.g., Yale Food Addiction Scale Version 2.0 [YFAS 2.0]). From an addiction perspective, developing intuitive/attuned eating patterns, and mindfulness-based interventions can be beneficial (Gearhardt et al., 2016). Moreover, given that weight-related concerns fluctuate, continual assessment and tailoring interventions are critical (Robinson et al., 2021).

READING BETWEEN THE SCARS: NONSUICIDAL SELF-INJURY (NSSI)

> *People take drugs to make it [the pain] disappear, and they cut themselves to make it disappear, and they starve themselves to make it disappear . . . and once you have these horrible sensations in your body, you'll do anything to make it go away.*
>
> BESSEL VAN DER KOLK

Nonsuicidal self-injury (NSSI) involves "the direct and deliberate destruction of one's own body tissues without suicidal intent" (Andersson et al., 2013, p. 2). NSSI is distinct from suicide as many who self-injure do not become suicidal; however, burgeoning research indicates that NSSI and suicide planning are related and that high NSSI engagement corresponds with higher suicide planning over time (Muehlenkamp et al., 2022). A meta-analysis examining the relationship between self-harming cognitions and behaviors with suicide attempts reveals that NSSI contributes to the highest risk of future suicide attempts, even more than suicidal ideation and past suicide attempts (Ribeiro et al., 2016). While NSSI is higher among females, a meta-analysis of gender differences in NSSI reveals that males are more likely to engage in burning, self-battery, and banging (Bresin & Schoenleber, 2015). Moreover, CSA (and other forms of child maltreatment) is an established risk factor for NSSI (Ernst et al., 2022; Malet-Karas et al., 2022; Watters & Yalch, 2022).

While not everyone who self-injures is addicted to NSSI (just as not everyone who drinks is addicted to alcohol), impulsive self-injury (e.g., cutting, burning) often involves a preoccupation with the harming behavior and self-harming cravings (Favazza, 2011). There are many reasons NSSI may develop. NSSI, like other addictive behaviors such as SUD and EDs, is frequently used to regulate feelings of distress (Malet-Karas et al., 2022). Here, NSSI attempts to manage the internal secret, burning to be told, heard, and understood. For others, NSSI is like a best friend in the form of a razor or lighter. This companion *gets* the pain and will take all the unwanted internal emotions pent up inside and will bleed or burn it out.

Shame, panic, rage, and grief intensify, and then with the slice of a blade, the rushing river of emotions is washed away. In the same way, NSSI can be an attempt to become unsullied and washed clean (Watters & Yalch, 2022). The sense of dirtiness stemming from CSA frequently engenders a desire to scrub the soul clean, using hair pulling, burning, or other types of self-mutilation as a type of bleach. For others, NSSI is painted with paradoxical brush strokes:

> The act of wounding oneself *embodies*—literally—an implicit connotation of something unbearable, unutterable, that is communicated in this act. . . . One of the most distressing features of abuse is its demand for secrecy and silence; victims who wish and long to be heard are forbidden from speaking by various means. . . . Self-inflicted injuries, while telling an "unspeakable secret," can also be used to deflect from it. Thus self-mutilation can be used to speak and not to speak. (Babiker & Arnold, 1997, p. 1)

Cutting can also be a way of reminding myself that I am still alive. Individuals who engage in NSSI have frequently learned to dissociate and become like strangers to their bodies and emotions (Nester et al., 2022), and cutting is a way of associating, signaling a return to life. Self-injurious behavior can also be a way of activating the pain pathway whereby natural opioids in the brain (e.g., endorphins) are released to soothe physical pain (Giordano, 2022). Thus, self-injurious behavior attempts to trick the body into numbing the deeper emotional pain.

While a salient aim of NSSI is to regulate emotions, ultimately, these broken solutions fail to deal with the hole in the soul. Thus, when working with survivors, therapists are wise to assess for the presence of NSSI (e.g., the Non-Suicidal Self-Injury Disorder Scale [NSSIDS; Victor et al., 2017]; Alexian Brothers Urge to Self-Injure Scale [ABUSI; Washburn et al., 2010]). At the outset, it is important to assess a survivor's desire to give up NSSI. I (Tammy) recall working hard to help a survivor that I was journeying with to relinquish her cutting. In fact, I was working much harder than my client. I came to realize this survivor was not interested in stopping her NSSI, as it was her lifeline. We had other work to do before considering relinquishing her "best friend."

Speaking of "best friends," there is also an increasing awareness of the social contagion effect of NSSI via social media platforms (and, potentially, treatment facilities), whereby self-harm is desensitized and normalized, and a sense of belonging can be fostered with others who self-injure (Moss et al., 2023; Twenge, 2020). Moreover, it is increasingly common for individuals who wrestle with self-injury to post pictures of NSSI wounds and scars (Arendt et al., 2019). Thus, Giordano (2022) recommends that clinicians ask clients about their social media usage regarding viewing and sharing NSSI information. In addition, given that NSSI is a significant risk factor for suicide, clinicians need to regularly assess and monitor suicide risk among survivors who self-injure (Muehlenkamp et al., 2022).

There are many more types of addictive ways of wrestling with CSA. Since many clinicians have not been trained to simultaneously attend to trauma and addictions, we elaborate on several integrative approaches. We begin with general recommendations and then turn to specific integrative approaches.

OVERALL THERAPEUTIC RECOMMENDATIONS

Giving up smoking is the easiest thing in the world. I know because I've done it thousands of times.

MARK TWAIN

One of the leaders in the field of trauma and addictions is Lisa M. Najavits, who was on the faculty of Harvard Medical School for twenty-five years and was a research psychologist at the Veterans Affairs Healthcare System, Boston, for twelve years. A major focus of her research is substance abuse and trauma. Najavits's (2015) words of wisdom for clinicians working with individuals who have experienced trauma and have SUD or behavioral addictions are wise. Thus, we include them here. Thereafter, we will discuss more specific approaches for working with CSA survivors who have addictions:

1. Attend to how PTSD and SUD/behavioral addictions appear in clients. Just as a physician working with a patient with cancer and high blood pressure needs to be aware of both medical concerns, clinicians must also be attuned to both PTSD and addictions. Clinicians need to be trauma-informed and addiction-informed. Moreover, since both PTSD and SUD affect each other, successful therapeutic approaches are "like a seesaw that needs careful balancing to prevent tipping too far to one side" (Najavits, 2015, p. 317).
2. Good clinical work involves accurate assessment. Clients may be wrestling with a myriad of trauma symptoms and SUD/behavioral addictions. Casting a wide net with initial assessment using free, psychometrically reliable/valid screening for PTSD symptoms such as the PCL-5 (Weathers et al., 2013) and SUDs such as the Tobacco, Alcohol, Prescription Medication, and other Substance Use tool (TAPS; McNeely et al., 2016) allows clinicians to assess a baseline and re-evaluate changes throughout treatment as clients may be increasingly willing to discuss addictions over the course of therapy. It is widely understood that clients underreport trauma and substance use. Thus, re-evaluation and returning to trauma and substance use assessments are critical. Giordano (2022) recommends inviting survivors to create an addictions genogram to examine three generations of their family and identify addictions (SUD and behavioral). This can also spark discussions about vulnerabilities to specific addictive behaviors. We also recommend that clinicians consider the potential benefit of assessing areas of well-being (and not only psychopathology). A short and sweet example (only 5 items) is one of the most widely used measures of well-being called the WHO-5 (Topp et al., 2015).

3. Work together with the client collaboratively to explore which therapeutic approaches might work best for that individual. Najavits emphasized that "my way or the highway" and needing to "hit bottom" clinical stances rarely are effective (Najavits 2015, p. 322). The motivational interviewing (MI) literature consistently reveals that clinical hospitality (i.e., compassionate interaction) is most effective for SUD (Frey & Hall, 2021) and trauma aftermath effects versus a confrontational approach.
4. Compassion, compassion, compassion. Traumatized clients wrestling with SUD are often imbued with shame. Family members often feel robbed of relationships and may harbor resentments. Survivors are sensitive to criticism and judgmental demeanors. Thus, warm and nonjudgmental therapists are gold. However, Najavits underscored that a compassionate therapeutic approach does not mean anything goes, making excuses, or enabling clients. Rather clinical hospitality involves warmth and kindness as treatment goals while maintaining boundaries.
5. Survivors with SUD/behavioral addictions are not a homogenous population. Survivors vary regarding the type of symptoms they are experiencing and the type of strengths they have. Like snowflakes, no two survivors are alike.
6. The severity of PTSD and SUD symptoms needs primary attention when determining the course of therapy versus the order of onset. While some therapists maintain that if the trauma occurred first, PTSD treatment needs to come first, Najavits (2015) asserted that the severity of symptoms and consequences of both concerns should determine the treatment plan.
7. Regularly assess substance use every session. Clearly written contracts using lucid goals regarding substance use are important (e.g., no more than one drink daily, measured by a shot glass; no substance use at all).
8. Do not pressure clients with past-focused trauma approaches (e.g., If you stop avoiding CSA, you will get to the root of your problems and not need substances). Rather, providing clients with choices about trauma approaches without pressure empowers clients. Provide options for therapeutic approaches with realistic aspects (e.g., individual and/or

group work; EMDR or CPT). A client's financial situation (i.e., whether an individual has insurance coverage or Medicaid) impacts options.

9. Keep current on both SUD and PTSD treatment by clinicians and researchers who understand the need for integrative approaches.

Twelve-step programs.

Came to believe that a Power greater than ourselves could restore us to sanity.

STEP 2 OF THE TWELVE STEPS

Alcoholics Anonymous (AA) and other twelve-step programs have aided countless people despite the fact that it doesn't "work" for everyone and has received skepticism from some therapists (Kelly et al., 2020). AA is a low-cost (free) mutual aid group available in 181 countries (Alcoholics Anonymous, 2001). Twelve-step groups can also be an excellent adjunct for therapy, particularly when clients lack social support and when family and friends support continued SUDs and behavioral addictions (Breuninger et al., 2020). When the world shut down due to the COVID-19 global pandemic, I (Hannah) remember how devastating it was to our local recovery community when twelve-step meetings were only available online, which provided a barrier for those without internet access. Relapses and overdoses skyrocketed in our community. Vicki, fourteen years sober, still attends meetings. She has a sponsor who has a sponsor, and she has several sponsees. She "gives it away to keep it."

As clinicians, it is helpful to be aware of treatment centers that are trauma-informed and twelve-step meetings that are unsafe (e.g., sexual advances are made to individuals; therapy is negated; Marich, 2020). It is also worth noting that there are twelve-step programs for various nonsubstance-related addictive struggles, including Al-Anon (for friends and family members of those struggling with a SUD), Co-Dependents Anonymous, Overeaters Anonymous, Narcotics Anonymous, and Sex and Love Addicts Anonymous.

Motivational interviewing (MI).

I never met a feeling that wouldn't be a god if you let it.

ANDREE SEU

The MI approach provides an alternative to confrontational approaches that were the cornerstone in many substance abuse centers for decades. It is a complementary approach designed to be integrated with other evidence-based approaches and a way of being with clients (Frey & Hall, 2021). It includes using "common" factors (i.e., therapeutic alliance, therapist empathy, positive regard, genuineness, and client expectation) based on an analysis of seventy years of literature concerning what helps therapists be effective (Miller & Moyers, 2021). Problematically, implementing the common factors is not all that common despite therapists' beliefs about their own skills. The MI approach involves the application of multiple principles (e.g., expressing empathy, rolling with resistance, avoiding arguments, attuning to ambivalence, and highlighting discrepancies). Ultimately, the MI approach has been described as less exhausting than wrestling and breaking down resistance and more effective (Frey & Hall, 2021). While MI is not the "bricks" of treatment (i.e., evidence-based treatment for SUD and PTSD), it serves as the mortar that not only holds the bricks in place but also makes the entire intervention stronger. MI guides clients toward changes or goal acquisition but does not demand the change. It facilitates empathy and empowerment.

Integrating an MI approach may begin with the OARS skills from this paradigm: **O**pen-ended questions, **A**ffirmations, **R**eflections (of feeling and meaning), and **S**ummaries. MI facilitates empathy and empowerment. Here are a few examples of use of the OARS skills when journeying with Vicki:

- *Open-ended questions:* "Can you tell me more about when you realized drugs weren't the solution?" and "What do you wish was different?"
- *Affirmations:* "You've been through unspeakable hurts and found ways to survive," and "It's remarkable you had the wisdom to realize your solution was causing more problems."
- *Reflecting feelings:* "It seems this deeply saddens you as you say it out loud"; "It sounds like your whole life you sought comfort from someone or something that eventually harmed or betrayed you"; "You desperately sought the safety and security you missed out on with your family through drugs, and it was another source of pain."
- *Reflecting meaning:* "So you are still searching for comfort that no relationship or substance could satisfy?" and "It sounds like you've concluded that substances cannot offer the comfort you so deeply long for."
- *Summary:* "What I heard you say is that the drugs worked as a temporary form of comfort but eventually became problematic."

Seeking Safety.

Hardships often prepare ordinary people for an extraordinary destiny.

C. S. LEWIS

Seeking Safety is a low-cost integrative therapeutic model that simultaneously addresses PTSD and SUD by the same therapist within an individual or group format (Najavits, 2002). This model has become the most popular empirically studied treatment model for clients with trauma histories and SUD (Hien et al., 2019; Najavits, 2020; Roberts et al., 2022). It contains twenty-five topics for individuals experiencing co-occurring PTSD and SUD (e.g., asking for help, when substances control you, creating meaning) (Najavits, 2002). Each topic includes a different coping skill pertaining to both trauma and addictions (Hien et al., 2019). This present-focused CBT approach focuses on the impact of the trauma versus the details of the trauma narratives. Attention is given to the underlying thoughts and assumptions that impact feelings and behaviors. This strength-based model utilizes everyday language and emphasizes empowerment, the inspiration of hope, and implementation of practical solutions.

Vicki benefited from the *Seeking Safety* curriculum while incarcerated. She had been accepted into a specialized docket through the local court system while waiting for an opening at a treatment facility. Clinicians in the specialized docket staff lead therapeutic support groups in the jail, and the *Seeking Safety* manual was most helpful to Vicki and many others. One of the most helpful pieces for Vicki was the list of over eighty safe coping skills shared in chapter two of the curriculum. Vicki needed new "solutions" in this early season of healing. In fact, because she was incarcerated (in a stressful situation) and did not have access to her drugs of choice (alcohol, drugs), she was desperate for some new practices.

Concurrent treatment of PTSD and SUD using prolonged exposure (COPE). COPE is a past-focused approach for both SUD and PTSD that utilizes elements of prolonged exposure, psychoeducation, and relapse prevention in a twelve-session (weekly) protocol (Back et al., 2014; Roberts et al., 2022). This manualized treatment includes education and goal setting associated with both PTSD and SUD in sessions one through three. In sessions four through eleven, imaginal exposure (i.e., visualization) is implemented to address trauma memories. Throughout the protocol, clients are taught skills to manage triggers for SUD. Similar to traditional prolonged exposure, each session is audio recorded to be listened to after the conclusion of the live session. COPE provides a framework for the concurrent treatment of PTSD and SUD and is a well-researched form of concurrent therapy.

Utilizing COPE for Vicki provided an evidence-based approach to address both PTSD and SUD symptoms concurrently (Ruglass et al., 2017). In our clinical experience, there is a lot to contend with when a client has an extensive trauma background and SUD. This manualized evidenced-based approach can provide wise structure and guidance and build confidence in a clinician to attend to both salient concerns (Back et al., 2014). This may be a particularly helpful approach if a client has a history of noncompliance or drop-out with other SUD approaches. Moreover, attending to PTSD and SUD simultaneously results in better client therapeutic outcomes (Ruglass et al., 2017).

EMDR. A research review of the efficacy of EMDR for trauma survivors who also have comorbid SUD suggests that EMDR is more effective in treating trauma symptoms and less impactful for SUD (Tapia, 2019). Although the impact on SUD was less evident, this scoping review of eight representative studies suggests that a multifaceted approach to treatment is important for those who suffer with both PTSD and SUD. We have long understood that a trauma-informed approach to SUD treatment results in measurable improvements in clients fully engaging in therapy and overall outcomes (LeTendre & Reed, 2017). Other studies suggest that EMDR as an add-on increases the overall benefit of treatment for clients with a dual diagnosis, with particular relevance for those who have experienced childhood trauma (Carletto et al., 2018). Thus, EMDR, when paired with evidence-based SUD treatments, seems to bolster outcomes.

In clinical settings, a credentialed EMDR therapist may be heartened to know that add-on EMDR benefits trauma survivors battling SUD. Because avoidance is a hallmark symptom for both trauma survivors and individuals battling SUD, the therapist who utilizes EMDR for trauma symptoms would be wise to simultaneously offer SUD treatment and other SUD options as needed (e.g., recovery support groups, intensive outpatient programs, consulting with a licensed alcohol and drug counselor, fidelity to pharmacological interventions) and monitor substance use or relapse throughout the treatment process. For clinicians who do not have addiction training, additional training and working closely with an addiction counselor are essential. At this juncture, more research is needed regarding the concurrent usage of EMDR and SUD treatments (Najavits et al., 2020).

In conclusion, several studies have evaluated concurrent SUD and trauma therapeutic approaches over the past several years (Roberts et al., 2022). Since survivors with PTSD and SUD comorbidity have higher symptomatology, more severe coping challenges, and poorer therapy outcomes, ongoing research considering therapeutic approaches that integrate SUD and PTSD treatment concurrently are needed. When comparing treatment models for individuals with PTSD and SUD, Najavits and colleagues (2020, p. 8) explain:

> Decades of both PTSD and SUD research show that manualized treatments perform similarly overall and that occasional small findings for one model or another don't represent a consistent larger pattern, especially for complex patients. PTSD/SUD research is at an early stage but here too no one treatment is the winner; instead there are various models from which to choose. This has been called the "no wrong door" approach.

Ultimately, working with survivors with addictions requires a client-centered approach that considers client-specific needs and preferences. The ability to tolerate emotionally intense material, drop-out rates, individual versus group options availability, pacing, and socio-economic realities is crucial (Najavits et al., 2020; Roberts et al., 2022). Moreover, graduate programs that include training regarding the need for integrative therapeutic approaches for clients experiencing PTSD and SUD are vital.

PATHWAYS FULL OF POSSIBILITIES

> *Once you have tasted flight, you will forever walk the earth with your eyes turned skyward, for there you have been, and there you will always long to return.*
>
> LEONARDO DA VINCI

We continue to learn more about which evidence-based trauma and SUD approach might best suit specific survivors. With this consideration in mind, we also believe that approaches that consider the body, mind, *and* soul are essential. Worthington et al., (2011, p. 212) conducted a meta-analysis of forty-six studies that reveals "clear findings about the effectiveness of religious and spiritual accommodation." These researchers explained that some examples of ethical faith accommodations include providing therapy consistent with Christian values, giving space for the client to pray in session, and discussing theological questions. Their findings reflect the idea that, for some individuals, *something more* is needed to weather the storm of addictions stemming from the abuse. While clinicians must avoid exploiting the therapy relationship, which includes refraining from imposing their own beliefs on clients, Christian clinicians can draw on the wisdom in the Scriptures at judicious moments. As the cofounder of Alcoholics Anonymous Bill Wilson realized after trying many faulty cures,

> the divine paradox that strength rises from weakness, that humiliation goes before resurrection: that pain is not only the price but the very touchstone of rebirth. The irony continues throughout recovery. Although an alcoholic may pray desperately for the condition to go away, very few alcoholics or other addicts report sudden, miraculous healing. Most battle temptation every day of their lives. They experience grace not as a magic potion, rather as a balm whose strength is activated daily by conscious dependence on God. (Wilson, n.d., as cited in Yancey, 2000)

Vicki needed some better "solutions" for a time but eventually needed *the Solution.* We need something far more powerful to enable us to "stand up and walk" (Acts 3:6). Because the power of addiction is tenacious, we need something or someone who can break through the magnetic force of addictive substances, behaviors, and thoughts.

In the book of Exodus, God's people, having been rescued by God out of bondage, repeatedly express that they want to return to Egypt, to bondage. In Jeremiah, these addictions are referred to as "cracked cisterns" (Jer 2:13). In Ecclesiastes, they are our "schemes" (Eccles 7:29). In the book of Hosea, God calls these things our "lovers" (Hos 2:13). Throughout Scripture, these addictions are referred to as our idols (Ex 20:4; Lev 19:4; Ps 96:5; Acts 15:20; 1 Jn 5:21).

So pervasive are addictions that we wonder which disordered attachments Tamar clung to: "So Tamar remained, a desolate woman, in her brother Absalom's house" (2 Sam 13:20). The Scriptures do not provide details about what Tamar's particular flavor of *desolate* meant. We do not know if she had flashbacks or nightmares. She may have experienced PTSD or depression, and she may have developed various addictions. We cannot say how Tamar coped with her plight, but collectively we have worked with so many Tamars in this world, many of whom find themselves addicted to *something* or *someone*. And a life controlled by and enslaved to a substance, a habit, or anything other than what God intended is a desolate one. Thus, tending to our clients' bodies, minds, *and* souls is work made lighter by the ironic truth that God's power is made perfect in weakness.

COUNSELING CONSIDERATIONS

- **National Institute on Drug Abuse** features a website with reliable, validated screening tools for clinicians seeking to assess substance use for adolescents and adults.
- **PTSD Checklist for *DSM-5* (PCL-5)** is a twenty-item self-report measure based on how much an individual has been bothered by the symptoms. PCL-5 total scores range from 0 to 80, with higher scores indicating greater PTSD severity. It is offered for free on the Veterans Affairs National Center for PTSD website.
- **WHO-5 (Topp et al., 2015)** comprises five straightforward, noninvasive questions associated with well-being. It is available for free online and has been translated and studied in over thirty languages worldwide. We firmly believe that clinicians should assess for not only pathology but also areas of strength and well-being both at the outset of therapy and throughout the process.
- **Yale Food Addiction Scale (YFAS; Gearhardt et al., 2016)** is a commonly used assessment for food addiction. Gearhardt and colleagues (2016) viewed high-fat and high-sugar foods from an addiction perspective using a thirty-five-item scale.
- **The Non-Suicidal Self-Injury Disorder Scale (NSSIDS; Victor et al., 2017)** is a brief self-report scale based on NSSI criteria in the *DSM-5*.
- **Alexian Brothers Urge to Self-Injure Scale (ABUSI; Washburn et al., 2010)** measures the frequency, duration, and type of NSSI and assesses cravings and urges for NSSI.
- **Seeking Safety:** Resources and training links for Seeking Safety, an evidence-based treatment that helps people with trauma and SUD, can be accessed through the Substance Abuse and Mental Health Services Administration (SAMHSA) website.

CHILDREN'S CORNER

- ***When a Family Is in Trouble: Children Can Cope with Grief from Drug and Alcohol Addiction*** (Heegaard, 1993): This frequently recommended workbook for children ages 6-12 leans into the fact that when someone carries an addiction, all loved ones are affected and provides ways of naming sorrows and healing pathways.
- ***Broken Crayons Still Color*** (Hitz & Waddle, 2017): Children growing up in homes with trauma and addictions frequently know despair in deep and wide ways. While this hopeful book is not centered on addictions, it is a helpful reminder to children that, like broken crayons that can create beautiful pictures, God can take broken-down people and the broken-down places in our lives and create masterpieces.
- ***The Book of Mistakes*** (Luyken, 2017). "A little spill could be a small mistake . . . or the start of a big idea." This beautifully illustrated book reveals the journey of an artist's mistakes that are transformed over time into a masterpiece. This story may serve as a helpful metaphor for an addict in recovery who wonders how their "mistakes" might be woven into the overall tapestry of their lives and stories. It's not to suggest that the mistakes were beautiful but that, indeed, "he has made everything beautiful in its time" (Eccles 3:11 NIV).

REFERENCES

Alcoholics Anonymous (2001). *Alcoholics Anonymous: The story of how thousands of men and women have recovered from alcoholism.* Alcoholics Anonymous World Services.

Andersson, M. J. E., Tannå, H., & Nordin, S. (2013). Self-image in adolescents with deliberate self-harm behavior: Self-image and deliberate self-harm. *PsyCh Journal, 2*(3), 209-16. https://doi.org/10.1002/pchj.38

Arendt, F., Scherr, S., & Romer, D. (2019). Effects of exposure to self-harm on social media: Evidence from a two-wave panel study among young adults. *New Media & Society, 21*, 2422-42. https://doi.org/10.1177/1461444819850106

Babiker, G., & Arnold, L. (1997). *The language of injury: Comprehending self-mutilation.* British Psychological Society.

Back, S. E., Foa, E. B., Killeen, T. K., & Mills, K. L. (2014). *Concurrent treatment of PTSD and substance use disorders using prolonged exposure (COPE): Therapist guide.* Oxford University Press.

Beaulieu, M., Tremblay, J., & Bertrand, K. (2022). Adjustments to service organization in specialized addiction services and clinical strategies for better meeting the needs of people with a persistent substance use disorder. *International Journal of Mental Health and Addiction*. https://doi.org/10.1007/s11469-022-00982-z

Blum, K., Soni, D., Badgaiyan, R. D., & Baron, D. (2022). Overcoming reward deficiency syndrome by the induction of "dopamine homeostasis" instead of opioids for addiction: Illusion or reality? *Journal of Osteopathic Medicine, 122*(7), 333-37. https://doi.org/10.1515/jom-2021-0026

Braun, T. D., Green, Z., Meshesha, L. Z., Sillice, M. A., Read, J., & Abrantes, A. M. (2023). Self-compassion buffers the internalized alcohol stigma and depression link in women sexual assault survivors who drink to cope. *Addictive Behaviors, 138*, 107562. https://doi.org/10.1016/j.addbeh.2022.107562

Bresin, K., & Schoenleber, M. (2015). Gender differences in the prevalence of nonsuicidal self-injury: A meta-analysis. *Clinical Psychology Review, 38*, 55-64. https://doi.org/10.1016/j.cpr.2015.02.009

Breuninger, M. M., Grosso, J. A., Hunter, W., & Dolan, S. L. (2020). Treatment of alcohol use disorder: Integration of Alcoholics Anonymous and cognitive behavioral therapy. *Training and Education in Professional Psychology, 14*(1), 19.

Brewerton, T. D., O'Neil, P. M., Dansky, B. S., & Kilpatrick, D. G. (2015). Extreme obesity and its associations with victimization, PTSD, major depression and eating disorders in a national sample of women. *Journal of Obesity, 1*(2), 6. https://doi.org/10.21767/2471-8203.100010

Carletto, S., Oliva, F., Barnato, M., Antonelli, T., Cardia, A., Mazzaferro, P., Raho, C., Ostacoli, L., Fernandez, I., & Pagani, M. (2018). EMDR as add-on treatment for psychiatric and traumatic symptoms in patients with substance use disorder. *Frontiers in Psychology, 8*, 2333. https://doi.org/10.3389/fpsyg.2017.02333

Colaianni, A. (2021). Exploring the potential shared pathology of eating disorders and addiction: A behavioral neuroscience approach. *Behavioral Neuroscience, 5*, 1-5.

Degenhardt, L., Bharat, C., Glantz, M. D., Bromet, E. J., Alonso, J., Bruffaerts, R., Bunting, B., de Girolamo, G., de Jonge, P., Florescu, S., Gureje, O., Haro, J. M., Harris, M. G., Hinkov, H., Karam, E. G., Karam, G., Kovess-Masfety, V., Lee, S., Makanjuola, V., . . . Wojtyniak, B. (2022). The associations between traumatic experiences and subsequent onset of a substance use disorder: Findings from the World Health Organization World Mental Health surveys. *Drug and Alcohol Dependence, 240*, 109574. https://doi.org/10.1016/j.drugalcdep.2022.109574

Dube, S. R., Anda, R. F., Felitti, V. J., Edwards, V. J., & Croft, J. B. (2002). Adverse childhood experiences and personal alcohol abuse as an adult. *Addictive Behaviors, 27*(5), 713-25. https://doi.org/10.1016/S0306-4603(01)00204-0

Dube, S. R., Felitti, V. J., Dong, M., Chapman, D. P., Giles, W. H., & Anda, R. F. (2003). Childhood abuse, neglect, and household dysfunction and the risk of illicit drug use: The adverse childhood experiences study. *Pediatrics, 111*(3), 564-72. https://doi.org/10.1542/peds.111.3.564

Ernst, M., Brähler, E., Kampling, H., Kruse, J., Fegert, J. M., Plener, P. L., & Beutel, M. E. (2022). Is the end in the beginning? Child maltreatment increases the risk of non-suicidal self-injury and suicide attempts through impaired personality functioning. *Child Abuse & Neglect, 133*, 105870. https://doi.org/10.1016/j.chiabu.2022.105870

Favazza, A. R. (2011). *Bodies under siege: Self-mutilation, nonsuicidal self-injury, and body modification in culture and psychiatry* (3rd ed.). Johns Hopkins University Press.

Felitti, V. J., Anda, R. F., Nordenberg, D., Williamson, D. F., Spitz, A. M., Edwards, V., Koss, M. P., & Marks, J. S. (1998). Relationship of childhood abuse and household dysfunction to many of the leading causes of death in adults. *American Journal of Preventive Medicine, 14*(4), 245-58. https://doi.org/10.1016/S0749-3797(98)00017-8

Foote, J., Wilkens, C., Kosanke, N., & Higgs, S. (Eds.). (2014). *Beyond addiction: How science and kindness help people change*. Scribner.

Frey, J., & Hall, A. (2021). *Motivational interviewing for mental health clinicians: A toolkit for skills enhancement.* PESI Publishing.

Galanter, M., White, W. L., Khalsa, J., & Hansen, H. (2023). A scoping review of spirituality in relation to substance use disorders: Psychological, biological, and cultural issues. *Journal of Addictive Diseases*, 1-9.

Gearhardt, A. N., Corbin, W. R., & Brownell, K. D. (2016). Development of the Yale Food Addiction Scale Version 2.0. *Psychology of Addictive Behaviors, 30*(1), 113-21. https://doi.org/10.1037/adb0000136

Giordano, A. L. (2022). *A clinical guide to treating behavioral addictions: Conceptualizations, assessments, and clinical strategies.* Springer.

Guarino, H., Mateu-Gelabert, P., Sirikantraporn, S. J., Ruggles, K., Syckes, C., Goodbody, E., & Friedman, S. R. (2017). The role of adverse childhood experiences in initiation of substance use and sexual behaviors among opioid-using young adults. *Abstracts/Drug and Alcohol Dependence, 171*, e2-e226. https://doi.org/10.1016/j.drugalcdep.2016.08.224

Hailes, H. P., Yu, R., Danese, A., & Fazel, S. (2019). Long-term outcomes of childhood sexual abuse: An umbrella review. *The Lancet Psychiatry, 6*(10), 830-39. https://doi.org/10.1016/S2215-0366(19)30286-X

Heegaard, M. E. (1993). *When a family is in trouble: Children can cope with grief from drug and alcohol addiction*. Woodland.

Hien, D., Litt, L., & Cohen, L. R. (2019). Seeking Safety: A present-focused integrated treatment for PTSD and substance use disorders. In A. A. Vujanovic & S. E. Back (Eds.), *Posttraumatic stress and substance use disorders: A comprehensive clinical handbook* (pp. 183-207). Routledge.

Hitz, S., & Waddle, J. (2017). *Broken crayons still color.* Body and Soul.

Johnson, R. H., Pitt, H., Randle, M., & Thomas, S. L. (2023). A scoping review of the individual, socio-cultural, environmental and commercial determinants of gambling for older adults: Implications for public health research and harm prevention. *BMC Public Health, 23*(1), 1-15.

Kelly, J. F., Abry, A., Ferri, M., & Humphreys, K. (2020). Alcoholics anonymous and 12-step facilitation treatments for alcohol use disorder: A distillation of a 2020 Cochrane review for clinicians and policy makers. *Alcohol and Alcoholism, 55*(6), 641-51. https://doi.org/10.1093/alcalc/agaa050

Knapp, C. (1996). *Drinking: A love story*. Dial Press.

Leigh, S. J., & Morris, M. J. (2018). The role of reward circuitry and food addiction in the obesity epidemic: An update. *Biological Psychology, 131*, 31-42. https://doi.org/10.1016/j.biopsycho.2016.12.013

LeTendre M. L., & Reed M. B. (2017). The effect of adverse childhood experience on clinical diagnosis of a substance use disorder: Results of a nationally representative study. *Substance Use Misuse, 52*, 689-97. https://doi.org/10.1080/10826084.2016.1253746

Luyken, C. (2017). *The book of mistakes*. Penguin.

Malet-Karas, A., Bernard, D., Piet, E., & Bertin, E. (2022). Disordered eating as a repercussion of sexual assault: A consequence to consider. *Eating and Weight Disorders—Studies on Anorexia, Bulimia and Obesity, 27*(6), 2095-2106. https://doi.org/10.1007/s40519-021-01356-5

Marich, J. (2020). *Trauma and the 12 steps, revised and expanded: An inclusive guide to enhancing recovery*. North Atlantic Books.

Marlatt, G. A. (1996). Harm reduction: Come as you are. *Addictive Behaviors, 21*(6), 779-98. https://doi.org/10.1016/0306-4603(96)00042-1

Maté, G. (2020). *In the realm of hungry ghosts: Close encounters with addiction*. Random House Digital.

May, G. (2007). *Addiction and grace: Love and spirituality in the healing of addictions*. HarperCollins.

McLean, C. P., Asnaani, A., & Foa, E. B. (2015). Prolonged exposure therapy. In U. Schnyder & M. Cloitre (Eds.), *Evidence based treatments for trauma-related psychological disorders: A practical guide for clinicians* (pp. 152-59). Springer.

McNeely, J., Wu, L. T., Subramaniam, G., Sharma, G., Cathers, L. A., Svikis, D., Sleiter, L., Russell, L., Nordeck, C., Sharma, A., O'Grady, K. E., Bouk, L. B., Cushing, C., King, J., Wahle, A., & Schwartz, R. P. (2016). Performance of the Tobacco, Alcohol, Prescription Medication, and Other Substance Use (TAPS) Tool for substance use screening in primary care patients. *Annals of Internal Medicine, 165*(10), 690-99. https://doi.org/10.7326/M16-0317

McNeill, J. T. (Ed.). (1960). *Calvin: Institutes of the Christian religion*. John Knox Press.

Michaels, T. I., Stone, E., Singal, S., Novakovic, V., Barkin, R. L., & Barkin, S. (2021). Brain reward circuitry: The overlapping neurobiology of trauma and substance use disorders. *World Journal of Psychiatry, 11*(6), 222. http://doi.org/10.5498/wjp.v11.i6.222

Miller, W. R., & Moyers, T. B. (2021). *Effective psychotherapists: Clinical skills that improve client outcomes*. Guilford.

Mitchell, K. S., Mazzeo, S. E., Schlesinger, M. R., Brewerton, T. D., & Smith, B. N. (2012). Comorbidity of partial and subthreshold PTSD among men and women with eating disorders in the national comorbidity survey-replication study. *International Journal of Eating Disorders, 45*(3), 307-15. https://doi.org/10.1002/eat.20965

Moss, C., Wibberley, C., & Witham, G. (2023). Assessing the impact of Instagram use and deliberate self-harm in adolescents: A scoping review. *International Journal of Mental Health Nursing, 32*(1), 14-29. https://doi.org/10.1111/inm.13055

Muehlenkamp, J. J., Brausch, A. M., & Littlefield, A. (2022). Concurrent changes in non-suicidal self-injury and suicide thoughts and behaviors. *Psychological Medicine*, 1-6. https://doi.org/10.1017/s0033291722001763

Najavits, L. M. (2002). *Seeking safety: A treatment manual for PTSD and substance abuse.* Guilford.

Najavits, L. M. (2009). Psychotherapies for trauma and substance abuse in women: Review and policy implications. *Trauma, Violence, & Abuse, 10*(3), 290-98. https://doi.org/10.1177/1524838009334455

Najavits, L. M. (2015). Trauma and substance abuse: A clinician's guide to treatment. In U. Schnyder & M. Cloitre (Eds.), *Evidence based treatments for trauma-related psychological disorders: A practical guide for clinicians* (pp. 317-30). Springer.

Najavits, L. M. (2019). *Finding your best self: Recovery from addiction, trauma, or both*. Guilford.

Najavits, L. M., Clark, H. W., Diclemente, C. C., Potenza, M. N., Shaffer, H. J., Sorensen, J. L., Tull, M. T., Zweben, A., & Zweben, J. E. (2020). PTSD/substance use disorder comorbidity: Treatment options and public health needs. *Current Treatment Options in Psychiatry, 7*, 544-58. https://doi.org/10.1007/s40501-020-00234-8

National Institute of Mental Health. (2024, March). *Substance use and co-occurring mental disorders.* www.nimh.nih.gov/health/topics/substance-use-and-mental-health#:~:text=Substance%20use%20disorder%20(SUD)%20is,drugs%2C%20alcohol%2C%20or%20medications

Nester, M. S., Brand, B. L., Schielke, H. J., & Kumar, S. (2022). An examination of the relations between emotion dysregulation, dissociation, and self-injury among dissociative disorder patients. *European Journal of Psychotraumatology, 13*(1), 2031592. https://doi.org/10.1080/20008198.2022.2031592

Norcross, J. C., Krebs, P. M., & Prochaska, J. O. (2010). Stages of change. *Journal of Clinical Psychology, 67*(2), 143-54. https://doi.org/10.1002/jclp.20758

Parisi, A., Jordan, B., Jensen, T., & Howard, M. O. (2022). The impact of sexual victimization on substance use disorder treatment completion: A systematic review and meta-analysis. *Substance Abuse, 43*(1), 131-42. https://doi.org/10.1080/08897077.2020.1748168

Pietrzak, R. H., Goldstein, R. B., Southwick, S. M., & Grant, B. F. (2011). Prevalence and axis I comorbidity of full and partial posttraumatic stress disorder in the United States: Results from wave 2 of the National Epidemiologic Survey on Alcohol and Related Condition. *Journal of Anxiety Disorders, 25*, 456-65. http://doi.org/10.1016/j.janxdis.2010.11.010

Prochaska, J. O., & DiClemente, C. C. (1983). Stages and processes of self-change of smoking: Toward an integrative model of change. *Journal of Consulting and Clinical Psychology, 51*(3), 390. https://doi.org/10.1037//0022-006x.51.3.390

Ribeiro, J. D., Franklin, J. C., Fox, K. R., Bentley, K. H., Kleiman, E. M., Chang, B. P., & Nock, M. K. (2016). Self-injurious thoughts and behaviors as risk factors for future suicide ideation, attempts, and death: A meta-analysis of longitudinal studies. *Psychological Medicine, 46*(2), 225-36. https://doi.org/10.1017/S0033291715001804

Roberts, N. P., Lotzin, A., & Schäfer, I. (2022). A systematic review and meta-analysis of psychological interventions for comorbid post-traumatic stress disorder and substance use disorder. *European Journal of Psychotraumatology, 13*(1), 2041831. https://doi.org/10.1080/20008198.2022.2041831

Robinson, L. D., Kelly, P. J., Larance, B. K., Griffiths, S., & Deane, F. P. (2021). Eating disorder behaviours and substance use in women attending treatment for substance use disorders: A latent class analysis. *International Journal of Mental Health and Addiction*, 1-18. https://doi.org/10.1007/s11469-021-00497-z

Rohr, R. (2011). *Breathing under water: Spirituality and the twelve steps*. Franciscan Media.

Ruglass, L. M., Lopez-Castro, T., Papini, S., Killeen, T., Back, S. E., & Hien, D. A. (2017). Concurrent treatment with prolonged exposure for co-occurring full or subthreshold posttraumatic stress disorder and substance use disorders: A randomized clinical trial. *Psychotherapy and Psychosomatics, 86*(3), 150-61. https://doi.org/10.1159/000462977

Center for Substance Abuse Prevention, Substance Abuse and Mental Health Services Administration. (2023, April 24). *Harm reduction framework*. https://www.samhsa.gov/find-help/harm-reduction/framework

Tapia, G. (2019). Review of EMDR interventions for individuals with substance use disorder with/without comorbid posttraumatic stress disorder. *Journal of EMDR Practice and Research, 13*(4), 345-53. https://doi.org/10.1891/1933-3196.13.4.345

Tatarsky, A., & Marlatt, G. A. (2010). State of the art in harm reduction psychotherapy: An emerging treatment for substance misuse. *Journal of Clinical Psychology, 66*(2), 117-22. https://doi.org/10.1002/jclp.20672

Toates, F. (2022). A motivation model of sex addiction—relevance to the controversy over the concept. *Neuroscience & Biobehavioral Reviews, 142*, 104872. https://doi.org/10.1016/j.neubiorev.2022.104872

Topp, C. W., Østergaard, S. D., Søndergaard, S., & Bech, P. (2015). The WHO-5 Well-Being Index: A systematic review of the literature. *Psychotherapy and Psychosomatics, 84*(3), 167-76. https://doi.org/10.1159/000376585

Trickett, P. K., Noll, J. G., & Putnam, F. W. (2011). The impact of sexual abuse on female development: Lessons from a multigenerational, longitudinal research study. *Development and Psychopathology, 23*(2), 453-76. https://doi.org/10.1017%2FS0954579411000174

Tripp, J. C, Jones, J. L, Back, S. E, & Norman, S. B. (2019). Dealing with complexity and comorbidity: Comorbid PTSD and substance use disorders. *Current Treat Options Psychiatry*, 6(3):188-97. https://doi.org/10.1007/s40501-019-00176-w

Twenge, J. M. (2020). Increases in depression, self-harm, and suicide among US adolescents after 2012 and links to technology use: Possible mechanisms. *Psychiatric Research and Clinical Practice*, 2(1), 19-25. https://doi.org/10.1176/appi.prcp.20190015

Vanderlinden, J., & Vandereycken, W. (1996). Is sexual abuse a risk factor for developing an eating disorder? In M. F. Schwartz, & L. Cohn (Eds.), *Sexual abuse and eating disorders*. New Brunner/Mazel.

Victor, S. E., Davis, T., & Klonsky, E. D. (2017). Descriptive characteristics and initial psychometric properties of the non-suicidal self-injury disorder scale. *Archives of Suicide Research*, 21(2), 265-78. https://doi.org/10.1080/13811118.2016.1193078

Volkow, N. D., & Boyle, M. (2018). Neuroscience of addiction: Relevance to prevention and treatment. *American Journal of Psychiatry*, 175(8), 729-40. https://doi.org/10.1176/appi.ajp.2018.17101174

Washburn, J. J., Juzwin, K. R., Styer, D. M., & Aldridge, D. (2010). Measuring the urge to self-injure: Preliminary data from a clinical sample. *Psychiatry Research*, 178(3), 540-44. https://doi.org/10.1016/j.psychres.2010.05.018

Watters, K. N., & Yalch, M. M. (2022). Relative effects of sexual assault and other traumatic life events on self-harm. *European Journal of Trauma & Dissociation*, 6(1), 100244. https://doi.org/10.1016/j.ejtd.2021.100244

Weathers, F. W., Litz, B. T., Keane, T. M., Palmieri, P. A., Marx, B. P., & Schnurr, P. P. (2013). *The PTSD checklist for DSM-5 (PCL-5)*. The National Center for PTSD.

Wise, R. A. (2013). Dual roles of dopamine in food and drug-seeking: The drive-reward paradox. *Biological Psychiatry*, 73(9), 819-26. https://doi.org/10.1016%2Fj.biopsych.2012.09.001

Wiss, D. A., Brewerton, T. D., & Tomiyama, A. J. (2022). Limitations of the protective measure theory in explaining the role of childhood sexual abuse in eating disorders, addictions, and obesity: An updated model with emphasis on biological embedding. *Eating and Weight Disorders—Studies on Anorexia, Bulimia and Obesity*, 27(4), 1249-67. https://doi.org/10.1007/s40519-021-01293-3

Worthington, E. L., Jr., Hook, J. N., Davis, D. E., & McDaniel, M. A. (2011). Religion and spirituality. *Journal of Clinical Psychology*, 67(2), 204-14. https://doi.org/10.1002/jclp.20760

Yancey, P. (2002). *Reaching for the invisible God: What can we expect to find?* Zondervan.

6

COMPLEX TRAUMA, COMPLEX MEMORIES

My memories of the abuse were like a spot on the highway behind me, which I watched recede in the rearview mirror; it became smaller and smaller until it vanished.

RICHARD BERENDZEN

It takes enormous trust and courage to allow yourself to remember.

BESSEL A. VAN DER KOLK

In the poignant film *The Tale* (Fox, 2018), writer and director Jennifer grapples with her memories of being groomed and sexually abused by her running coach when she was thirteen years old. Previously, she had viewed her relationship with her forty-something-year-old coach as romantic. Jennifer's story speaks to the intricacies of remembering her abuse. As the autobiographical film unfolds, we see Jennifer come to reinterpret some of the many details she remembers. What she initially described as making love was later redefined as rape.

Jennifer's arduous journey of recalling her abuse began when her mom discovered an essay Jennifer had written for a school assignment at fifteen. She wrote about a relationship she had previously had with an "older man." Her mother's discovery sparked Jennifer's investigation, and the film reveals her discoveries. According to a *New York Times* interview with Jennifer, now a filmmaker and professor in her forties, years after the film aired, she disclosed the identity of her perpetrator and more details about that essay she wrote decades earlier:

> In the assignment, Jennifer described having a loving relationship with two adults. She wrote that a man had invited her into his bedroom and touched her body and her breasts as she remained frozen. . . . Her teacher simply changed "me" to "my" and later commented: "If what you talk about here were accurate, I would say that you have been taken advantage of by older people." The teacher wrote, "thank you for sharing—imaginatively conceived piece of writing," and gave the paper an A-minus. (Macur, 2023)

Reinterpreting earlier specifics surrounding CSA is one type of experience in the sinuous landscape of remembering. Some survivors always remember and realize early on that the CSA was harmful. Others yearn for their uninvited memories in the form of flashbacks and night terrors to be banished from consciousness. Alternatively, some survivors endeavor to recall the black spots of their formative years, incomplete and fragmentary memories that seem like sandcastles washed away by the tides. Still, for others, remembering is insulated in ambivalence—wanting to remember punctuated by not wanting to remember. The attempt to understand memories of interpersonal trauma more fully has been encompassed in academic inquiry, significant debate, and political movement over the past century. We briefly explore the polarizing views on consolidating and retrieving memories of traumatic events.

THE DIALECTIC OF REMEMBERING ABUSE

The conflict between knowing and not knowing,
speech and silence, remembering and forgetting,
is the central dialectic of psychological trauma.

JUDITH HERMAN

Over the years, I (Tammy) have journeyed with survivors who carried fragments of intense sensations, feelings, and sparse or absent narratives related to their childhood trauma. Still, others hold some vivid recollections, while other specific memories are sequestered from ordinary awareness. The topic of delayed recall for abuse has intrigued a lot of people, including survivors, therapists, researchers, family members, and lawyers, triggering a thorny and polarizing controversy and acrimonious discourse over the last couple of decades that persist to the present day (Brewin, 2021; Dalenberg et al., 2020; Lynn et al., 2023; Otgaar et al., 2022).

On one side of the delayed memories debate are researchers and clinicians who maintain that individuals sexually abused as children can experience a lack of recall for childhood abuse "as a protective response to traumatic or overwhelming experiences" (Lowenstein, 2018, p. 229). The mechanism for the inability to remember childhood traumatic events may stem from a variety of reasons (e.g., ordinary forgetting, failure to encode information in long-term memory, drug intoxication, viewing the CSA as unimportant, intentional cognitive avoidance of the abuse) (Brewin, 2021; Lowenstein, 2018). Dissociation is another mechanism cited as the basis of reduced recall for CSA. Dissociation is the inability to remember stressful or traumatic autobiographical experiences that is not due to ordinary forgetting, cognitive avoidance, the effects of substance abuse, traumatic brain injury, neurocognitive disorders, factitious disorder, or malingering (Mangiulli et al., 2021).

On the other end of the debate continuum, experts argue that delayed memories of abuse are a myth and documented traumatic experiences are rarely, if ever, forgotten (Pope et al., 1999). Instead, delayed memories are believed to stem from therapists using techniques (e.g., leading questions, guided imagery) that produce false or pseudo-memories or clients reading or hearing others talk about their own abuse, prompting them to falsely believe the trauma happened to them (Lynn et al., 2023). This view further suggests that some individuals are "fantasy prone and suggestible," and cultural influences prompt susceptibility to imagining abuse that did not occur (Bailey & Brand, 2017, p. 173). Thus, the debate centers on whether some individuals can develop a lack of recall from traumatic experiences through dissociation or whether these are confabulated trauma memories (Lowenstein, 2018).

Truth is often clouded in contentious polemics for those peering from different sides of the spectrum. Learning from varying perspectives is vital so that researchers, therapists, and survivors have a more accurate understanding, and so we can respond with wisdom and compassion when clients discuss memories of abuse. In this chapter, we examine both sides of the debate briefly, and then we discuss best practices with clients with memory disturbances, drawing information from both sides of the discussion.

TRAUMA CAN LEAD TO MEMORY DISTURBANCES

Clinicians and researchers who contend that some traumatized individuals can develop memory disturbances for CSA underscore clinical and research accounts documented over the past century of a lack of recall for abuse that has occurred (Herman, 2022). For example, the findings from nine thousand HMO members who participated in the Adverse Childhood Experiences Study (ACEs Study) (Felitti & Anda, 2010) reveal that childhood autobiographical memory disturbances are related to cumulative traumatic childhood experiences, specifically sexual abuse, physical abuse, and combined physical and sexual abuse (Brown et al., 2007). Patihis and Pendergrast (2019) surveyed 2,316 US adults. They indicated that five percent (n = 122) reported that during therapy they remembered being abused as a child after previously having no memory of the abuse. A study of 1,312 French participants revealed six percent (n = 33) reported that during therapy they remembered being abused as a child after previously having no memory of the abuse (Dodier et al., 2019). In a separate large French general public study (n = 3,346), nine percent (n = 82) disclosed recovered memories of abuse that they had no memory of beforehand. In addition, 90 percent of this subgroup reported delayed memories while they were not in therapy (e.g., after discussions with peers or media exposure) (Dodier et al., 2019). Thus, over several decades, a subpopulation of individuals report having recalled abuse following no previous memories of abuse (Dodier & Patihis, 2020).

According to the *DSM-5-TR* (American Psychiatric Association, 2022), a hallmark of PTSD is the oscillation between symptoms of re-experiencing and the avoidance of difficult memories, while alterations in memory primarily characterize dissociative disorders. Numerous studies have highlighted the changes in the volume of the hippocampus and the amygdala in PTSD and dissociative disorders and their impact on memory impairment among individuals who have been traumatized (Blihar et al., 2021; Bidzan, 2017; Weis et al., 2021; Zhang et al., 2021). Despite the inclusion of memory disturbances as symptoms of both PTSD and dissociative disorders in the *DSM* and neuroscientific evidence related to changes in the hippocampus and amygdala for those experiencing these disorders, false memory researchers argue that "traumatic amnesia appears to be a myth" (Kihlstrom et al., 2005, p. 1183). However, Ross (2022, p. 490) explained, "Dissociative amnesia and DID have been accepted as valid disorders by the two most relevant scientific communities—the American Psychiatric Association and the World Health Organization—for many decades." Thus, the dismissal of dissociation as one reason for delayed memories of abuse fails to acknowledge extensive empirical evidence on dissociative amnesia (Ross, 2022, 2023).

Betrayal trauma theory (BTT), developed by Jennifer Freyd (previously discussed in the "Trust and Treachery" chapter), acknowledges the importance of attachment figures in children's lives and suggests that some individuals may develop "betrayal blindness," which is the "unawareness, not-knowing, and forgetting of betrayal traumas" to maintain closeness with abusive attachment figures when physical escaping is impossible (Gómez et al., 2023, p. 157). Thus, according to this theory, betrayal traumas create circumstances that may increase the likelihood of memory disturbances due to the utility of not remembering the abuse when the victim is dependent on the perpetrator (Freyd, 1996).

For example, when a little girl is repeatedly sexually abused by her father who sits across from her at the breakfast table the next day, she is faced with an untenable situation as the perpetrator is the same person she depends on for food, clothing, and shelter. Thus, while many victims may have continuous memories of being abused, for some, remembering the abuse can endanger their well-being (DePrince et al., 2012). Some children may learn to cope by escaping internally from the awareness of body sensations, emotions, and memories through dissociation. Months or years later, sensations may trigger memories of the abuse. Triggers such as reading or hearing news events about other individuals' abuse, the smell of a specific type of cologne or gasoline, an old song on the radio, sexual intimacy, and experiencing troubling current events can prompt traumatic events to come surging back through flashbacks, nightmares, and intrusive thoughts (Damis, 2022). Thus, when individuals experience danger, they often develop critical survival tactics. These tactics can impact memory formation and later retrieval when a survivor depends on an abuser for their survival need (e.g., shelter, food) or higher-order needs (belonging/love).

Despite numerous suggestibility and false memory studies that have demonstrated participants are susceptible to creating false memories (e.g., being lost in the mall), the reviews of these studies omitted significant findings when the studies included suggestive questioning about "taboo acts of a sexual nature" (Goodman et al., 2019, p. 29). For example, Pezdek and colleagues (1997) attempted to lead adult participants to believe they had experienced being lost in a mall while others were told that they had experienced a childhood rectal enema. In this study, the scenario of receiving an enema was specifically selected, as it may be shameful or embarrassing, like CSA. However, while some participants agreed with more plausible possibilities of being lost in a mall, none agreed that they had experienced a childhood rectal enema. More recently, Goldfarb and colleagues (2019) conducted a longitudinal study with adults who experienced a documented child maltreatment medical examination that included genital touch when the participants were three to seventeen years old and then interviewed later as adults. No participants incorporated beliefs of reportable abuse that did not occur, even when false suggestions about childhood events occurred (Goldfarb et al., 2019). Thus, while many studies reveal that participants incorporated false beliefs when suggestive leading pressure and questions were utilized, other studies showed that participants were resistant to incorporating false beliefs with inquiries about sexual taboo acts (Goodman et al., 2019).

Proponents of the idea that trauma can result in a lack of memories for a time highlight that memory disturbances have been documented in the literature related to war trauma (e.g., Grinker & Spiegel, 1945; Sargant & Slater, 1941; Thom & Fenton, 1920). However, memory recovery was not suspected until female survivors of CSA reported memory disturbances and later recall. Van der Kolk and colleagues (1996) explain that the emphasis on false allegations versus false denials of abuse is most accurately understood as gender politics versus science.

> It appears that as long as men were found to suffer from delayed recall of atrocities committed either by a clearly identifiable enemy or themselves, the issue was not controversial. However when similar memory problems started to be documented in girls and women in the context of domestic abuse, the news was unbearable; when female victims started to seek justice against their alleged perpetrators, the issue moved from science into politics. (van der Kolk et al., 1996, p. 566)

During an interview with James Hopper, psychologist and teaching associate at Harvard Medical School, he framed this dismissal of memory disturbances and later recall by survivors of CSA as a gender-political double standard: "Every day in courtrooms around the country, [defense attorneys] attack and question the credibility of victims of sexual assault for having the same kind of memories that soldiers have for their combat experiences" (Hopper, 2021, as cited in Caiola, 2021).

In response to questions about the veracity of delayed memories of abuse, proponents from this perspective point out that numerous survivors have obtained external corroboration (e.g., police and medical reports, court records, eyewitnesses, confessions by perpetrators) for the delayed memories of abuse. While many survivors are unable to obtain external corroboration due to formidable circumstances (e.g., neither the survivor nor the alleged perpetrator told anyone about the abuse at the time of the occurrence; the victim did not have a physical exam), the Recovered Memory Project (Cheit, 2023) is an internet-based collection of corroborated clinical and legal cases of CSA. The project is maintained by Ross Cheit, a political scientist at Brown University who researches public policy on CSA in the United States. For example, one legal case cited in the Recovered Memory Project is the case of Frank Fitzpatrick. At the age of forty-one years he had no memory of CSA but began having flashbacks about being sexually abused by Father James Porter thirty years before when he was an altar boy. Fitzpatrick initiated a personal investigation whereby he phoned, confronted, and recorded Porter, who acknowledged that he abused Fitzpatrick (and later admitted to dozens of other victims). Porter was successfully prosecuted and pleaded guilty (Cheit, 2023). Moreover, Harvard psychiatrist Stuart Grassian surveyed forty-three Porter victims. He indicated that 19 percent had no thoughts or memories of the CSA until the abuse was reported in the media (Cheit, 2023).

In summary, the view that trauma can result in the inability to remember is based on extensive empirical research documenting reports of memory disturbances; the acceptance of PTSD and dissociative disorders that include symptoms of memory disturbances as valid disorders by the American Psychiatric Association and the World Health Organization for several decades; and betrayal trauma theory, which explains traumatic betrayal experiences that foster memory disturbance due to conflicting survival mechanisms, support the notion that some individuals experience delayed memories following CSA. Moreover, many survivors who have no recall of the CSA for a period have obtained external corroboration, validating the reality of their delayed memories. We now turn our attention to a contrasting view of traumatic memory, arguing that trauma rarely, if ever, results in a lack of recall.

TRAUMA RARELY RESULTS IN MEMORY DISTURBANCES

Proponents of the view consist primarily of eyewitness memory and forensic researchers. Some advocates contend that "genuinely traumatic events—those experienced at the time as overwhelmingly terrifying and life-threatening—are seldom, if ever, truly forgotten" (Kihlstrom et al., 2005, pp. 1183). This perspective is based on several reasons.

First, over two decades of laboratory research have revealed that individuals are susceptible to creating false memories. Approximately 30 percent of individuals in these laboratory contexts developed false memories of autobiographical experiences (Wade et al., 2018). For example, Loftus and Pickrell (1995) devised the now-famous "Lost in the Mall" study in which participants were given summaries of four experiences from their childhood. Three of the stories were true, and the false story was about the participant being lost in the mall until the participant was eventually found and returned to the parents. Participants were suggestively interviewed over time, and approximately 25 percent reported clear memories of the fictional "memory" (Loftus & Pickrell, 1995). Over the past two decades, variations of these studies have prompted participants to recall illusory childhood hospital visits, animal attacks, classroom pranks, hot-air balloon rides, and crimes (Brewin & Andrews, 2017; Wade et al., 2018). These studies reveal that in contexts where experiences are complicated or ambiguous, use of suggestive pressure and imagination exercises can prompt people to generate false autobiographical memories (Brewin et al., 2020; Otgaar et al., 2022; Shaw & Porter, 2015; Wade et al., 2018).

Another critical point supported by this perspective is that the diagnostic label of dissociation is often inappropriately used to describe a lack of memory for the abuse before other reasons are ruled out (e.g., ordinary forgetting, encoding failure, prolonged stress, traumatic brain injury, cognitive avoiding, malingering) (Dalenberg et al., 2020; Mangiulli et al., 2021). An additional explanation is that some individuals are ashamed of the traumatic experience, and what may have been labeled as forgetting may instead be shame and the desire not to talk about the abuse. Alternatively, individuals may not have forgotten the abuse; rather, events may not have been viewed as traumatic at the time and only later reinterpreted as traumatic (Otgaar et al., 2022). Thus, further assessment is needed to accurately determine symptoms and diagnoses (Dalenberg et al., 2020). Moreover, from this vantage point, dissociation is frequently understood as the by-product of suggestive pressure by clinicians in which leading questions and visual imagery exercises result in false memories (Otgaar et al., 2022). Instead, proponents point out that it is essential to examine other plausible explanations for the apparent forgetting of CSA (Otgaar et al., 2023).

Advocates of the perspective that trauma rarely results in the inability to remember emphasize that distressed individuals seeking help for sizeable concerns (e.g., depression, eating disorders) meet with therapists who maintain that CSA is the basis for these concerns (McNally, 2003) and consequently use misguided techniques (e.g., guided imagery, leading questions) to produce highly implausible memories (Lynn et al., 2023). This viewpoint further underscores that some clinicians hold erroneous perspectives on how memory works (e.g., memory works as a photo or a video camera versus understanding that memory is reconstructive and malleable), which can impact how clients believe they are to remember childhood experiences and increase the presence of false or inaccurate memories associated with traumatic events (Otgaar et al., 2021, 2022). For example, Otgaar and colleagues (2022) examined and summarized studies indicating that therapists utilizing EMDR or any other exposure approaches for therapy (e.g., imagery rescripting) can play a role in a client misremembering or even developing false memories based on faulty memory frameworks. For example, their report summarizing a criminal case from Italy revealed the circumstances surrounding a therapist who was found guilty of implanting false memories of abuse in a young girl (Otgaar et al., 2022). The therapist frequently utilized suggestive pressure, leading assumptions, and included details about previously undisclosed traumatic experiences that resulted in confusion and eventual acquiescence by the client. In cases of suggestive approaches, therapists may use more words than the client and construct a narrative of past events through manipulative questioning (Otgaar et al., 2022).

In summary, this viewpoint posits that humans are highly unlikely to experience an inability to recall traumatic events and disputes the mechanism of dissociative amnesia. Instead, proponents assert that suggestive pressure and questioning increase the likelihood of false memories emerging. Furthermore, therapist bias or familial/cultural influences contribute to misattributions of CSA for other problematic behaviors (e.g., eating disorders, relational problems). In these ways, these individuals can construct false memories of CSA that are reinforced by therapists or others.

After several decades of lab research and talking with clients in therapeutic settings, we have learned a lot about the intricacy of factors related to the lack of recall of CSA. It is important to note that a subpopulation of survivors of CSA consistently report a lack of memory and later recall of abuse (DePrince et al., 2012). These voices are essential in this dialogue. We have also learned important factors that can influence the development of false beliefs and false memories in therapeutic settings. Clinicians must be aware of the implications of this research so that we engage in best practices with vulnerable clients. Let us turn our attention to wise clinical practices when working with clients who come to therapy with partial memories of CSA, extensive memories, or no memories yet have a sense that something untoward has happened to them during childhood.

GUIDELINES FOR WORKING WITH CLIENTS WITH COMPLEX TRAUMA AND MEMORY DISTURBANCES

God does not take away our past; God gives it back to us—fragments gathered, stories reconfigured, selves truly redeemed, people forever reconciled.

MIROSLAV VOLF

We begin this section with several premises:

1. It is possible for individuals to experience CSA, develop memory disturbances, and later remember the CSA (Dalenberg et al., 2020).
2. Delayed memories of CSA "can be subject to all the fallibilities of memory—bias and decay" (Dalenberg et al., 2020, p. 150).
3. It is harmful to individuals (a) when others believe no CSA happened to them when CSA did occur, (b) to believe that CSA happened when it did not, and (c) to be falsely accused of perpetrating CSA.

Ambiguity tolerance.

Your future depends on how you decide to remember your past.

HENRI NOUWEN

I (Tammy) worked with Sarah, who had lengthy gaps in memories from her formative years. At the outset of therapy, she asked me if I would hypnotize her so she would know what happened to her as a child. I explained that I was not trained in hypnosis and therefore I did not use this intervention. Then I asked Sarah what she hoped would happen if I could hypnotize her. She told me that she would finally understand the reasons for so many of the struggles she had endured. She remembered numerous dysfunctional patterns in her family of origin, a family member in prison for abuse of her sibling, and no memories of significant portions of her childhood. She also reported no brain injuries, no history of substance abuse, and did not appear to be experiencing delusions or thought disorders. Sarah deeply desired to know about her life—a legitimate longing. She wanted to have a sense of herself as a child. So often, when we are in pain, we want to know the *what* and *why*. I have worked with other clients who had no childhood pictures and an absence of family stories. Thus, it is essential that we as clinicians acknowledge and affirm the good longing that we were made to have to know our histories.

As clinicians, it is also important to ask our clients at wise junctures: "What might occur if you never know what happened to you as a child?" Therapists are tasked with holding a ton of ambiguity involving situations that are unclear, inconsistent, or have too little information to be precisely understood. Ambiguity tolerance involves holding complex and nuanced understandings and meanings of the world (Furnham & Ribchester, 1995). Therapy can be an opportunity to learn to live with the uncertainties of life and ways to respond more flexibly to challenging life circumstances. Methods of developing ambiguity tolerance include gradually and regularly introducing uncertain activities in daily practice (e.g., initiating a conversation with someone unknown, wearing clothes that are different in style, and sitting in a different place in a classroom). Therapy with Christian clients can also be a space to grow in the certainty that God does know what happened and that he may reveal more of our clients' stories according to his timetable, or he may not.

Ambiguity tolerance is also a muscle to be exercised by clinicians regarding some of the harrowing narratives of CSA that clients may share in therapy. Some abuse stories may be difficult to believe. Sometimes, it is difficult to comprehend the horrific evils some individuals do to others. Alternatively, clients could be malingering; they could be experiencing thought disorders or delusions (Ross, 2023). Moreover, since memory is not a tape recorder, there may be various reasons for a lack of memories. We will never know with absolute conviction the specifics of what happened in our clients' lives. We do know that clinicians are not designed to be investigative reporters for *Dateline,* ferreting out the details so that we can reach certainty about the past. Moreover, an atmosphere of skepticism or disbelief in clinical settings can re-enact the client's family dynamics of not being believed by significant others. Developing ambiguity tolerance about many uncertainties in life and certainty in our good God's character is a high calling.

Exposure, phase-based, or modular approaches? Clients who have experienced complex posttraumatic stress disorder (CPTSD), a recognized diagnosis in the International Classification of Diseases 11th revision (ICD-11; World Health Organization, 2019), experience significant symptom complexity, extensive emotional dysregulation, and fewer coping strategies (de Boer et al., 2023). There is debate about whether exposure-based or phase-based approaches are more prudent in order to avoid symptom decompensation in clients when processing memories occurs (Brand et al., 2019; International Society for the Study of Trauma and Dissociation, 2020). Dorahy and colleagues (2017, p. 207) explain one perspective:

> Treatment guidelines and clinical experience have suggested that as patients' presentations become more complicated, exposure therapies are best withheld until a period of stabilization has been achieved, enabling patients to acquire internal and external resources before facing the magnitude of their trauma.

However, more recent research using randomized controlled trials (RCTs) reveals that therapy with an added initial stabilization phase to trauma-focused treatment approaches for CPTSD is effective but unnecessary (Oprel et al., 2021; Raabe et al., 2022; Van Vliet et al., 2021). De Jongh and Hafkemeijer (2023) indicate that there is currently significant empirical support for the use of immediate trauma-focused therapy for the treatment of CPTSD (e.g., EMDR, TF-CBT, CPT), according to general PTSD treatment guidelines, versus needing a preparatory stabilization phase. De Jongh and Hafkemeijer (2023) provide helpful suggestions regarding ways to tailor EMDR with a client with significant dissociation. Specifically, some clients may dissociate and only partially activate memories associated with a traumatic event due to fears of being overwhelmed. In this case, therapists using EMDR do well to educate and motivate clients to actively engage as much of their trauma memories as possible to purposefully tax working memory for as long as possible to facilitate desensitization and complete consolidation of memories (De Jongh & Hafkemeijer, 2023).

Alternatively, the phasic-based approach adheres to the mindset that processing complex trauma memories too quickly is like jumping into the deep end of the pool when you do not know how to swim. Thus, the emphasis is on learning to wade in the shallow end of the pool and developing skills with a trustworthy swimming coach before approaching deeper waters. Briefly, a phase-based approach includes the following:

Phase one. The goals of phase one include using psychoeducation, developing safety, and learning to manage clients' emotional thermostats. This phase involves learning to identify and experience emotions versus seesawing between emotional extremes (e.g., numbness, rage, despair) and the acquisition of healthy coping skills to replace dependence on unhealthy behaviors (e.g., substance sobriety, ability to refrain from self-injurious behaviors). As clients improve awareness and tolerance of emotions without becoming overwhelmed, decrease dissociation, master basic symptom management skills and intrapersonal and interpersonal safety, they may (optionally) advance to the next phase.

Phase two. This phase involves wisely paced processing of trauma memories while staying present and attentive to safety (e.g., using exposure-based therapies while carefully titrating to the needs of clients). It also entails grieving the loss of loving relationships and the evil that has occurred. Symptoms of emotional overload can signal the clinician to tap on the brakes and return to additional skill building.

Emancipation from clients' painful pasts comes as they face the specific memories of abuse and experience a shift in perspective as lies are replaced with truth. Clients realize that they are no longer merely victims of their past. Rather, they have suffered significantly, but they are also someone who has been delivered by God and given a new life. Miroslav Volf (2021), director of the Yale Center for Faith and Culture, explains that there is increasing freedom as individuals begin to see themselves like the ancient Israelites, not first and foremost as victims of Pharaoh but as people *delivered* by their God and who walked out of Egypt with their heads held high, (see Lev 26:13).

This phase can also include holding up the specific traumatic memory in front of the gaze of God so he can speak and bring truth in place of lies. Ultimately, we want God's perspective regarding past events and help with what we have learned to believe because of the past. Volf (2021, p. 79) further explains that true healing comes when the painful memories have been "dislodged from the center of our identity and assigned a proper place on its periphery, and that its hold over how we live in the present and how we project ourselves into the future has been broken."

Phase three. Here, the long walk toward relationship connection is predominant. Faith-based clients increasingly focus on the present and taking healthy risks, believing that God is strong enough to catch them even when the risk-taking does not turn out the way they hoped. Forgiveness is integral to this phase (see "Flying Above the Fray" chapter). Grief work continues as individuals face the cumulative losses attached to abuse over their lifetime.

Over the past few years, there has also been an increasing call for a trauma-informed modular approach, which is a personalized treatment approach that includes a flexible style and the tailoring of interventions to individual clients depending on their unique symptoms and circumstances (Elsaesser et al., 2022). A modular approach considers the severity of symptoms clients are experiencing and the client's readiness to grapple with specific client concerns (Owczarek et al., 2023). Thus, it may spend extended time using a phasic approach (focus on phase one skill building and emotional regulation skills) before using an exposure-based approach, depending on the client's needs (Karatzias & Cloitre, 2019).

Differentiating therapeutic inquiries to avoid suggestive pressure. Several lawsuits have been levied against clinicians who have worked with clients who have reported delayed memories of abuse (Otgaar et al., 2022). A central complaint in these cases was therapists who used suggestive pressure and leading questions that contained information that influenced client memories of childhood events. We distinguish three types of questions used in clinical settings to develop wise practices with clients reporting abuse or delayed memories of abuse.

Open-ended questions invite a response of more than one to two words and pave the way for the client's candid thoughts, feelings, attitudes, or opinions. Open-ended questions can empower clients to speak truthfully and without bias/influence. These questions may begin with the words *how, what,* or *who.* Examples of open-ended questions include "How were you feeling?" or "What sensory memories do you recall from that day (e.g., things you saw, heard)?"

Closed-ended questions are often answered in one to two words or invite clients to affirm or disaffirm the content. These types of questions can be helpful when gathering much information during intake sessions, obtaining specific information, narrowing the topic of discussion, and helping clients share detailed information. Examples of closed-ended questions include "Were you scared?"

Leading questions are problematic in therapy because they prompt a specific response. Using leading questions or statements can be harmful because they are assumptive and suggestive. Some examples:

- You have mentioned an unhealthy attachment with men for most of your life. Sometimes, this traces to abuse between daughters and their fathers. (*assumptive*)
- If you are willing, I want you to go back to your earliest memories with your father. Is it possible he ever abused you? (*suggestive*)
- Do you have any traumatic memories with your mother? (*assumption and suggestive*)
- Sometimes, survivors bury memories very deeply. (*assumption*)
- Trauma often occurs in the home during everyday activities. Did he ever penetrate you sexually when changing your diaper or during bath time? (*suggestive*)
- There is probably something you did not understand then but can understand now. (*assumptive*)

As previously discussed, therapists must be cautious and patient with clients with unclear or uncertain memories of possible trauma. It is critical to educate and remind clients that it is acceptable not to be able to recall certain aspects of their history and to say "I don't know" or "I cannot recall" when asked questions they do not know the answers to. In this way, therapists educate and empathize that memories can be complicated, incomplete, or unknown.

In summary, the therapeutic relationship involves a power dynamic between a vulnerable and exposed client and a powerful professional. It is a painful experience for clients who have experienced abuse and have not been believed by loved ones. Thus, as clinicians we need to provide spaces that honor clients and their experiences and opportunities to develop ambiguity tolerance regarding memories that may not be recalled for a time or indefinitely. Moreover, it is essential that when clients indicate delayed memories, we explore the multiple reasons for delayed memories. As we gather information, open-ended questions allow clients to tell their stories without being influenced by the question itself. While we might have therapeutic hunches about clients' histories, it is crucial to give space for clients to tell their stories absent of suggestive pressure.

ESTABLISHING EBENEZERS

Samuel took a single rock and set it upright between Mizpah and Shen. He named it "Ebenezer" (Rock of Help), saying, "This marks the place where God helped us."

1 SAMUEL 7:12 MSG

We conclude this chapter by underscoring that clinicians need to attend to clients' painful memories *and* hopeful remembrances (e.g., times when God has worked in their lives). This work corresponds with flourishing and post-traumatic growth concepts (see the "Living Beyond Desolate" chapter).

Though not specific to CSA, it might be helpful to draw on the wisdom of those who mourn and the practices suggested for commemorating loss. Establishing memorials is a common way of helping individuals and entire communities who have had loved ones die. For example, Rwanda genocide survivors have aided in developing national and local memorials throughout the country (Ibreck, 2010); white "ghost" bikes have been installed at sites where cyclists have been killed (Costantini, 2019). One group of researchers explored the idea that "roadside memorials function as holy grounds" (Klaassens et al., 2007), a place where a person was last alive. Perhaps survivors of CSA, too, need a kind of memorial—a way of signaling that *this happened, it mattered,* and *I am different because of it.*

Building monuments out of stones was a frequent practice of the Hebrew nation in the Old Testament (Arnold, 2003). Jacob used a stone to commemorate that God met him at Bethel in an "awesome" way (Gen 28:17). Joshua placed twelve stones to remember where God led the Israelites across the parted Jordan River (Josh 4:1-9). Later, we see Samuel continue this monument-building tradition. Following a time of fasting and genuine repentance, the Israelites defeated the Philistines. "Then Samuel took a stone and set it up between Mizpah and Jeshanah and named it Ebenezer, for he said, 'Thus far the LORD has helped us'" (1 Sam 7:12).

Stone upon stone was placed as a permanent reminder that God had been faithful and acted on behalf of his people. These monuments served as a visual reminder that their victory was not due to their power or brilliance but because of their great God. Moreover, future generations saw these stones and were reminded that God helps his people. Building Ebenezers was an act of worship.

Imagine if survivors commemorated the ways God has helped, times when God led them to freedom, turning-point experiences he has brought them to, and ways God specifically remembered them. Some may not remember all the abuse experiences, but what clients can remember is even more critical: God's grace, which is placed stone upon stone in their lives.

Once again, we do not know what Tamar's experience was with her memories of being assaulted. We live with the ambiguity of her story and wonder and hope that she and others could honor what she lost and somehow cling to the goodness of God. It is a privilege to aid a person in harvesting the work of God in their life—and to *remember*.

Some of our clients' Ebenezers may be their dad's tattered old Bible that symbolized how he prayed for them. It may be a picture of someone who told them about Jesus. It may be an object that reminds them of when someone offered them a safe harbor in a raging storm. Perhaps it is the words written on a slip of paper that Jesus whispered when they asked him how he feels about them.

May our clients keep a collection of these items—on a wall, in a journal, or in a box. Together, may we echo Samuel's words, "Thus far the LORD has helped us." And may we sing from deep inside of us the lyrics of the classic hymn "Come, Thou Fount of Ev'ry Blessing":

> Here I raise my Ebenezer; hither by thy help I've come;
> and I hope, by thy good pleasure, safely to arrive at home.
> Jesus sought me when a stranger, wandering from the fold of God;
> he, to rescue me from danger, interposed with precious blood.

COUNSELING CONSIDERATIONS

Recent randomized control trial data suggests that some clients with complex trauma do not necessarily require extensive resourcing/stabilization prior to trauma-related or purely exposure-based treatment (Oprel et al., 2021; Raabe et al., 2022; Van Vliet et al., 2021). Additionally, for some clients a phasic-based approach can be helpful when wading into complex or incomplete memories. Just as the memory retrieval process is idiosyncratic for each survivor, so too approaches to treatment need to be flexible enough to "fit" the specific client. A major takeaway we hope to impart in this chapter is how critical education, awareness/sensitivity, and risk management are for clinicians working with clients who have experienced complex trauma.

- *Education:* From the outset of the therapy relationship with clients with complex trauma-related memories, it is critical that a therapist takes a patient, nonleading, noncoercive approach providing ample education on how traumatic memories can be encoded and how some aspects of traumatic memory may be hazy or not recalled. This can help normalize the challenging nature of trauma memories and the spectrum of possible memory-related experiences.
- *Awareness/sensitivity:* Evidence-based practice marries research-informed therapeutic intervention with client preferences and clinician training. Clinicians can glean contemporary clinical practice

guidelines for the treatment of traumatic stress and refine the trajectory of therapy based on client needs/preferences. For example, some clients may benefit from a slower, phasic-based approach with careful grounding skills work to prevent dissociation, whereas others may move more quickly through the therapy process with fewer instances of dissociation. In our experience, each client is different, and yet, the common elements inherent in most trauma-informed care can be implemented.

- *Risk management:* Consultation with colleagues and use of research-informed therapy interventions go a long way to ensure clinicians serve ethically within their scope of practice.

CHILDREN'S CORNER

- ***A Terrible Thing Happened*** (Holmes, 2000): Sherman, a young raccoon, saw something disturbing. He tried to forget about it, but eventually, he experienced scary dreams and became aggressive to other children. The author does not specify the nature of the trauma that Sherman experienced. Sherman meets Ms. Maple, who helps him discuss what happened, and Sherman eventually feels better.
- ***Once I Was Very Very Scared*** (Ghosh Ippen, 2016): The story tells about many little animals who experienced some difficult experiences and ways they tried to cope. The turtle hides and gets a tummy ache, the monkey clings tightly, the dog barks, and the elephant does not want to talk about what happened. They need help from an adult to help them feel safe and find ways to cope with their feelings.

REFERENCES

American Psychiatric Association. (2022). *Diagnostic and statistical manual of mental disorders* (5th ed., text rev.). https://doi.org/10.1176/appi.books.9780890425787

Arnold, B. T. (2003). *The NIV 1 & 2 Samuel application commentary.* Zondervan.

Bailey, T. D., & Brand, B. L. (2017). Traumatic dissociation: Theory, research, and treatment. *Clinical Psychology: Science and Practice, 24*(2), 170-85. https://doi.org/10.1111/cpsp.12195

Bidzan, M. (2017). Biological bases of dissociative amnesia. *Acta Neuropsychologia, 15*(1), 1-11. https://doi.org/10.5604/12321966.1233199

Blihar, D., Crisafio, A., Delgado, E., Buryak, M., Gonzalez, M., & Waechter, R. (2021). A meta-analysis of hippocampal and amygdala volumes in patients diagnosed with dissociative identity disorder. *Journal of Trauma & Dissociation*, *22*(3), 365-77. https://doi.org/10.1080/15299732.2020.1869650

Brand, B. L., Loewenstein, R. J., Schielke, H. J., Van Der Hart, O., Nijenhuis, E. R. S., Schlumpf, Y. R., Vissia, E. M., Jepsen, E. K. K., & Reinders, A. A. T. S. (2019). Cautions and concerns about Huntjens et al.'s Schema Therapy for Dissociative Identity Disorder. *European Journal of Psychotraumatology*, *10*(1), 1631698. https://doi.org/10.1080/20008198.2019.1631698

Brewin, C. R. (2021). Tilting at windmills: Why attacks on repression are misguided. *Perspectives on Psychological Science*, *16*(2), 443-53. https://doi.org/10.1177/1745691620927674

Brewin, C. R., & Andrews, B. (2017). Creating memories for false autobiographical events in childhood: A systematic review. *Applied Cognitive Psychology*, *31*(1), 2-23. https://doi.org/10.1002/acp.3220

Brewin, C. R., Andrews, B., & Mickes, L. (2020). Regaining consensus on the reliability of memory. *Current Directions in Psychological Science, 29*(2), 121-25. https://doi.org/10.1177/0963721419898122

Brown, D. W., Anda, R. F., Edwards, V. J., Felitti, V. J., Dube, S. R., & Giles, W. H. (2007). Adverse childhood experiences and childhood autobiographical memory disturbance. *Child Abuse & Neglect*, *31*(9), 961-69. https://doi.org/10.1016/j.chiabu.2007.02.011

Caiola, S. (2021, September 1). *How rape affects memory, and why police need to know about that brain science.* KFF Health News. https://kffhealthnews.org/news/article/how-rape-affects-memory-and-why-police-need-to-know-about-that-brain-science

Cheit, R. (2023). Recovered Memory Project: Case archive, commentary, and scholarly resources. https://blogs.brown.edu/recoveredmemory/

Constantini, N. (2019). Bikes and bodies: Ghost bike memorials as performances of mourning, warning, and protest. *Text and Performance Quarterly, 39*(1), 22-36. https://doi.org/10.1080/10462937.2019.1576919

Dalenberg, C. J., Brand, B. L., Loewenstein, R. J., Frewen, P. A., & Spiegel, D. (2020). Inviting scientific discourse on traumatic dissociation: Progress made and obstacles to further resolution. *Psychological Injury and Law*, *13*, 135-54. https://doi.org/10.1007/s12207-020-09376-9

Damis, L. F. (2022). The role of implicit memory in the development and recovery from trauma-related disorders. *NeuroSci*, *3*(1), 63-88. https://doi.org/10.3390/neurosci3010005

de Boer, K., Arnold, C., Mackelprang, J. L., Williamson, D., Eckel, D., & Nedeljkovic, M. (2023). Outcomes from a pilot study to evaluate phase 1 of a two-phase approach to treat women with complex trauma histories. *Australian Psychologist*, 1-11. https://doi.org/10.1080/00050067.2023.2192335

De Jongh, A., & Hafkemeijer, L. C. S. (2023). Trauma-focused treatment of a client with complex PTSD and comorbid pathology using EMDR therapy. *Journal of Clinical Psychology, 80*(4), 824-35. https://doi.org/10.1002/jclp.23521

DePrince, A. P., Brown, L. S., Cheit, R. E., Freyd, J. J., Gold, S. N., Pezdek, K., & Quina, K. (2012). Motivated forgetting and misremembering: Perspectives from betrayal trauma theory. In R. Belli (Ed.), *True and false recovered memories: Toward a reconciliation of the debate* (pp. 193-242). Nebraska Symposium on Motivation. Springer. https://doi.org/10.1007/978-1-4614-1195-6_7

Dodier, O., & Patihis, L. (2020). Recovered memories of child abuse outside of therapy. *Applied Cognitive Psychology*, *35*(2), 538-47. https://doi.org/10.1002/acp.3783

Dodier, O., Patihis, L., & Payoux, M. (2019). Reports of recovered memories of childhood abuse in therapy in France. *Memory*, *27*(9), 1283-98. https://doi.org/10.1080/09658211.2019.1652654

Dorahy, M. J., Lewis-Fernández, R., Krüger, C., Brand, B. L., Şar, V., Ewing, J., Martínez-Taboas, A., Stavropoulos, P., & Middleton, W. (2017). The role of clinical experience, diagnosis, and theoretical orientation in the treatment of posttraumatic and dissociative disorders: A vignette and survey investigation. *Journal of Trauma & Dissociation*, *18*(2), 206-22. https://doi.org/10.1080/15299732.2016.1225626

Elsaesser, M., Herpertz, S., Piosczyk, H., Jenkner, C., Hautzinger, M., & Schramm, E. (2022). Modular-based psychotherapy (MoBa) versus cognitive-behavioural therapy (CBT) for patients with depression, comorbidities and a history of childhood maltreatment: Study protocol for a randomised controlled feasibility trial. *BMJ Open*, *12*(7), e057672. http://doi.org/10.1136/bmjopen-2021-057672

Felitti, V. J., & Anda, R. F. (2010). The relationship of adverse childhood experiences to adult medical disease, psychiatric disorders, and sexual behavior: Implications for healthcare. In R.A. Lanius, E. Vermetten, & C. Pain. (Eds.), *The hidden epidemic: The impact of early life trauma on health and disease* (pp. 77-87). Cambridge University Press.

Fox, J. (Dir.). (2018). *The Tale.* [Film]. HBO Films.

Freyd, J. J. (1996). *Betrayal trauma: The logic of forgetting childhood abuse*. Harvard University Press.

Furnham, A., & Ribchester, T. (1995). Tolerance of ambiguity: A review of the concept, its measurement and applications. *Current Psychology: A Journal for Diverse Perspectives on Diverse Psychological Issues, 14*(3), 179-99. https://doi.org/10.1007/BF02686907

Goldfarb, D., Goodman, G. S., Larson, R. P., Eisen, M. L., & Qin, J. (2019). Long-term memory in adults exposed to childhood violence: Remembering genital contact nearly 20 years later. *Clinical Psychological Science*, *7*(2), 381-96. https://doi.org/10.1177/2167702618805742

Gómez, J. M., Freyd, J. J., Delva, J., Tracy, B., Mackenzie, L. N., Ray, V., & Weathington, B. (2023). Institutional courage in action: Racism, sexual violence, & concrete institutional change. *Journal of Trauma & Dissociation*, *24*(2), 157-70. https://doi.org/10.1080/15299732.2023.2168245

Goodman, G. S., Gonzalves, L., & Wolpe, S. (2019). False memories and true memories of childhood trauma: Balancing the risks. *Clinical Psychological Science*, *7*(1), 29-31. https://doi.org/10.1177/2167702618797106

Grinker, R. R., & Spiegel, J. P. (1945). *Men under stress.* Blakiston. https://doi.org/10.1037/10784-000

Herman, J. L. (2022). *Trauma and recovery: The aftermath of violence—from domestic abuse to political terror*. Basic Books.

Holmes, M. M. (2020). *A terrible thing happened: A story for children who have witnessed violence or trauma*. American Psychological Association.

Ibreck, R. (2010). The politics of mourning: Survivor contributions to memorials in post-genocide Rwanda. *Memory Studies*, *3*(4), 330-43. https://doi.org/10.1177/1750698010374921

International Society for the Study of Trauma and Dissociation. (2020). *Getting treatment for complex trauma and dissociation.* www.isst-d.org/wp-content/uploads/2020/03/Fact-Sheet-V-Getting-Treatment-for-Complex-Trauma-and-Dissociation-1-1.pdf

International Society for Traumatic Stress Studies. (2023). *Recovered memories of childhood trauma.* https://istss.org/public-resources/trauma-basics/what-is-childhood-trauma/remembering-childhood-trauma

Ippen, C. G., & Ippen, C. H. (2017). *Once I was very very scared*. Piplo Productions.

Karatzias, T., & Cloitre, M. (2019). Treating adults with complex posttraumatic stress disorder using a modular approach to treatment: Rationale, evidence, and directions for future research. *Journal of Traumatic Stress*, *32*(6), 870-76. https://doi.org/10.1002/jts.22457

Kihlstrom, J. F., McNally, R. J., Loftus, E. F., & Pope, H., Jr. (2005). The problem of child sexual abuse. *Science, 309*(5738), 1182-84.

Klaassens, M., Groote, P., & Breen, V. (2007). *Roadside memorials: Public places of private grief.* [Unpublished manuscript]. Department of Spatial Sciences, University of Groningen, Groningen, Netherlands.

Loewenstein, R. J. (2018) Dissociation debates: Everything you know is wrong. *Dialogues in Clinical Neuroscience, 20*(3), 229-42. https://doi.org/10.31887/DCNS.2018.20.3/rloewenstein

Loftus, E. F., & Pickrell, J. E. (1995). The formation of false memories. *Psychiatric Annals*, *25*(12), 720-25. https://psycnet.apa.org/doi/10.3928/0048-5713-19951201-07

Lynn, S. J., McNally, R. J., & Loftus, E. F. (2023). The memory wars then and now: The contributions of Scott O. Lilienfeld. *Clinical Psychological Science*, *11*(4). https://doi.org/10.1177/21677026221133034

Macur, J. (2023, March 20). Jennifer Fox said a coach abused her. Now she has named a legend. *The New York Times*. www.nytimes.com/2023/03/20/sports/olympics/jennifer-fox-sexual-abuse-the-tale.html

Mangiulli, I., Otgaar, H., Jelicic, M., & Merckelbach, H. (2021). A critical review of case studies on dissociative amnesia. *Clinical Psychological Science*, *10*(2), 191-211. https://doi.org/10.1177/21677026211018194

McNally, R. J. (2003). Recovering memories of trauma: A view from the laboratory. *Current Directions in Psychological Science, 12*(1), 32-35. https://doi.org/10.1111/1467-8721.01217

Oprel, D. A. C., Hoeboer, C. M., Schoorl, M., Kleine, R. A., Cloitre, M., Wigard, I. G., van Minnen, A., & van der Does, W. (2021). Effect of prolonged exposure, intensified prolonged exposure and STAIR + prolonged exposure in patients with PTSD related to childhood abuse: A randomized controlled trial. *European Journal of Psychotraumatology,12*(1), 1-13. https://doi.org/10.1080/20008198.2020.1851511

Otgaar, H., Curci, A., Mangiulli, I., Battista, F., Rizzotti, E., & Sartori, G. (2022). A court ruled case on therapy-induced false memories. *Journal of Forensic Sciences, 67*(5), 2122-29. https://doi.org/10.1111/1556-4029.15073

Otgaar, H., Howe, M. L., Dodier, O., Lilienfeld, S. O., Loftus, E. F., Lynn, S. J., Merckelbach, H., & Patihis, L. (2021). Belief in unconscious repressed memory persists. *Perspectives on Psychological Science: A Journal of the Association for Psychological Science, 16*(2), 454-60. https://doi.org/10.1177/1745691621990628

Otgaar, H., Howe, M. L., Patihis, L., Mangiulli, I., Dodier, O., Huntjens, R., Krackow, E., Jelicic, M., & Lynn, S. J. (2023). The neuroscience of dissociative amnesia and repressed memory: Premature conclusions and unanswered questions. *Legal and Criminological Psychology*. https://openaccess.city.ac.uk/id/eprint/30341/

Owczarek, M., Karatzias, T., McElroy, E., Hyland, P., Cloitre, M., Kratzer, L., Knefel, M., Grandison, G., Ho, G. W. K., Morris, D., & Shevlin, M. (2023). Borderline personality disorder (BPD) and complex posttraumatic stress disorder (CPTSD): A network analysis in a highly traumatized clinical sample. *Journal of Personality Disorders, 37*(1), 112-29. https://doi.org/10.1521/pedi.2023.37.1.112

Patihis, L., & Pendergrast, M. H. (2019). Reports of recovered memories of abuse in therapy in a large age-representative US national sample: Therapy type and decade comparisons. *Clinical Psychological Science, 7*(1), 3-21. https://doi.org/10.1177/2167702618773315

Pezdek, K., Finger, K., & Hodge, D. (1997). Planting false childhood memories: The role of event plausibility. *Psychological Science, 8*(6), 437-41. https://doi.org/10.1111/j.1467-9280.1997.tb00457.x

Pope, H. G., Jr., Oliva, P. S., & Hudson, J. I. (1999). Repressed memories: The scientific status. In D. L. Faigman, D. H. Kaye, M. J. Saks, & J. Sanders (Eds.), *Modern scientific testimony: The law and science of expert testimony* (Vol. 1, pp. 115-55). West Publishing.

Raabe, S., Ehring, T., Marquenie, L., Arntz, A., & Kindt, M. (2022). Imagery rescripting as a stand-alone treatment for posttraumatic stress disorder related to childhood abuse: A randomized controlled trial. *Journal of Behavior Therapy and Experimental Psychiatry,77,* 1-13. https://doi.org/10.1016/j.jbtep.2022.101769

Ross, C. A. (2022). False memory researchers misunderstand repression, dissociation, and Freud. *Journal of Child Sexual Abuse, 31*(4), 488-502. https://doi.org/10.1080/10538712.2022.2067095

Ross, C. A. (2023). The false memory debate: A reply to Otgaar. *Journal of Child Sexual Abuse, 32*(1), 127-29. http://doi.org/10.1080/10538712.2023.2166887

Sargant, W., & Slater, E. (1941). Amnesic syndromes in war. *Proceedings of the Royal Society of Medicine, 34*(12), 757-64.

Shaw, J., & Porter, S. (2015). Constructing rich false memories of committing crime. *Psychological Science, 26*(3), 291-301. https://doi.org/10.1177/0956797614562862

Thom, D. A., & Fenton, N. (1920). Amnesias in war cases. *American Journal of Psychiatry, 76*(4), 437-48.

van der Kolk, B. A., McFarlane, A. C., & Weisaeth, L. (Eds.). (1996). *Traumatic stress: The effects of overwhelming experience on mind, body, and society.* Guilford.

Van Vliet, N. I., Huntjens, R. J. C., van Dijk, M. K., & De Jongh, A. (2021). Phase-based treatment versus immediate trauma-focused treatment for post-traumatic stress disorder due to childhood abuse: Randomised clinical trial. *British Journal of Psychiatry Open, 7*(e211), 1-7. https://doi.org/10.1192/bjo.2021.1057

Volf, M. (2021). *The end of memory: Remembering rightly in a violent world.* Eerdmans.

Wade, K. A., Garry, M., & Pezdek, K. (2018). Deconstructing rich false memories of committing crime: Commentary on Shaw and Porter (2015). *Psychological Science*, 29(3), 471-76. https://psycnet.apa.org/doi/10.1177/0956797617703667

Weis, C. N., Webb, E. K., Huggins, A. A., Kallenbach, M., Miskovich, T. A., Fitzgerald, J. M., Bennett, K. P., Krukowski, J. L., deRoon-Cassini, T. A., & Larson, C. L. (2021). Stability of hippocampal subfield volumes after trauma and relationship to development of PTSD symptoms. *NeuroImage, 236*, 118076. https://doi.org/10.1016/j.neuroimage.2021.118076

World Health Organization. (2019). *International statistical classification of diseases and related health problems* (11th ed.). https://icd.who.int/

Zhang, L., Lu, L., Bu, X., Li, H., Tang, S., Gao, Y., Liang, K., Zhang, S., Hu, X., Wang, Y., Li, L., Hu, X., Lim, K. O., Gong, Q., & Huang, X. (2021). Alterations in hippocampal subfield and amygdala subregion volumes in posttraumatic subjects with and without posttraumatic stress disorder. *Human Brain Mapping*, *42*(7), 2147-58. https://doi.org/10.1002/hbm.25356

7

INDOMITABLE HOPE

In·dom·i·ta·ble (adj.):
Incapable of being overcome, subdued, or vanquished; unconquerable.

Hope is being able to see that there is light despite all of the darkness.

DESMOND TUTU

And hope does not disappoint.

ROMANS 5:5 NASB

HOPE IS A DANGEROUS THING

Andy Dufresne was sentenced to life in prison for a crime he did not commit—a hopeless situation (Darabont, 1994). Yet there was something different about Andy. From day one, he involved himself in personal hobbies and made a few friends along the way. As time passed, Andy, a banker on the outside, became even more involved by assisting inmates and staff with their taxes and helping inmates achieve their high school equivalency. He also wrote letters to request books for the new library at Shawshank Prison, and after years of writing letters, he received a myriad of books and a few records. Andy loved music. So, in a moment of pure rebellion, he played an Italian opera on the speaker system for the entire prison to hear after locking one of the guards in the bathroom. Andy's fellow inmate and close friend, Red, described hearing that beautiful music in prison. As he listened to the music, his heart soared as he was free for a brief moment.

After Andy spent two weeks in solitary confinement, he entered the cafeteria with an unusual glow, and the guys began to ask him how he did it. How was he undisturbed after two weeks of solitary confinement? He took the music with him, was his reply. Confusion sprawled over their faces since the warden would not have permitted a record player in solitary confinement. Andy explained that he carried the music in his heart, that the music awakened his hope. Red became unglued. Hope only makes a man go insane; he shot back. Hope has no use in prison . . . it is a dangerous thing.

Hope is not a game many survivors play anymore, as *"hope is a dangerous thing"* (Darabont, 1994). As one survivor said, "When daddy lifted me onto his lap, I hoped this time he would just hold me, spend time with me, and love me." Yet when incest trails, hope and the desire for love frequently become despised enemies. For many, hope feels like foreplay to a violation. Consequently, survivors may train themselves to avoid hope, not to desire, and not to allow themselves to yearn for something more to protect themselves from one more grand let-down. Eventually, many survivors learn not to hope from others and God as well. As John Eldredge (2007, p. 20) states, "Hope rouses the desire from its slumber and makes us even more vulnerable to disappointment."

While many survivors learn to avoid hope, Victor Frankl, a Jewish psychiatrist, neurologist, Holocaust survivor, and significant pioneer in the mental health field, discovered that hope was critical for life (Frankl, 1985). Frankl developed this belief in what seems the most unlikely of places: a dark and dehumanizing World War II concentration camp, a place where his wife, father, and mother died. Frankl witnessed that while he and fellow inmates couldn't make sense of their abject suffering, those who had nothing to live for quickly died. Yet those who did not lose hope survived.

Burgeoning mental health research has also revealed that hope is critical to therapeutic effectiveness (Irving et al., 2004; Schrank et al., 2011). Clients bring differing degrees of hope about whether therapy can be helpful and whether change can occur. Schrank and colleagues (2011, p. 427) state that hope is "a potent predictor of quality of life and other positive outcome domains in a wide range of health conditions . . . [and an] important health outcome in its own right." Moreover, a meta-analytical study reviewing the relationship between posttraumatic stress symptoms, hope, optimism, and self-efficacy found that each positive expectancy was associated with lower levels of posttraumatic stress symptoms (Gallagher et al., 2020).

Given the centrality of hope as a component of flourishing in the aftermath of egregious trauma (Munoz et al., 2020), this chapter examines the essence of hope discussed in the mental health literature and in Scripture. We also explore and illustrate ways to nurture hope in therapy. We include using lament with a client as a religion-specific way to cope with CSA. Hope is not exclusive to clients, so we also look at clinicians' hope to conclude the chapter.

THE ESSENCE OF HOPE

Positive psychology commenced in the 1990s as mental health research pivoted from an exclusive focus on psychopathology/illness toward individuals' strengths, virtues, and adaptive aspects. This shift marked a time of empirical attention on flourishing rather than failing, well-being versus woe, and hope versus hopelessness. In this context, Snyder and colleagues (1991) developed a cognitively based theory of hope that entails more than wishful thinking and seeing hope as exclusively an emotion. Hope theory consists of well-defined goals and two cognitive components: (a) agency and (b) pathway thinking.

Agency thinking involves the motivation to pursue an identified goal, such as, "I believe I can do this because . . ." and "I want to do this because . . ." Thus, according to Snyder, hopeful individuals focus their energies on specific, challenging goals fueled by their beliefs in their abilities to persist and succeed in accomplishing the goals. Agency thinking can be bolstered by a person's awareness of her signature strengths, wisdom and mastery from past experiences, and confidence that one's abilities can foster change or growth. Hope theory asserts that highly hopeful individuals are conscious of their agency. In contrast, pathway thinking involves one's perceived abilities to develop numerous routes to overcome obstacles when barriers emerge in pursuit of a goal. Multiple pathways can help goals become more attainable. According to Snyder, both pathway and agency thinking are necessary to maintain hope.

Colla et al. (2022), however, noted the acontextual limitations of Snyder's original hope theory and the cultural biases inherent in a theory largely crafted and studied in individualistic Western cultures. Colla et al. (2022) highlight ways to expand on Snyder's initial agency and pathway constructs, including interpersonal nuances and intrapersonal factors. For example, agency may well be bolstered by individual strengths and someone's family, community, and essential groups. Intrapersonal factors highlight the roles of coherence and purpose underneath the goal-directed pathway processes associated with hope. Simply put, expanding the agency/pathway approach with careful attention to how humans comprehend and assign meaning to various goals expands the traditional model and illuminates new facets of bolstering hope.

From a theological integration perspective, there are benefits and limitations to Snyder's agency and pathway hope theory. Using a theological lens, a more nuanced understanding of hope recognizes that God is sovereign and can strengthen individuals to engage in flourishing behaviors that they have not previously imagined. Hoover-Kinsinger's (2018) perspective can be helpful for survivors who maintain helpless and hopeless beliefs regarding personal abilities. For example, agency thinking based on an awareness of God's strength can include statements in specific circumstances, such as "God can do this" or "God can help me do this." This more nuanced understanding of hope recognizes that God is sovereign, and he can strengthen individuals to engage in flourishing behaviors that they have not previously imagined.

Further, from an applied theological perspective, Rueger and colleagues (2022) expand Snyder's agency and pathway conceptualization of hope with an essential third facet. This component includes a transcendent component named *persevering hope*. They explain that this aspect of hope is germane to individuals in "seemingly impossible circumstances, enduring multiple losses, or living with protracted uncertainty" (Rueger et al., 2022, p. 69). Throughout Scripture, we are invited to ask God for "impossible" requests, yet the outcomes of these circumstantial changes are not guaranteed, as God does not always promise to change our circumstances, or he may ask us to wait. In five separate studies, Rueger and colleagues found evidence of persevering hope distinct from Snyder's agency and pathway thinking. Thus, these researchers (2022, p. 68) conceptualized agency thinking as "will-power," pathway thinking as "way-power," and persevering hope as "wait-power."

This persevering, future-oriented hope (i.e., wait-power) is founded on how hope is defined in both the Old and New Testaments. The first use of the word "hope" in the Old Testament is in the book of Ruth when Naomi reveals that she has no hope (Ruth 1:12). The Hebrew word translated as hope means to expect (Strong, 2010). The New Testament provides a fuller understanding as the Greek word for hope connotes a firm or confident expectation that what God has promised in his Word is true, has occurred, or will happen

(Strong, 2010). The eschatological aspect of hope is anchored in Someone (2 Cor 1:10). This strand of hope is relational, rooted in God's steadfast character and promises. God loves and is with the brokenhearted in their darkest hours; nothing that happen to individuals is outside his awareness, and abuse will one day not have the last word. This hope is the inheritance of Christians that is impossible to subdue or defeat. It is indomitable.

So, how do we as clinicians cultivate hope in therapy with survivors who have a relationship with God and for survivors who do not? To be sure, clinicians cannot conjure up hope in clients. As therapists, we are not like midwives who coax and draw hope from survivors who already have hope within. Thus, let's turn to what fostering hope in intentional and effective ways looks like in therapy.

NURTURING HOPE IN THERAPY

Tread carefully and thoughtfully. First and foremost, it is essential to remember that survivors may be wary of hope. Some who have been sexually abused, believe, like Nietzsche (1908), "hope is the worst of evils because it prolongs man's torments." From this perspective, numbing and ultimately annihilating the stirring of emotions and hope within can become a salient aim. Thus, clinicians would be wise to tread carefully as some survivors are likely to flee when others are near the flickering embers of hope in their souls. In a session, this can look like a client who begins pushing back in therapy, despite repeated demonstrations of a supportive and nurturing space, or avoiding therapeutic homework to avoid the disappointment that life will not change even if they give their all. Survivors may wonder when the other proverbial shoe will drop (e.g., the therapist secretly judges; the therapist will one day walk away when they get to know the survivor).

Simultaneously, survivors can also hold intense attachments to specific hopes that are not within their control (e.g., hoping that a partner will relinquish their attachment to illicit substances). Providing space for dialogue and helping survivors discern what they are hoping for can be beneficial (Larsen et al., 2014). Given that a picture is often worth a thousand words, clients can be invited to express "what gives you hope" through a collage, drawing, or sculpture using various artistic materials (e.g., crayons, charcoal, chalk, paint, fabric) (Koehn, et al., 2012; Larsen et al., 2007).

Perceiving authentic hope as complex (Neff & McMinn, 2020), a process, and a realistic assessment of painful circumstances (e.g., violence occurring within an intimate relationship) versus wishful thinking or denial of pain leads to a nuanced and multidimensional understanding of hope (Edwards & Jovanovski, 2016). This understanding prompts an awareness that for many survivors, it takes time to come to contend with specific relationships and dynamics, and what survivors are putting their hope in may "shift over time" (Larsen et al., 2014, p. 280).

Scott, a survivor of CSA, placed his hope in his wife for years. He largely abandoned other relationships and focused on caring for his wife. The day she had an affair with another man, Scott was devastated, as his source of hope and comfort had shattered and was now a source of pain. He and his wife began a years-long journey of repairing their marriage, but one of the last things Scott had to contend with was his misplaced hope. He had expected his wife to resolve his deepest wounds, though she could never do that. Unfortunately, this pressure contributed to the context in which his wife chose an affair.

Naming the brokenness. Sticks and stones and words can hurt us. The PTSD literature reveals that avoiding traumatic memories and the feelings attached to them is common (Caldas et al., 2022). While avoidance may be effective in the short term, it can cause more harm in the long term as avoidant behaviors are associated with increased PTSD symptoms. In a trusting relationship, clinicians can help survivors begin to express their feared memories. I (Hannah) attended a conference years ago where Dan Allender (2007) told a poignant story about an older woman naming her long-avoided brokenness for the first time. A former student of Allender's interacted with a client in a nursing home. The older woman had sailed on the *Lusitania*, and this student proceeded to ask some basic questions:

Student: How did you get on the boat, and what were you doing on that?

Elderly woman: I was thirteen, and I was coming to the United States. I was a musician and in that, I loved the opportunity to meet Americans and to play for the very first time in America. I don't play anymore. In fact, I didn't play after I came back from America.

Student: You used to play, and now you don't? And then you said you didn't play soon after you returned?

All this student did was restate what the elderly woman had said with a tone of compassion and concern, and the elderly woman began to look very uncomfortable. The woman explained that she had *never* talked about what happened so many years before.

Student: You've never talked about it . . . about why you stopped playing?

Elderly woman: My parents and friends asked at the time, but I couldn't say.

Student: What is it that brought you to a point where you made the decision [not to play]?

Elderly woman: My teacher went with me on the *Lusitania,* and he did things to me that ought to never have been done to a thirteen-year-old.

The woman who uttered this sentence was ninety-two years old. From age thirteen to ninety-two, no one had asked the simple question as to why she stopped making music. Yet, when someone finally asked, she sincerely said, "That day, when he did those things, the music died." Survivors of CSA need relational spaces to tell sordid stories of sorrow and suffering and opportunities to name the brokenness.

BOLSTERING WILL-POWER, WAY-POWER, AND WAIT-POWER THINKING

Hope is patience with the lamp lit.

TERTULLIAN

Therapists can process will-power, way-power, and wait-power thinking with clients. For many who have been violated and tasted powerlessness, deeply engrained beliefs develop, such as "I am powerless," even in situations where they can choose and act. Here, it may be particularly beneficial for a therapist to highlight will-power and way-power thinking as an intervention throughout therapy, such as, "Let's explore times in your past when you handled adversity effectively. What did you do, or what was different then?" to move toward agency thinking. The therapist may also collaborate with clients to determine initial steps toward flourishing (including therapy) to reinforce pathway thinking.

When working with a faith-based survivor of CSA, a clinician can invite wait-power dialogues, such as what it looks like to persist in asking God for the survivor's deepest needs (to keep knocking; cf. Lk 18:1-8) and what it looks like to actively wait for God's best timing (versus despair). Another way to bolster hope involves learning to engage in the biblical practice of lament.

LAMENTING LOSSES

Hope itself is like a star, not to be seen in the sunshine of prosperity, and only to be discovered in the night of adversity.

CHARLES H. SPURGEON

A significant yet seemingly paradoxical way of nurturing hope involves coping with the losses related to CSA through lament. Since anguish and hope can coexist, expressing and sorting through the despair can provide avenues to hope. In the foreword of a book of sermons for children's funerals, Nicholas Wolterstorff (as cited in Bush, 2006, p. 140) explained, "Though grief does not smother hope, neither does hope smother grief." For example, Neff and McMinn (2020, p. 39) explain that when referring to Jeremiah, the author of the book of Lamentations, it was in the "entering into and wrestling with the messiness of lament that he finds hope. Hope lives within the complexity of lament." Here, Jeremiah demonstrated his confidence that God loved and accepted him enough to express his rage and that God would not abandon him. Thus, authentic lament and an awareness of grace are wedded (Neff & McMinn, 2020).

Lewis Hall (2016) explained that lament differs from grief because lament involves taking personal grief to God. Moreover, lament is distinct from grumbling cloaked in spiritual jargon in our complaint-saturated culture. Instead, lament requires confidence (even minuscule and shaky confidence) that God is sovereign "else there would be no cause for lament" (Pemberton, 2012, p. 93). Thus, lamenting expresses pain to the One who can make a difference. In addition, grief may differ from lament, as lament expects God to respond. Pemberton (2012, p. 102) explains, "too many Christians never lament because they never really expect anything of God." Lament involves risk, daring to believe he hears and will respond.

Interestingly, within Scripture the structures of many spiritual practices are not explicitly outlined (e.g., how to forgive, how to fast, how to be grateful), yet repeatedly the steps of lament are included in Scripture, facilitating a "transformative movement" (Lewis Hall, 2016, p. 223). The five standard components displayed in a lament poured out in Psalm 13 are:

1. *Addressing God:* Lament is relational and involves turning to and calling on God (e.g., Ps 13:1: "LORD").
2. *Complaint:* To be in a genuine relationship with God, the deepest sorrows and the reason for suffering are expressed without denial or minimization, often using rhetorical questions (e.g., Ps 13: "How long . . . ?).
3. *Request:* The psalmist asks for deliverance from suffering and the meaninglessness of suffering (e.g., Ps 13:3, "Consider and answer me. . . . Give light to my eyes").
4. *Motivation:* The psalmist gives reasons God should answer the petition (e.g., Ps 13:3-4: "or I will sleep the sleep of death, and my enemy will say, 'I have prevailed'; my foes will rejoice because I am shaken").
5. *An expression of confidence in God:* A movement or shift on the part of the lamenter occurs here, frequently indicated with the sixth letter of the Hebrew alphabet, "vav." This conjunction marks a shift in thinking and posture, indicating a trajectory to trust, waiting, courage, or hope, regardless of how God responds. Here, the lamenter may exhaust himself in God's presence (i.e., like a small child in her parent's arms following bouts of anger and tears; e.g., Ps 13:6: "I will sing to the LORD, because he has dealt bountifully with me") (Lewis Hall, 2016; Pemberton, 2012).

Clinicians can invite clients to express a desire to engage in religion-specific ways to cope with CSA by reading examples of lament in Scripture and following the lament structure (e.g., Ps 13) with their personal anguish.

HIGHLIGHTING HOPE

"Hope" is the thing with feathers / that perches in the soul, / and sings the tune without the words, / and never stops at all.

EMILY DICKINSON

As many survivors of trauma come to therapy bereft of hope (Long, 2022), clinicians attuned to hope sightings, while avoiding a Pollyanna approach, can foster curiosity in clients and opportunities to notice hopeful glimpses they might have missed. What we pay attention to in therapy is essential. It is akin to watching for dolphins as we stand on the shoreline. We are searching to see if their bodies rise above the ocean's surface. If we are not watching, we might miss them. So, too, with hope in difficult sessions.

Schrank et al. (2011) discuss the importance of highlighting hope by conveying continued confidence that healing in therapy is not only possible but common for many. They further point out that many clients express gratitude when clinicians believe in them, even when the client does not believe in themselves. Here, the clinician lends hope when the client is not yet ready to do so.

Another effective strategy for nurturing hope is to engage clients in a deeper exploration of the concept. Larsen and colleagues (2007) suggest initiating a conversation about hope with the client's permission, such as: "Some clients find it beneficial to discuss hope. Would you be open to exploring this topic with me?" They also provided a list of hope-focused questions (Larson et al., 2007, p. 411):

- Who is someone you think of as being hopeful?
- If you placed a picture by your bed that symbolized hope, what would it be?
- If hope were a scent, what would it be? If hope were a song, what would it be? If hope was a color, what would it be?
- What most threatens your hope?

The very act of embarking on therapy is itself a hopeful movement. A helpful practice for clinicians might be to invite a hopeful vision of the future early in treatment. When starting each therapy relationship, I (Adam) often ask clients solution-focused questions, "If therapy was helpful for you, how might we know?" This often invites clients to share with me their hopes for the future. Frequently, individuals are both surprised and pleased with the question. Here they raise both intrapersonal issues (e.g., I would be less anxious) and interpersonal issues (e.g., I would be more connected to my intimate partner). This is also an important place to assist the client to begin to identify values and commit actions aligned with their values to move in a hopeful direction.

HOPE THAT IS CAUGHT VERSUS TAUGHT

Christian did not press on alone, for another pilgrim named Hopeful joined with him and, by means of a brotherly covenant, agreed to be his companion.

JOHN BUNYAN, *THE PILGRIM'S PROGRESS*

Repeatedly, survivors mention that while the abuse was painful, the response by others to what happened can be equally or even more unbearable. Indeed, Tamar needed words of hope from a faithful companion, and instead, her brother Absalom said to her after the rape, "Be quiet for now, my sister; he is your brother; do not take this to heart" (2 Sam 13:20). Social support (i.e., a sense of stability, being loved, cared for, and believed) is repeatedly mentioned in the literature as being a salient protective factor against the negative impact of CSA (Foley et al., 2022; Liu et al., 2022). Here, supportive individuals are pained by the survivor's pain; they give messages that the survivor's anguish matters and that they will accompany them in the healing journey. However, not only are supportive friends and family members' relationships influential, Schrank and colleagues (2011) highlighted the crucial role of meeting other survivors who have experienced similar circumstances and have become positive role models. Connecting with flourishing survivors can provide pictures and pathways that show healing is possible. As hopelessness is contagious, so is hopefulness passed on by others living it.

Emily, a clinical case manager, entered the Franklin County Corrections Center to help facilitate a group for the first time. The group was for incarcerated women who had experienced sexual exploitation and SUD. Emily assumed she would just observe the group on her first day, but the lead facilitator asked her if she wanted to tell her story. She agreed. Emily is a woman who spent twenty-six years on the street, experiencing homelessness, addiction, and sex trafficking. She eventually went to prison, where she was told about some helpful resources and began to change her mind and her life. As she was wrapping up, she shared the many gifts in her life. She spoke of having relationships with her kids, her new grandchild, owning a home, and her job that allowed her to "give back." And then she said, "What is today? Oh wow! *Today*, I have been seven years sober. I've also never told my story before." The room was full of women enraptured, some with tears in their eyes and some realizing they remembered Emily from the streets. Over and over, they said they couldn't believe it. Women said, "If you can do it, I can do it!" *This* is how hope gets passed on.

HOPE AND GRATITUDE

At times our own light goes out and is rekindled by a spark from another person. Each of us has cause to think with deep gratitude of those who have lighted the flame within us.

ALBERT SCHWEITZER

Gratitude is the awareness of receiving a good gift from someone (Watkins et al., 2009). Van Oyen Witvliet (2010) explains that despite the trauma, when individuals can attune to benefits experienced through facing the harm (e.g., meaning making, lessons learned), they can experience increased well-being. In a study of three hundred male and female young adults, hope and gratitude were protective factors against depression and suicidal ideation (Ohlan & Gera, 2022).

Cunha and colleagues (2019) conducted a noteworthy study that assessed the effect of a gratitude intervention with a randomized clinical trial of 1,337 participants (i.e., one intervention group and two control groups). All participants were asked to set aside ten to twenty minutes daily before sleeping to write about five experiences during that day (Cunha et al., 2019, p. 4).

- Control Group A was told: "In life, we sometimes encounter hassles and annoying situations that may bother and irritate us. They can occur in various realms of our lives (in personal relationships, workplace, university, home, or about finances or health). Think back over the past day and write down five hassles or annoying situations that you had to face."
- Control Group B was told: "During the day, there are events, both large and small, that end up affecting us. Think back over the past day and write down five events that somehow affected you."
- Gratitude Group was told: "There are many things in our lives, both large and small, that we might be grateful for. Think back over the past day and write down five things in your life that you are grateful for."

The study's main findings indicated that individuals in the gratitude group who intentionally focused on items they were thankful for experienced increased positive affect, subjective happiness, and life satisfaction, and reduced negative affect and depression symptoms. More gratitude and hope research is needed (Davis et al., 2016). For example, considering which factors might inhibit survivors from experiencing gratitude during gratitude exercises (e.g., shame) may be helpful. Significantly, if a survivor is in an abusive relationship (or engaged in dangerous behaviors), focusing on gratitude can be contraindicated. Yet, given the tendency for survivors to be neurobiologically attuned to threats in their environments, exercising gratitude muscles can be an area to explore in therapy. For example, acceptance-oriented therapies showcase how the avoidance of negative emotions, thoughts, memories, and bodily sensations can also prompt the general avoidance of the full spectrum of feelings, including desirable emotions.

The Science of Well-being is the title of a course taught by Yale University's Lori Santos that is offered for free. This course is the most attended one in the history of this prestigious university. A quintessential component of the course involves the regular practice of gratitude based on the behavioral science associated with the benefits of thankfulness. One of the assignments in the course involves a daily gratitude practice. After becoming familiar with the course content, I (Adam) began recommending the course for therapy clients in general and survivors of CSA to promote well-being. Inspired by the principle, my wife and I started filling a mason jar with slips of paper throughout the year with the date and a small sentence about something worthy of gratitude. In our home, we have mason jars for various years with slips of paper such as "June 2013: Started Commissioned Officer's Training at Maxwell Air Force Base," "Dec 2018: We are PREGNANT!" "March 2019: Shared a surprise meal with Tony," "Aug 2020: New job as Director of Emotional Wellbeing @ Notre Dame." These jars stand in prominent places in our home and serve as a visual reminder of the grace and goodness in our lives. They are also treasure troves to turn upside down and be reminded of God's generosity during times of discouragement.

COUNSELING SCENARIO

Rosie entered therapy with me (Hannah) when she was in her early sixties. She specifically expressed a desire that her Christian faith practices be incorporated into her therapeutic journey. She complained of social isolation and anxiety and that she had experienced tremendous suffering in childhood, including sexual abuse at the hands of her father. After several sessions of building rapport and resourcing Rosie, we used EMDR to work through some of her most painful childhood memories. At one point of being stuck, Rosie ended up pausing and asking, "What's the point?" She was experiencing a wave of hopelessness, wondering if all this hard work would pay off somehow. This ended up being a moment where I asked Rosie if she wanted to take that question ("What's the point?") to God together. After a moment or two of silence, Rosie prayed. I don't remember all her words that day, but I know the psalmist would be impressed. She addressed God as "Holy Friend" (addressing God) and asked him, "What was the point?" (complaint). She had many questions that day: "Why did this happen?" "Why me?" "What's wrong with me?" (complaint). She asked God to bring comfort and truth, to help her see clearly (request). She made it sound like her life depended on it. She also said that she knew he could do it (motivation). After she prayed (and cried and cried), something seemed to have shifted. I asked her question back to her, "What's the point?" And she said, "I know there's more for me. I know healing is possible. I know God wants me to have healing" (expression of confidence). Hope was on display once again.

CLINICIAN HOPE

Above all, trust in the slow work of God.

PIERRE TEILHARD DE CHARDIN,
HEARTS ON FIRE

Finally, the hope of clinicians is an important consideration. Vicarious trauma researchers McCann and Pearlman (1990) explain the importance of maintaining a sense of hope as a protective factor for clinicians. However, journeying with survivors of CSA is an endeavor that involves continual conversations about violations, sorrow, ambivalence, and betrayal. Larsen and colleagues (2013, p. 474) indicate that therapist attunement to "one's own fluctuating hope may be more important than never losing hope." Reasons for a diminished sense of hope among clinicians are varied (e.g., vicarious trauma, lack of institutional and personal support, an exclusive clientele of clients with complex trauma, personal stressors, and lack of understanding regarding the essence of hope). One factor that may contribute to discouragement among clinicians is the sometimes-slow therapy progress for survivors of complex trauma. While evidenced-based practices and the regular assessment of outcomes can enhance the clinical skills of clinicians and ultimately help survivors, healing is often messy, lengthy, and not usually linear.

Sandra attended an adult survivor's CSA group. She was quiet, present, and engaged but rarely spoke a word. It was evident to the rest of us that Sandra carried significant sorrow. Years later, I (Tammy) received an email from Sandra as she did an internet search and found me at Wheaton College. Her email began by stating that I might not remember her, but she was the woman who quietly wept most of the group. Then she shared some of her background. She was thirteen years old when her cousin raped her, and she became pregnant. Her home was imbued with shame and blame, and she was sent away to live with other family members until giving birth. She vividly recalled the day her mother walked with her to the little bedroom where she would be staying and then turned around without saying goodbye to her frightened and forlorn daughter. After giving birth, her parents demanded that she give up her baby daughter for adoption, leaving Sandra aching over abandoning her baby. For many years, Sandra struggled with nightmares, a sense of disconnection and invisibility from those around her, and a yearning for her daughter.

Years later, Sandra had seen the CSA group brochure, and she decided to attend with the encouragement of her individual therapist and all the determination she could muster. For many weeks, she did not want to return. Still, she paradoxically felt understood and less alone as other survivors shared their stories. In her email, she said the group had been a turning point. She was immensely grateful that she had been invited to share but was not required. Having a space to cry quietly as she listened to the information shared in the group and the stories of others had a healing impact on her soul. She continued her individual therapy after the group ended, kept in touch with several women in the group, read voraciously about the CSA healing journey, and increasingly took more risks in relationships and work. Yet the journey was frequently marked by two steps forward and one step back. One day, she was contacted by her daughter, whom she had been forced to give up so many years before. She had hoped and prayed for so many years for this reunion.

Sandra's story reminds us as clinicians that the roots of hope sometimes grow underground for a long time, not yet seen in the light of day. Her story is a poignant reminder to trust the slow work of God.

THE SANDY SHORELINE

Florence Chadwick was the first woman to swim across the English Channel in both directions. In 1952, she decided to swim from Catalina Island in the Pacific Ocean to the California coastline. Chadwick traveled with a team of individuals in boats who scoped for sharks and were available to assist her in the event of injury or fatigue. She swam for fifteen hours. The weather was extremely foggy, and there came the point Chadwick was physically and emotionally exhausted by the cold and swirling currents around her. All she could see was the fog, so she asked to be pulled out of the water. When Chadwick was in the boat, she realized she was less than half a mile from the shoreline. At the news conference the next day, she told reporters, "All I could see was the fog. I think if I could have seen the shore, I would have made it" (Alcorn, 2007. p. xx). On many days, survivors (and therapists too) need reminders of the shoreline. Not emotional or spiritual suppression. Not toxic positivity. Rather, deep and wide hope in the land of their suffering.

COUNSELING CONSIDERATIONS

- **Creative hopelessness.** In Acceptance and Commitment Therapy (ACT), a tongue-in-cheek label for an exercise fostering hope is called creative hopelessness (Harris, 2018). In this exercise, a therapist assists a client in identifying a yearning (such as the yearning to belong). Drawing on the assumption that our problem-solving mind has previously sought solutions, the therapist aids the client in articulating ways they have attempted to solve this issue and evaluating how effective those approaches were in satisfying the yearning. The creative hopelessness process occurs when the therapist (a) assists the client in seeing that their previous approaches were and will likely always be ineffective and (b) wonders aloud if these old, tired, ineffective strategies are to be left behind for alternative pathways. In essence, the therapist asks the client if "enough is enough," engendering the possibility that new ways of being and doing might emerge. In most cases, the therapist invites the client to consider different, courageous ways to satisfy the yearning. See also the appendix.
- **EMDR.** This approach allows clients to engage in bilateral stimulation while envisioning a future where courage is played out

stemming from adaptive core beliefs. Like an athlete who envisions a future event or competition, the trauma survivor envisions how she might walk into a first date, a crowded location, a family reunion, a funeral, and so on.

- **Hope sneaks into most approaches.** A lot of the evidence-based practice guiding therapy with clients experiencing PTSD invites individuals to recapture parts of their lives previously surrendered to avoidance. Specifically for survivors of CSA, education is offered about the normative responses to CSA and the beneficial effects of exposure (imaginal and in vivo). Here, therapists assist clients in reclaiming their lives. Even the creation of a hierarchy outlines a hopeful (and initially scary) vision of the future. Furthermore, in most approaches to effective therapy, a therapist collaborates with survivors to identify goals and outcomes throughout the clinical journey. The most effective means of therapy leads toward not only the amelioration of suffering but also the promotion of well-being that includes authentic hope. Finally, the existence of therapists in general and therapists with ample experience working with survivors is also a hopeful reality. A survivor contacts a therapist to start therapy precisely because there is hope that therapy can be effective (as it presumably has been for others).
- **Hope-Lit Database.** This database contains approximately 4,500 articles and books maintained by Hope Studies Central and the faculty of education at the University of Alberta for clinicians and researchers who want to research resources related to hope and clinical practices.

CHILDREN'S CORNER

- ***The Moon Is Always Round*** (2019) is a children's book written by seminary professor Jonathan Gibson. The author uses the moon as a metaphor, explaining that sometimes it looks like it is not round during its different phases. But it is always round, even when we cannot see everything. So too, is the goodness of God, even when we are sad, grieving, and circumstances do not make sense.

REFERENCES

Alcorn, R. (2011). *Heaven*. Tyndale House.

Allender, D. (2007, September 13-15). *Unknown conference session title* [conference session]. American Association of Christian Counselors World Conference, Nashville, TN.

Bartholomew, T. T., Gundel, B. E., Li, H., Joy, E. E., Kang, E., & Scheel, M. J. (2019). The meaning of therapists' hope for their clients: A phenomenological study. *Journal of Counseling Psychology, 66*(4), 496-507. http://doi.org/10.1037/cou0000328

Bush, M. D. (Ed.). (2006). *This incomplete one: Words occasioned by the death of a young person*. Eerdmans.

Caldas, S. V., Fondren, A., Batley, P. N., & Contractor, A. A. (2022). Longitudinal relationships among posttraumatic stress disorder symptom clusters in response to positive memory processing. *Journal of Behavior Therapy and Experimental Psychiatry, 76*, 101752. https://doi.org/10.1016/j.jbtep.2022.101752

Colla, R., Williams, P., Oades, L. G., & Camacho-Morles, J. (2022). "A new hope" for positive psychology: A dynamic systems reconceptualization of hope theory. *Frontiers in Psychology, 13*, 809053. https://doi.org/10.3389/fpsyg.2022.809053

Cunha, L. F., Pellanda, L. C., & Reppold, C. T. (2019). Positive psychology and gratitude interventions: A randomized clinical trial. *Frontiers in Psychology, 10*, 584. https://doi.org/10.3389/fpsyg.2019.00584

Darabont, F. (Dir.). (1994). *The Shawshank Redemption* [Film]. Castle Rock Entertainment.

Davis, D. E., Choe, E., Meyers, J., Wade, N., Varjas, K., Gifford, A., Quinn, A., Hook, J. N., Van Tongeren, D. R., Griffin, B. J., & Worthington, E. L. (2016). Thankful for the little things: A meta-analysis of gratitude interventions. *Journal of Counseling Psychology, 63*(1), 20-31. https://doi.org/10.1037/cou0000107

De Silva, D., & Liebscher, T. (2016). *SOZO saved healed delivered: A journey into freedom with the Father, Son, and Holy Spirit*. Destiny Image Publishers.

Dickie, J. F. (2019). Lament as a contributor to the healing of trauma: An application of poetry in the form of biblical lament. *Pastoral Psychology, 68*(2), 145-56. https://doi.org/10.1007/s11089-018-0851-z

Dickie, J. F. (2020). The practice of biblical lament as a means towards facilitating authenticity and psychological well-being. *Pastoral Psychology, 69*(5), 523-37. https//doi.org/10.1007/s11089-020-00928-z

Edwards, T. M., & Jovanovski, A. (2016). Hope as a therapeutic target in counselling—in general and in relation to Christian clients. *International Journal for the Advancement of Counselling, 38*(2), 77-88. https://doi.org/10.1007/s10447-016-9257-8

Eldredge, J. (2007). *Desire: The journey we must take to find the life God offers*. Thomas Nelson.

Foley, G., Fowler, K., & Button, P. (2022). Positive mental health in Canadian adults who have experienced childhood sexual abuse: Exploring the role of social support. *BMC Psychiatry*, 22(1), 1-11. https://doi.org/10.1186/s12888-022-04279-2

Frankl, V. E. (1985). *Man's search for meaning*. Simon and Schuster.

Gallagher, M. W., Long, L. J., & Phillips, C. A. (2020). Hope, optimism, self-efficacy, and posttraumatic stress disorder: A meta-analytic review of the protective effects of positive expectancies. *Journal of Clinical Psychology, 76*(3), 329-55. https://doi.org/10.1002/jclp.22882

Gibson, J. (2019). *The moon is always round.* New Growth Press.

Harris, R. (2018). Nuts and bolts of creative hopelessness: Practical tips for ACT therapists. https://contextualconsulting.co.uk/wp-content/uploads/2020/02/Creative-Hopelessness-Russ-Harris.pdf

Hoover-Kinsinger, S. E. (2018). Hoping against hope: An integration of the hope theology of Jürgen Moltmann and C. R. Snyder's psychology of hope. *Journal of Psychology & Christianity, 37*(4), 313-22.

Irving, L. M., Snyder, C. R., Cheavens, J., Gravel, L., Hanke, J., Hilberg, P., & Nelson, N. (2004). The relationships between hope and outcomes at the pretreatment, beginning, and later phases of psychotherapy. *Journal of Psychotherapy Integration, 14*(4), 419-43. https://doi.org/10.1037/1053-0479.14.4.419

Koehn, C., O'Neill, L., & Sherry, J. (2012). Hope-focused interventions in substance abuse counselling. *International Journal of Mental Health and Addiction, 10*(3), 441-52. https://doi.org/10.1007/s11469-011-9360-3

Larsen, D., Edey, W., & Lemay, L. (2007). Understanding the role of hope in counselling: Exploring the intentional uses of hope. *Counselling Psychology Quarterly, 20*(4), 401-16. https://doi.org/10.1080/09515070701690036

Larsen, D. J., Stege, R., & Flesaker, K. (2013). "It's important for me to not let go of hope": Psychologists' in-session experiences of hope. *International and multidisciplinary perspectives, 14*, 472-86. http://dx.doi.org/10.1080/14623943.2013.806301

Larsen, D. J., Stege, R., Edey, W., & Ewasiw, J. (2014). Working with unrealistic or unshared hope in the counselling session. *British Journal of Guidance & Counselling, 42*(3), 271-83. https://doi.org/10.1080/03069885.2014.895798

Lewis Hall, M. E. (2016). Suffering in God's presence: The role of lament in transformation. *Journal of Spiritual Formation and Soul Care*, 9(2), 219-32. https://doi.org/10.1177/193979091600900207

Liu, H., Wang, W., Qi, Y., & Zhang, L. (2022). Suicidal ideation among Chinese survivors of childhood sexual abuse: Associations with rumination and perceived social support. *Child Abuse & Neglect, 123*, 105420. https://doi.org/10.1016/j.chiabu.2021.105420

Long, L. J. (2022). Hope and PTSD. *Current Opinion in Psychology, 48,* 101472. https://doi.org/10.1016/j.copsyc.2022.101472

McCann, I. L., & Pearlman, L. A. (1990). Vicarious traumatization: A framework for understanding the psychological effects of working with victims. *Journal of Traumatic Stress, 3,* 131-49. https://doi.org/10.1007/BF00975140

Munoz, R. T., Hanks, H., & Hellman, C. M. (2020). Hope and resilience as distinct contributors to psychological flourishing among childhood trauma survivors. *Traumatology, 26*(2), 177-84. https://doi.org/10.1037/trm0000224

Neff, M. A., & McMinn, M. R. (2020). *Embodying integration: A fresh look at Christianity in the therapy room*. InterVarsity Press.

Nietzsche, F. (1908). *Human, all too human: A book for free spirits*. Newcomb Livraria.

Ohlan, A., & Gera, T. (2022). Character strength of hope and gratitude as protective factors of suicide. *Journal of Positive School Psychology*, 6(9), 2732-39.

Pemberton, G. (2012). *Hurting with God: Learning to lament with the psalms*. Abilene Christian University Press.

Rueger, S. Y., Worthington, E. L., Jr., Davis, E. B., Chen, Z. J., Cowden, R. G., Moloney, J. M., . . . Glowiak, K. J. (2022). Development and initial validation of the Persevering Hope Scale: Measuring wait-power in four independent samples. *Journal of Personality Assessment*, *105*(1), 58-73. https://doi.org/10.1080/00223891.2022.2032100

Schrank, B., Hayward, M., Stanghellini, G., & Davidson, L. (2011). Hope in psychiatry: A review of the literature. *Advances in Psychiatric Treatment*, *17*(3), 227-35. https://doi.org/10.1111/j.1600-0447.2008.01271.x

Snow, K. N., McMinn, M. R., Bufford, R. K., & Brendlinger, I. A. (2011). Resolving anger toward God: Lament as an avenue toward attachment. *Journal of Psychology and Theology*, *39*(2), 130-42. https://doi.org/10.1177/009164711103900204

Snyder, C. R., Harris, C., Anderson, J. R., Holleroan, S. A., Irving, L. M., Sigmon, S. T., Yoshinobu, L., Gibb, J., Langelle, C., & Harney, P. (1991). The will and the ways: Development and validation of an individual-differences measure of hope. *Journal of Personality and Social Psychology*, *60*(4), 570-85. https://doi.org/10.1037/0022-3514.60.4.570

Strong, J. (2010). *The new Strong's expanded exhaustive concordance of the Bible* (Red letter ed.). Thomas Nelson.

Van Oyen Witvliet, C. (2010). Understanding and approaching forgiveness as altruism: Relationships with rumination, self-control and a gratitude-based strategy. In M. R. Maamri, N. Verbin, & L. Everett Jr. (Eds.), *A journey through forgiveness* (pp. 99-107). Brill.

Watkins, P. C., Van Gelder, M., & Frias, A. (2009). Furthering the science of gratitude. In C. R. Snyder & S. J. Lopez (Eds.), *Oxford handbook of positive psychology* (pp. 437-45). Oxford University Press.

8

ATTACHED TO GOD

PRAYER PRACTICES IN THERAPEUTIC SETTINGS

At the profoundest depths of life, people talk not about God but with him.

D. E. TRUEBLOOD

You, God, who live next door—if at times, through the long night, I trouble you with my urgent knocking—this is why: I hear you breathe so seldom.

RAINER MARIA RILKE

God does his most stunning work where things seem hopeless. Wherever there is pain, suffering, and desperation, Jesus is.

JIM CYMBALA

WHO WILL PRAY FOR US NOW?

My (Tammy's) mom died on Mother's Day evening. She taught me more about talking to God than any study, seminar, or sermon. Conversing with God was the thread in the fabric of her life. She prayed fervently, believing she was her Father's loved child. As is true for many praying people, my mom learned to call on God because she sensed her enormous need for him. Difficult circumstances in my mom's life forced her to give up speaking to women's groups and teaching first graders. Instead, she began a quieter ministry—a ministry vital in its quietness. She spent her days praying for people.

The night my mom died, I began calling loved ones to share the news of her death. I spoke to Lori, who frequently came to see my mom. Lori did not know Jesus, but she knew that my mom enjoyed her, and often, after some conversation, my mom would ask Lori if she could pray for her and her concerns. That is how my mom loved Christians or non-Christians—she prayed for them. So, the night of my mother's death, I recall Lori's grief-filled question on the phone, "Who will pray for us now?" My friend's query echoed the words lodged in the hearts of my brother, me, and many others who knew my mom: who would pray for us now like my mom? She took seriously the words in 1 Samuel 12:23; she did not want to sin against the Lord by failing to pray for people in her life. Praying for others was her preeminent passion and precious privilege.

For years to come, my mom's steadfast commitment to praying for others in grueling situations prompted me to reflect on praying *with* clients in various clinical settings. This consideration continues to be examined empirically. Do some clients whose spirituality is embedded in their identities and way of life desire explicit prayer in therapy? If so, what does this look like for survivors who live riven with complicated concerns? In this chapter, we will examine the burgeoning empirical support for spiritually integrated approaches to psychotherapy while employing sensitivity to clients' worldviews and ethical principles associated with prayer. Reflections on research associated with how CSA can contaminate affectional bonds between people and God and God images that survivors hold support exploring these attachment concerns in therapy. Additionally, when a relationship with God is central, practical examples of prayer-based interventions are included.

SPIRITUALLY INTEGRATED THERAPEUTIC APPROACHES

Jesus himself always went where the pain was.

RICHARD ROHR

Effective therapy for trauma survivors addresses the body, mind, and soul. Koenig (2023) explains that a culturally sensitive, client-centered approach is now the standard of care in therapeutic settings. This includes attuning to the client's beliefs, worldview, and religious and spiritual values. Captari and colleagues (2018) conducted a meta-analysis of ninety-seven outcome studies (n = 7,181) examining the impact of accommodating treatments on clients' religious and spiritual values. They found that religious and spiritual adapted therapy resulted in increased mental health improvement and spiritual well-being compared to no treatment and nonreligious and spiritual therapies. Richards and colleagues (2023) indicate that since spirituality is a resource for many individuals, some clients want spiritually integrated therapy, increasing treatment efficacy.

Moreover, clients can intertwine spirituality with the challenges they are experiencing (e.g., interpreting Scripture as a justification for discrimination and physical abuse, compulsive prayer, and using prayer to bypass painful emotional, physical, and relational realities) (Leins & Williams, 2018). For example, Murray-Swank and Pargament (2005, p. 192) explain, "Sexual abuse also creates a fertile environment for the development of spiritual struggles." Thus, working through religious and spiritual challenges can potentially lead to more significant healing related to CSA (Dumulescu et al., 2022; Richards et al., 2023; Wan, 2021).

Potential ethical concerns necessitate consideration regarding using spiritually integrated interventions in therapy. While spiritually sensitive approaches in therapy have been shown to be beneficial to clients, integrating religious and spiritual practices in therapy does not entail proselytizing clients toward a specific religious practice or affiliation (Richards et al., 2023; Timbers & Hollenberger, 2022). As clinicians, it is unethical and harmful to foist our faith values and practices in overt or covert ways on clients (Miller & Chavier, 2013; Timbers & Hollenberger, 2022). Gaining client consent for spiritual interventions is vital (England & Klassen, 2023). Moreover, developing clinician competency regarding religious and spiritual clinical skills is needed. As Richards and colleagues (2023, p. 6) explain:

> Spiritually integrated psychotherapy rests instead on a respect for the patient's orientation to spirituality, whatever the orientation, and values the patient's right to make informed decisions about spiritual issues as in all dimensions of human functioning. . . . The therapist guards against overt or covert efforts to impose a particular worldview on the patient.

Thus, ethical and spiritually sensitive therapy involves a holistic understanding of clients, which includes creating safe spaces to discuss religious and spiritual concerns and integrating spiritual help (Richards et al., 2023). It does not mean pushing or pressuring clients toward God. For some clients wanting to attend to spiritual concerns in therapy, incorporating scriptural or sacred texts during discussions of values, core beliefs, or meaning making regarding the cause, purpose, or aftereffects of trauma can be helpful. Additionally, no discussion of posttraumatic growth is complete without an awareness that, for at least some survivors, a deepening connection to God is an adaptive form of transformation. Making room and inviting clients to explore these critical aspects in their personal lives (both past and present) can catalyze holistic healing.

PRAYING WITH CLIENTS IN THERAPY

For this reason, since the day we heard it, we have not ceased praying for you.

COLOSSIANS 1:9

Over the years, I (Tammy) have supervised students interning at both faith-sensitive and secular sites. During a supervision meeting, a mature and clinically gifted intern at a faith-sensitive site shared about one of his Christian clients who had experienced extensive CSA. This student had worked with this client during most of his internship experience, and they were soon ending their clinical work together. When my student asked this client if there was anything that he would have wished they had included in their therapeutic work together, his client gently said that he wished my student would have prayed with him about some of the concerns he was experiencing. This intern did not sense that this client was spiritually bypassing complex issues. Instead, prayer was an essential part of this client's walk with God, and he indicated that he would have liked to have engaged in prayer with his therapist at specific junctures during sessions.

There have been mixed findings regarding the appropriateness of praying explicitly with clients in therapy in the empirical literature. For instance, Gubi (2004) surveyed 578 accredited therapists in England to determine the prevalence and practice of prayer interventions in therapy. Gubi (2004) discovered that 11% of therapists prayed audibly with Christian clients, 37% had inaudibly prayed for direction during counseling sessions without the client's awareness, 49% prayed for clients outside of session, and 51% prayed in preparation for therapy sessions. Weld and Eriksen (2007) surveyed first-session Christian clients and their Christian therapists regarding prayer practices in therapy. They found that 82% of clients desired explicit prayer in counseling;

clients preferred that therapists introduce the topic of prayer; and clients who reported engaging in prayer in their personal lives held higher expectations of explicit prayer in therapy.

In contrast, a survey of religious interventions with 152 Mormon clients at a counseling center at a university sponsored by the Church of Jesus Christ of Latter-day Saints (LDS) revealed that therapist-client prayer was deemed inappropriate by participants (Martinez et al., 2007). Saenz and Waldo (2013) surveyed 109 university counseling center clients. They found that more than half of the clients did not want explicit prayer included in their counseling sessions and did not want their therapists to encourage prayer outside of the session. It was noteworthy that clients with higher self-reported religious and spiritual engagement wanted their therapist to explicitly pray in sessions compared with clients with lower levels of religious and spiritual engagement, who were less likely to want explicit prayer in therapy. Thus, a critical clinical implication is that therapists must assess faith beliefs, values, and practices to ascertain client preference regarding prayer in therapy (Koenig, 2023; Saenz & Waldo, 2013).

If a client has indicated that their Christian faith and prayer practices are important, I (Hannah) might ask near the end of a session: "You mentioned that prayer is an important spiritual practice for you. I have worked with some folks who appreciate prayer being incorporated into our therapeutic process and some who do not. Do you have a preference?" If the client wants to incorporate prayer into the therapy, I follow up with a few more questions about prayer practice preferences. "How do you feel about praying out loud during our time together?" If the client desires audible prayer in the session, I inquire, "Would you like me to be the one to pray, or might you like to pray sometimes?"

An in-depth qualitative study with five Christian women in therapy revealed noteworthy themes regarding explicit prayer experiences in therapy (England & Klassen, 2023). Participants indicated that prayer was essential to them as they were experiencing significant suffering and that this anguish was often lonely and consuming and the catalyst to obtain therapy. In this context, the participants noted that intentional praying with their therapist provided an "invitation to be present" and a calming, undistracted, and embodied opportunity to acknowledge God amid suffering (England & Klassen, 2023, p. 56). Participants further noted that praying with their therapists provided a "deepening of the therapeutic bond," a sense of being "accompanied" in their anguish, and "an intimacy that healed" (p. 57). Explicit praying in therapy also fostered "engagement with God" and experiencing God as "being-with-them" (p. 58). Finally, another salient theme noted was that even though some of the specific client circumstances did not change, clients experienced being seen and cared for by God, which facilitated transformative hope-filled perspectives (England & Klassen, 2023). Thus, in this study, these participants saw explicit prayer in therapy as a relational experience engendering closeness with God and their therapist, consistent with their values and beliefs, that fostered transformational perspectives.

GOD IMAGE AND PRAYER

What comes into our minds when we think about God is the most important thing about us.

A. W. TOZER

Long before we think in words, we think in images. To some, the word *father* connotes intimate images of warm embraces, belly laughs, protective arms, walking in the woods, helpful advice, wrestling and more wrestling, early mornings on his knees, and loving conversations. In stark contrast, for others, *father* conjures up graphic depictions of shouting arguments, cold and angry stares, drunken slurs, and sexual violations. Kosarkova and colleagues (2020, p. 1) define the image of God as "a subjective experience of what an individual or community perceives as God, based on the way in which a person unconsciously interacts with God at an emotional, nonverbal and often implicit level." Trauma can negatively impact our image of God. In a study of 1,800 Czech adults, individuals who experienced childhood trauma were "less likely to describe God as loving, always present and forgiving" (Kosarkova et al., 2020, p. 1). Other studies have also revealed that CSA survivors experience decreased spiritual well-being and maintain more negative images of God than individuals without a history of CSA (Murray-Swank & Pargament, 2005; Rudolfsson & Tidefors, 2014; Upenieks & Ford-Robertson, 2022).

Significant research indicates that when attachment figures perpetrate CSA and other forms of trauma, this can impact a survivor's development and formation of secure relationships and their image of God (Bowlby, 1988; Dumulescu et al., 2022; Karatzias et al., 2022). Consequently, instead of young children feeling safe and secure with parental figures, they may alternate between feeling deep-seated fear and engaging in withdrawal behavior while simultaneously seeking out reassurance and clinging behavior to stave off the fear of abandonment (Hollman & Marmarosh, 2023). Parents were designed to foster a secure sense of attachment and safety when in close proximity (Bolwby, 1988; Hollman & Mararosh, 2023). However, abusive and neglectful parental figures can teach the antithesis of these lessons (Dumulescu et al., 2022). Researchers have also suggested that attachment dynamics in a parent-child relationship can have corresponding implications in the attachment relationship with God (Granqvist, 2020; Hollman & Marmarosh, 2023).

On an eternal landscape, parental relationships are intended to help us capture a glimpse of a heavenly Father who is connected, comforting, and available in all circumstances (Hollman & Marmarosh, 2023). When parental figures are unavailable, neglectful, or abusive, this can prompt individuals to believe that God will also not meet their needs and that God is angry, abandoning, inconsistent, unreliable, unpredictable, punishing, and violent. Thus, feelings of unworthiness and shame can result in a "projection of a negative parental image onto the image of God" (Pressley & Spinazzola, 2017, p. 211). Moreover, Kirkpatrick and Shaver (1992) found that individuals who develop avoidant or anxious attachment relationships with God are likelier to experience loneliness, depression, and anxiety, and indicate diminished health and life satisfaction compared to individuals who are securely attached to God.

A negative image of God and a ruptured attachment relationship with God have significant implications for communing with God through prayer (Richards et al., 2023; Schutz; 2021). Just as infants seek proximity to attachment figures during distress, many individuals seek proximity to God through prayer (Granqvist, 2020). Yet, seeking proximity to God through prayer may be conflictual when early trauma has occurred, as God may be viewed as unresponsive, ignoring, and uncaring (Exline et al., 2015, 2021). How, then, do clinicians help survivors who desire spiritually integrated therapy sort through their relationship and conversations with God when he has seemed untrustworthy?

IMAGE OF GOD PROCESSING

The best prayers often have more groans than words.

JOHN BUNYAN

I (Tammy) journeyed with Aysun, a Christian client who had experienced a spate of sorrows during her formative years. During the middle phase of therapeutic work together, authentic and raw discussions about her deep-rooted perception of God elbowed their way through the soils of our conversations:

Tammy: "Aysun, we have processed how the abuse by your uncle has impacted you and your relationship with your husband. I'm wondering how the abuse has affected your relationship with God?"

Aysun: "Even though I'm involved in church, I can go for months without talking with him at all . . . It's like I am ignoring him . . . mad at him . . . pushing him away."

Tammy: "What do you think the distance between you and God is about?"

Aysun: "Well, where was he when I was being abused? I was nine years old, and I pleaded with Jesus when my uncle took me to the shed. I begged him to stop the abuse, just like I begged my uncle. But the abuse went on for years. . . . If my child was being raped and I could protect her in any way, I would do whatever it took. But he didn't stop my uncle from abusing me when he could have. What kind of God lets a little girl be abused over and over again? [begins to weep]

Tammy: "The abuse was a horrible thing to happen to a little girl." [silence as she continues to cry] "Aysun, what is it like to share this with me?"

Aysun: "This is the first time I have expressed these thoughts about God out loud. I'm a little embarrassed to share this with you. Yet I'm so mad at him. But I miss him too." [cries again]

Tammy: "You have a lot of complicated and confusing feelings about God. You seem mad at him, yet you miss him. And you are a little ashamed of letting me know about your mixed feelings with God, wondering, perhaps, what I might think of you. Will I back away too?"

Aysun: [nods her head] "For so much of my life, he was all I had."

This conversation initiated further processing with Aysun about the deep well of hurt with God underlying her anger and simultaneous yearning for God. We had previously engaged in EMDR work together regarding some of her abuse memories. This conversation led to some further EMDR work surrounding some of her abuse memories and her perceptions and relationship with God. A critical piece included processing how God felt about her, given that he didn't stop the abuse despite her repeated appeals as a little girl. She had believed for many years that God had abandoned her out in that shed and that he had hidden his face from her throughout her life. In adulthood, she experienced an anxious attachment with God as she longed for him and pursued connection but then became fearful that he would not care about her enough to be responsive to her at the time of her most profound need. Our work together involved EMDR, God image processing, and prayers of lament. Increasingly, Aysun came to perceive God tenderly gazing on her with love as the One who wept over the abuse she experienced. As her image of God continued to transform, her ambivalence with him increasingly dissipated. Instead of a God with an aloof demeanor and a turned back, she increasingly came to know him as the God who saw her, and the God who was gutted by what he saw happen to her. Our therapeutic journey together was permeated with starts and stops, backtracking as former beliefs resurfaced, and tastes of growing trust and closeness with God.

Thus, as part of the discussion of a client's image of God and prayer it is pivotal for clinicians to assess not only *if* a client prays and if they want this spiritual integration but also who or what kind of God they perceive they are praying to (Tait et al., 2016). As clinicians, we can tap into the image of God when survivors discuss the CSA specifics. I (Tammy) often invite clients to ask God where he was when the abuse happened, how he felt about them, and what the look on his face was when the abuse occurred.

Another way to assess a client's image of God is through drawing. Olson and colleagues (2016) invited individuals to draw a picture of God and themselves. Clinicians can invite deeper reflections by asking clients to draw:

1. a picture of you and God
2. a picture of how God looks when you do something wrong. Draw what you feel, not what you think
3. a picture of how you desire God to look on you when you do something wrong

We have often wondered about Tamar's view of God. Did the impact of her brother raping her and her father's passivity and lack of justice-seeking behavior on her behalf lead her to view God as passive, unresponsive, and uncaring? What did she experience in her brother Absalom's home that might have brought healing to her image of God or further harm? We know that

Tamar offered her lament immediately after her rape. Did she continue to voice her laments to God? Did Tamar find in God a bent ear and a strong shoulder? Did she come to know in her lifetime what Aysun discovered?

PRAYER PRACTICES WITH SURVIVORS IN THERAPY

Prayer is a vast territory, with room for silence and shouting, for creativity and repetition, for original and received prayers, for imagination and reason.

TISH HARRISON WARREN

As mentioned, while CSA can prompt some survivors to turn away from God or develop conflicted relationships with God, some survivors seek out support from God through prayer (Pargament & Exline, 2022). Thus, assessing how survivors perceive attachment relationships with God is essential. Gaining this information can help therapists be culturally sensitive with clients who are receptive and desirous of praying as part of their healing journey. It can also be helpful to provide information regarding various forms of prayer that can help survivors deepen intimacy with God (e.g., lamenting prayers, journaling prayers, contemplative, written liturgical prayers, and breath prayers) (Pargament, 2011). Clients may need guidance about praying in the same way they need guidance for other interventions. Pargament (2011, p. 254) explains, "Rather than simply encouraging their clients to pray, clinicians can help their clients locate those prayers that are best suited to their needs." Thus, we examine various forms of prayer as essential resources in therapy.

Lamenting prayer.

The caged bird sings with a fearful trill of things unknown but longed for still and his tune is heard on the distant hill for the caged bird sings of freedom.

MAYA ANGELOU,
I KNOW WHY THE CAGED BIRD SINGS

In the film *Forrest Gump*, Jenny takes Forrest by the hand and runs as fast as their little legs will carry them away from her drunken, molesting father (Zemeckis, 1994). They come to a hidden place in the cornfields. As Jenny's dad hunts for her, she kneels with Forrest on the ground. She repeatedly prays that God will make her a bird so she can fly far, far away. Yet God did not make Jenny a bird in this fictional film. And she did not fly away. So, too, in the nonfictional lives of many survivors who prayed and pleaded in faith that God would stop the abuse, he did not stop it. Rage, doubts, confusion, and pointed questions are gathered and brought before God.

In the "Indomitable Hope" chapter, we discussed lamenting prayers. As a brief reminder, lamenting prayers are a complaint or an expression of sorrow, often composed as a song, hymn, or prayer (Lewis Hall, 2016; Neff & McMinn, 2020). Several central questions are frequently embedded in lamenting prayers, including, God, are you there? Are you fair? Do you care (Card, 2014)? Given that CSA is frequently shrouded in secrecy, invitations to survivors to break their silence about the CSA with God through lamenting prayers can counter the surrounding secrecy and isolation and be a vehicle of wrestling with God over not stopping the abuse. Breaking the silence on a spiritual stratum is exemplified using poetry in *Survivor Prayers: Talking with God About Childhood Sexual Abuse* by Catherine Foote (Foote, 1994, p. 72):

> Hear the stories I tell. Hear the silence, words I cannot even whisper yet. . . .
> Be with me when I freeze in fear.
> Be with me when I cry out from remembered forgotten anguish.
> Be with me when I rage, when I strike out, when my fist squeezed tight
> swings into the
> nothing that is now in front of me.
> Be with me when it seems that healing will never come.
> Be with me when I wonder where you were.
> Be with me when I wonder where you are.
> Be with me as I heal.

Expressive writing prayers and liturgical prayers.

> *Aren't your eyelids tired of keeping prisoners?*
> *those tears are precious minerals.*
> *lap them up like a medicine;*
> *it's called healing.*
>
> COLE ARTHUR RILEY, *BLACK LITURGIES*

In Alice Walker's Pulitzer Prize–winning novel *The Color Purple*, Celie is raped by her stepfather. He admonishes her never to tell anyone, especially not her mother, as, according to her stepfather, "It'd kill your mammy" (Walker, 1992, p. 1). Paradoxically, perhaps, much of the book includes Celie's tender and vulnerable written conversations with God as if he were her loving and compassionate friend. Many of these talks are about the repeated abuse she experienced.

Much has been written about the potential benefits of expressive writing as a reflective tool in therapy (Guo, 2023; Smyth et al., 2008). In like manner, a way to integrate prayer in clinical work as a demonstration of culturally competent clinical care and encouraging religious coping can be through expressive written dialogue or prayer journaling with God. This practice can facilitate connecting with God, expressing concerns, requests for comfort, self-examination, and receptive listening to God (Collins, 2005; England & Klaassen, 2023; Meisenhelder et al., 2016; Mosher et al., 2021; Pargament, 2011). Moreover, journaling with God using words, drawings, collages, and music can develop a roadmap of one's spiritual journey, provide glimpses of ways God has responded to prayers in the past, and cultivate gratitude.

In *Journaling as a Spiritual Practice*, Helen Cepero (2008, pp. 27-28) explains: "If we think of psalms as letters to God . . . tell God where you are in your story; tell God where you wish you were. Tell God how you see yourself and how you see God." The psalms and other written prayers portray an intensity of emotion and language that reminds us *we can say anything to God.* For some time, one of my (Hannah) favorite psalms has been Psalm 13: "How long, O LORD? Will you forget me forever?" It's a bleak passage. Years ago, as I sat with that passage, I imagined David's back and forth with God as he penned those words. And what I love is that God did not say, "Nope, you can't say that because it is not true. I did not forget you." Instead, I imagine God saying something like, "This is good, son. Write that down. Make sure people know they can say *anything* to me."

Some survivors may be less comfortable with expressing spontaneous written prayers in a journal. Discomfort with spontaneous, less structured, written prayers may be due to preferences about different prayer traditions. It may also partly stem from concerns that someone could read conversations with God in a journal without the survivor's permission. Just as a survivor's emotions, mind, and body were invaded during the CSA, a fear of someone invading intimate reflections with God can impact this prayer practice.

Some clients may be drawn to praying more liturgical or prewritten prayers. Some of these prayers have survived for centuries, reminding us that we sometimes need help being guided through the brambly and bruising underbrush of life. Liturgical prayers in books like *Every Moment Holy, Volume I, Every Moment Holy, Volume II: Death, Grief, and Hope,* and *The Lives We Actually Have* can lead some to more profound prayer conversations with God. As we pray scripted prayers, Warren (2021, p. 125) explains, "we read our own lives back into the words we pray. Our own biographies shape our understanding of these prayers as much as these prayers shape us and our own stories."

Michelle was a client who loved to journal and had been journaling for many years since her experience with CSA. Michelle indicated to me (Hannah) that she grew up in a family that prayed before meals and bedtime, but she had not established a prayer practice of her own. She desired a connection with God and wanted to learn more about talking to God openly. I paid attention to her desire to pray and her already-honed gift for writing and suggested that she merely orient her journal entries to God. We talked about how this might help her express herself to God freely in her journal and to listen for any response from God. This process began a vibrant prayer practice that continues to carry Michelle through the vicissitudes of her life.

Asking others to pray.

> *If we truly love people, we will desire for them far more than it is within our power to give them, and this will lead us to prayer.*
>
> RICHARD FOSTER

Clinicians regularly assess the extent of social support in clients' lives, as the empirical literature is replete with benefits stemming from strong social support for individuals as they contend with concerns in their life, including CSA (e.g., feeling understood, increased social connectedness, inspiration to heal, gaining shared resources and coping strategies from others, diminished shame and stigma, and increased resilience) (Fuller-Thomson et al., 2020; Gregory et al., 2022; Machisa et al., 2018). Likewise, there are benefits of prayer support (Lynn et al., 2014; Schaefer, 2013; Skipper et al., 2018; Torbjørnsen et al., 2021). Asking others to pray for one's current concerns is an important type of emotional, relational, and spiritual support with benefits such as a source of encouragement to persevere in personal prayer; help to develop a more optimistic outlook; a means of buffering stress; an aid to developing spiritual connectedness with others; and a sense of being valued by others who pray for them (Lynn et al., 2014; Krause, 2011; Schafer, 2013; Skipper et al., 2018; Torbjørnsen et al., 2021).

If a client is connected with a church and the prayer ministry within the church, some may seek this additional prayer support. As with all other involvements, this type of support for clients outside of therapy can be beneficial. It can also be misused and abused (e.g., prayer as a cover for giving advice, inserting opinions). We include the following example of a survivor who sought prayer support in her church. While this story is not part of clinical practice, we thought that it is instructive, and it could be an experience that a survivor may want to process in therapy. Olivia tells her story of receiving care from her church's prayer ministry:

> I was sexually assaulted by a man posing as a doctor in the hospital when I was five. I always had a vivid memory of this event. . . . In the months that followed [in therapy], I noticed my body was activated whenever I was alone with a man. Previously safe friends, family members, and coworkers felt vaguely threatening to me. The breaking point was a panic attack in an elevator with a male coworker. I knew I needed extra help processing this trauma, so I filled out an application to go through the intensive prayer ministry at my church. Unfortunately, the waiting list was four months long.
>
> I shared this with a married couple that were dear friends of mine, and the husband said that his team was available to pray. The only problem was that this meant processing the sexual assault in a room alone with four men. The more I thought about this possibility, the more it seemed like a sign from God that the only team available to pray for me was made up entirely of men. I decided to accept their offer to pray for me. These teams typically meet with a person for 90 minutes weekly for four consecutive weeks. For the first two weeks, it was all I could do to stay in the room. I wanted to run away the entire time and had to really fight to be present and speak. I made the four of them sit together on the couch on the opposite side of the room from me. I kept my eyes open during prayer and sat right by the door. They also weren't allowed to touch me at all, not even to shake my hand. By the third week, I was able to relax and close my eyes, sharing even more vulnerably and really grieving the assault openly. In the fourth week, they each prayed a father's blessing over me. One man even wrote a song for me and sang it over me. I joyfully hugged them all in gratitude at the end.

> Two weeks later, I needed urgent surgery. I was admitted to the very same hospital where my assault had taken place. My entire medical team was male, even the nurse who was responsible for getting me to and from the bathroom and helping me change my clothing was a man. Yet, I felt safe. I really believe that God knew what was going to happen to me, and he used this kind of team of men to bring me deep healing in prayer.

This poignant example is not offered as a prescription, and of course, not every church will have a robust and trauma-sensitive prayer ministry. Yet we share it here as encouragement of ways that faith leaders and lay people can support the healing journey of CSA survivors.

Earlier in the chapter, we wondered about Tamar's view of God. We also find ourselves curious about Tamar's prayer experience. Did she pen her conversations with God in a prayer journal (whatever this looked like during Tamar's time in history)? We wonder if Tamar had people who prayed for her in her desolation. Or if she did not have people praying for her during her darkest days, perhaps she connected with God through her very breath.

Breath prayers.

> *But our Lord Jesus Christ . . . would not surely exhort us so strongly to ask, if He were not willing to give.*
>
> SAINT AUGUSTINE

Breath prayers are ancient, short prayers connected to the rhythm of deep breathing (Knabb, 2021). Deep breathing reduces sympathetic nervous system (SNS) arousal, encourages affect regulation, and counteracts the fight-or-flight response (Aideyan et al., 2020). Calling out to God in prayer positions an individual toward the Lord (Tucker, 2022). Thus, breath prayers merge our focus on breathing as we connect with God, the Author of life and breath itself, through prayers of meditation on God's Word (Koenig, 2023; Tucker, 2022).

Many breath prayers are six to eight syllables, corresponding with our inhales and exhales. The timeless Jesus Prayer, in varying versions, involves inhaling "Jesus, Son of God," then exhaling a request of God, "Be merciful to me, a sinner" (Knabb, 2021). This simple breath prayer traces its origins to Diadochos in the early sixth century, who taught that repetition of this prayer leads to inner peace. A primary aim of breath prayers is not to eliminate pain or suffering (although that may occur) but to more deeply press in to the nearness of God amid a suffering moment.

Knabb (2021) explains that other passages of Scripture might also be utilized in breath prayers. For example, with Psalm 7:1, we inhale and inwardly profess, "Lord, my God," and with a slow exhale, we declare inwardly, "I take refuge in you." While secular and Buddhist mindfulness meditation involves emptying the mind or looking within the self to discover peace, breath prayers fill the mind with the Word of God and look toward the Lord to quiet us (Tucker, 2022).

It's important to note that breath prayers are not just for adults. Children, too, can be taught how to engage in breath prayers. Using bubbles to express breath prayers or teaching "Smell the flowers, blow out the candles" are two ways to help children engage in breath prayers (Borgo, 2020; Tucker, 2022). Therapists can lead and model meditative and other prayer practices and invite clients to engage in directed exercises between sessions. I (Hannah) like to imagine a breath prayer for the clients that you, our reader, serve:

Inhale: Comfort them, Lord.

Exhale: May they be freed from desolation.

Creative prayer practices with children.

The task of nourishing spirituality is one of releasing, not constricting, children's understanding and imagination.

DAVID HAY

Sensory-based creative and expressive therapies that help individuals grapple with trauma have significant therapeutic benefits (Homeyer & Sweeney, 2022). Children may not be able to communicate with God in words. Thus, in therapeutic settings, at a wise juncture, children can be invited to engage in various types of prayer expressions (Borgo, 2020). Play with an expressive medium such as sand can increase personal awareness, provide a means of communication, provide opportunities to verbalize spiritual concerns, provide a safe space to work through spiritual matters, and deepen connectivity with God (Baggerly, 2018; Hagedorn et al., 2018; Homeyer & Sweeney, 2022). In *Spiritual Conversations with Children*, spiritual director Lacy Finn Borgo (2020, p. 15) invites children to sit on a white blanket as a symbol of holy listening to God. Using reflection cards, she asks children to consider a time they "knew God was with them" (p. 16). She uses sand trays to help children express their stories with God without words.

Alternatively, a child can sculpt their sadness over abuse with God using silly putty, paint, or a prayer collage (Borgo, 2020). Clinicians can display different ways to express thoughts and feelings to God and asked children how they might like to communicate with God. More research is needed regarding this type of spiritual formation activity and other prayer practices within therapeutic settings sensitive to Christians' faith beliefs and practices (Wilder et al., 2020).

I (Adam) had a recent experience of offering prayer to God with my four-year-old daughter. We drove to a nearby grotto, where we approached the scene with quiet reverence, acquired an unlit candle, lit the candle as we whispered a prayer to God on behalf of a sick loved one, and then placed the candle on display. Although there are many regular, daily moments where we might teach our children to talk with God (e.g., at the dining room table, watching the sunset, before bed, or on the drive to preschool), it seemed significant to make prayer a destination activity. In so doing, we experienced anticipatory enthusiasm (like other intriguing destinations such as a swimming pool or trampoline park) and participated in something sacred and communal. There were other prayerful people there, and this communicated to my daughter that prayer is a shared phenomenon and that many people come to that location to speak with God. Each flickering candle seemed to suggest that others take prayer seriously and that God listens to many different prayers. The sensory experience and novelty of pairing prayer with a candle seemed to enhance our shared sacred time with God.

"If you can" prayers.

Prayer is an expression of who we are. . . .
We are a living incompleteness. We are a gap,
an emptiness that calls for fulfillment.

THOMAS MERTON

There are too many days when I (Hannah) want to pray on behalf of the clients I care for, but my whispers to God are meek and timid, filled with doubt. On these days, when evil looms large on the horizon, the list of clients mesmerized with meth is long, and client relationships have run amok, my prayer life frequently mirrors the words of the father of the demon-possessed son, who said to Jesus, "but if you are able to do anything, help us!" (Mk 9:22).

Despite this father's little faith, Jesus, the best of counselors, responded with words that elicited faith rather than a rebuke. Jesus did not stomp out the smoldering wick waiting to be ignited. "If you are able!" said Jesus. "All things can be done for the one who believes." So, the father responded, "I believe; help my unbelief!" (Mk 9:23-24). Perhaps you see his prayer as a giant contradiction, but we think it is a most excellent prayer.

> Help me to believe more, Jesus.
> Help me to believe more, Jesus,
> that you are the healer of my clients.
> Help me to believe more, Jesus, that without you,
> all my "brilliant" counseling is just words.
> Help me to believe more, Jesus,
> that you love my client more than I could ever love her.
> Help me to believe more, Jesus,
> that you will never love me more than you do right now.
> We do believe. Help us to believe more, Jesus.

Finally, an instructive entry in Philip Yancey's thought-provoking book *Prayer: Does It Make Any Difference?* comes from attorney, CEO, and founder of International Justice Mission, Gary Haugen. Haugen spent his time investigating genocide in Rwanda, as well as in twelve other countries, specializing in human trafficking, slavery, illegal detention, torture, and helping widows and orphans. His words about how prayer became the quintessential element of their work have potentially wise implications for therapists walking with clients who have faced evil.

> From the very beginning, I believed we needed reminders that the work of justice is God's work. . . . Otherwise, we might get overwhelmed by the enormity of the evil we confront. I feared a slide toward what I call *prayerless striving*. So, every day our entire staff begins with thirty minutes of silence, in which we encourage prayer and meditation. We don't talk, we don't work. We sit at our desks and pray. In addition, every day we get together at eleven o'clock and spend thirty minutes praying for each other and the cases we're involved in. Our staff members often report this is the most meaningful part of their day. (Yancey, 2006, p. 110)

Reading this, we let our imaginations run wild. Imagine if clinicians who worked with survivors began their day with a time of silence in prayer and, later in the day, spent time praying for other clinicians on our teams and the clients we see. Imagine all the client productivity we would be losing. Imagine all the eternal productivity we would be gaining. Imagine.

COUNSELING CONSIDERATIONS

- ***Christian Meditation in Clinical Practice: A Four-Step Model and Workbook for Therapists and Clients*** (Knabb, 2021) offers researched applications of rich and varied prayer practices in therapy and adjunct to therapy. For example, it includes steps to centering prayer that cultivate awareness of God and welcoming prayer that involves surrendering repeatedly and inviting Jesus to be in our inner world. See also the spiritually oriented interventions section in the appendix.
- **Spiritually accommodated prayer, meditation, and mindfulness resources** are abundant and available to be downloaded. In addition to being free or very low cost, these technologies invite consumers to cultivate disciplines away from the therapy room. At the time of the authoring of this book, popular and well-done Christian prayer, mindfulness, and meditation apps include Abide, Hallow, One Minute Pause, Soultime, and Pray. These tools equip clients with resources to practice between sessions. Orienting a client to one of these platforms and collaborating on a goal for daily/weekly engagement can be an important discipline to cultivate during and after the therapy journey.
- **Praying for clients in therapy sessions** can be a compelling way to model regulating emotions with prayer. When clients are open to beginning or ending a therapy session with prayer, the therapist functions in a priestly role, leading a client into the presence of God where healing and union might be found.
- **Exploring ways to cultivate prayerful habits** is another way a therapist might offer education, insight, or even personal reflections on the science and theology of cultivating gratitude or thanksgiving. Connecting clients with sacred or secular resources associated with the benefits of gratitude, clinicians can explore with individuals on how they might lean into gratitude on a more regular basis. Gratitude exercises

invite clients (and possibly families) to develop a regular rhythm of gratitude. One of my (Adam) family's favorite examples is using a glass gratitude jar (or other container) placed in a visible, ideally central, place in the home. Small slips of colorful paper and a writing instrument provide a visual cue to be mindful of targets for gratitude. Over time, the jar becomes filled to the brim with written moments of gratitude. Eventually, the jar itself becomes a memorial to diverse blessings.

CHILDREN'S CORNER

- ***Tell God How You Feel: Helping Kids with Hard Emotions*** (2021) by Christina Fox provides five snapshots of experiences that kids face. Some are joyful but most are challenging. This book offers vivid pictures of how we (children and adults) can talk to God about various experiences and emotions.
- ***Drawing God*** (2019). Emma, a little girl, wonders how to draw God. Using artful words and expressive drawings, this children's book by Karen Kiefer can spawn conversations or spark drawings, sculptures, and collages to express children's and adults' subjective and emotional images of God.
- ***Am I Praying?*** (2003) by Jeannie St. John Taylor is a creative book that illustrates various ways little Erik expresses his concerns to God.

REFERENCES

Aideyan, B., Martin, G. C., & Beeson, E. T. (2020). A practitioner's guide to breathwork in clinical mental health counseling. *Journal of Mental Health Counseling*, *42*(1), 78-94. https://doi.org/10.17744/mehc.42.1.06

Baggerly, J. (2018). Religious faith in play therapy: Survey findings. *International Journal of Play Therapy*, *27*(2), 114-23. https://doi.org/10.1037/pla0000070

Borgo, L. F. (2020). *Spiritual conversations with children: Listening to God together*. InterVarsity Press.

Bowlby, J. (1988). *A secure base: Parent-child attachment and healthy human development*. Basic Books.

Captari, L. E., Hook, J. N., Hoyt, W., Davis, D. E., McElroy-Heltzel, S. E., & Worthington, E. L., Jr. (2018). Integrating clients' religion and spirituality within psychotherapy: A comprehensive meta-analysis. *Journal of Clinical Psychology*, *74*(11), 1938-51. https://doi.org/10.1002/jclp.22681

Card, M. (2014). *A sacred sorrow: Reaching out to God in the lost language of lament*. Tyndale House.

Cepero, H. (2008). *Journaling as a spiritual practice: Encountering God through attentive writing*. InterVarsity Press.

Collins, W. L. (2005). Embracing spirituality as an element of professional self-care. *Social Work & Christianity, 32*(3), 263-74.

Dumulescu, D., Nečula, C. V., Sarca, D. M., & Cristea, G. W. (2022). Spiritual practice in psychological counseling: The return to the self. *Journal for the Study of Religions and Ideologies, 21*(62), 20-36.

England, M., & Klaassen, D. (2023). Clients' experiences of praying during therapy sessions. *Journal of Psychology and Theology, 51*(1), 48-66. https://doi.org/10.1177/00916471221095108

Exline, J. J., Grubbs, J. B., & Homolka, S. J. (2015). Seeing God as cruel or distant: Links with divine struggles involving anger, doubt, and fear of God's disapproval. *The International Journal for the Psychology of Religion, 25*(1), 29-41. https://doi.org/10.1080/10508619.2013.857255

Exline, J. J., Wilt, J. A., Harriott, V. A., Pargament, K. I., & Hall, T. W. (2021). Is God listening to my prayers? Initial validation of a brief measure of perceived divine engagement and disengagement in response to prayer. *Religions, 12*(2), 80. https://doi.org/10.3390/rel12020080

Foote, C. J. (1994). *Survivor prayers: Talking with God about childhood sexual abuse*. Westminster/John Knox Press.

Fox, C. (2021). *Tell God how you feel: Helping kids with hard emotions*. CF4Kids.

Fuller-Thomson, E., Lacombe-Duncan, A., Goodman, D., Fallon, B., & Brennenstuhl, S. (2020). From surviving to thriving: Factors associated with complete mental health among childhood sexual abuse survivors. *Social Psychiatry Psychiatric Epidemiology, 55*(6), 735-44. https://doi.org/10.1007/s00127-019-01767-x

Granqvist, P. (2020). *Attachment in religion and spirituality: A wider view*. Guilford.

Gregory, A., Johnson, E., Feder, G., Campbell, J., Konya, J., & Perôt, C. (2022). Perceptions of peer support for victim-survivors of sexual violence and abuse: An exploratory study with key stakeholders. *Journal of Interpersonal Violence, 37*(15-16), NP14036-NP14065. https://doi.org/10.1177/08862605211007931

Gubi, P. M. (2004). Surveying the extent of, and attitudes towards, the use of prayer as a spiritual intervention among British mainstream counsellors. *British Journal of Guidance & Counselling, 32*(4), 461-76. https://doi.org/10.1080/03069880412331303277

Guo, L. (2023). The delayed, durable effect of expressive writing on depression, anxiety and stress: A meta-analytic review of studies with long-term follow-ups. *British Journal of Clinical Psychology, 62*(1), 272-97. https://doi.org/10.1111/bjc.12408

Hagedorn, W. B., Pennock, E., & Finnell, L. R. (2018). Addressing spiritual and religious themes with play, creativity, and experiential interventions. In C. S. Gill & R. R. Freund (Eds.), *Spirituality and religion in counseling* (pp. 189-206). Routledge. https://doi.org/10.4324/9781315211046

Hollman, S. N., & Marmarosh, C. (2023). Providing a secure base: Facilitating a secure attachment to God in psychotherapy. In. P. Richards, G. E. Allen, & D. K. Judd (Eds.),

Handbook of spiritually integrated psychotherapies (pp. 57-75). American Psychological Association. https://doi.org/10.1037/0000338-003

Homeyer, L. E., & Sweeney, D. S. (2022). *Sandtray therapy: A practical manual.* Taylor & Francis. https://doi.org/10.4324/9781003221418

Karatzias, T., Shevlin, M., Ford, J. D., Fyvie, C., Grandison, G., Hyland, P., & Cloitre, M. (2022). Childhood trauma, attachment orientation, and complex PTSD (CPTSD) symptoms in a clinical sample: Implications for treatment. *Development and Psychopathology, 34*(3), 1192-97. https://doi.org/10.1017/S0954579420001509

Keifer, K. (2019). *Drawing God.* Paraclete.

Kirkpatrick, L. A., & Shaver, P. R. (1992). Attachment-theoretical approach to romantic love and religious belief. *Personality and Social Psychology, 18*(3), 266-75. https://doi.org/10.1177/0146167292183002

Knabb, J. J. (2021). *Christian meditation in clinical practice: A four-step model and workbook for therapists and clients.* InterVarsity Press.

Koenig, H. G. (2023). Person-centered mindfulness: A culturally and spiritually sensitive approach to clinical practice. *Journal of Religion and Health*, 1-13. https://doi.org/10.1007/s10943-023-01768-w

Kosarkova, A., Malinakova, K., van Dijk, J. P., & Tavel, P. (2020). Childhood trauma and experience in close relationships are associated with the god image: Does religiosity make a difference? *International Journal of Environmental Research and Public Health, 17*(23), 8841. https://doi.org/10.3390/ijerph17238841

Krause, N. (2011). The perceived prayers of others, stress, and change in depressive symptoms over time. *Review of Religious Research, 53*, 341-56. https://doi.org/10.1007/s13644-011-0016-3

Leins, C., & Williams, M. T. (2018). Using the Bible to facilitate treatment of religious obsessions in obsessive compulsive disorder. *Journal of Psychology and Christianity, 37*(2), 112-24.

Lewis Hall, M. E. (2016). Suffering in God's presence: The role of lament in transformation. *Journal of Spiritual Formation and Soul Care*, 9(2), 219-32. https://doi.org/10.1177/193979091600900207

Lynn, B., Yoo, G. J., & Levine, E. G. (2014). "Trust in the Lord": Religious and spiritual practices of African American breast cancer survivors. *Journal of Religion and Health, 53*(6), 1706-16. https://doi.org/10.1007/s10943-013-9750-x

Machisa, M., Christofides, N., & Jewkes, R. (2018). Social support factors associated with psychological resilience among women survivors of intimate partner violence in Gauteng, South Africa. *Global Health Action, 11*(Suppl 3), 1491114. https://doi.org/10.1080/16549716.2018.1491114

Martinez, J. S., Smith, T. B., & Barlow, S. H. (2007). Spiritual interventions in psychotherapy: Evaluations by highly religious clients. *Journal of Clinical Psychology, 63*(10), 943-60. https://doi.org/10.1002/jclp.20399

Meisenhelder, J. B., D'Ambra, C., & Jabaley, T. (2016). Spiritual coping at the end of life: A case study of a college student. *Journal of Hospice & Palliative Nursing, 18*(1), 66-73. https://doi.org/10.1097/NJH.0000000000000214

Miller, M. M., & Chavier, M. (2013). Clinicians' experiences of integrating prayer in the therapeutic process. *Journal of Spirituality in Mental Health, 15*(2), 70-93. https://doi.org/10.1080/19349637.2013.776441

Mosher, D. K., Hook, J. N., Captari, L. E., Hodge, A. S., Bellegarde, N., Davis, D. E., McElroy-Heltzel, S. E., Choe, E. J., Van Tongeren, D. R., Davis, E. B., & Aten, J. D. (2021). Spiritually oriented expressive writing and promoting positive outcomes after a natural disaster. *The Counseling Psychologist, 49*(6), 847-81. https://doi.org/10.1177/00110000211010499

Murray-Swank, N. A., & Pargament, K. I. (2005). God, where are you?: Evaluating a spiritually-integrated intervention for sexual abuse. *Mental Health, Religion & Culture, 8*(3), 191-203. https://doi.org/10.1080/13694670500138866

Neff, M. A., & McMinn, M. R. (2020). *Embodying integration: A fresh look at Christianity in the therapy room*. InterVarsity Press.

Olson, T., Tisdale, T. C., Davis, E. B., Park, E. A., Nam, J., Moriarty, G. L., Davis, D. E., Thomas, M. J., Cuthbert, A. D., & Hays, L. W. (2016). God image narrative therapy: A mixed-methods investigation of a controlled group-based spiritual intervention. *Spirituality in Clinical Practice, 3*(2), 77-91. https://doi.org/10.1037/scp0000096

Pargament, K. I. (2011). Religion and coping: The current state of knowledge. In S. Folkman (Ed.), *The Oxford handbook of stress, health, and coping* (pp. 269-88). Oxford University Press.

Pargament, K. I., & Exline, J. J. (2022). *Working with spiritual struggles in psychotherapy: From research to practice.* Guilford.

Pressley, J., & Spinazzola, J. (2017). Beyond survival: Application of a complex trauma treatment model in the Christian context. In H. D. E. Gingrich & F. C. Gingrich (Eds.), *Treating trauma in Christian counseling* (pp. 211-31). InterVarsity Press.

Richards, P. S., Pargament, K. I., Exline, J. J., & Allen, G. E. (2023). Introduction: Bringing spiritually integrated psychotherapies into the health care mainstream. In. P. Richards, G. E. Allen, & D. K. Judd (Eds.), *Handbook of spiritually integrated psychotherapies* (pp. 3-29). American Psychological Association. https://doi.org/10.1037/0000338-001

Rudolfsson, L., & Tidefors, I. (2014). I have cried to him a thousand times, but it makes no difference: Sexual abuse, faith, and images of God. *Mental Health, Religion & Culture, 17*(9), 910-22. https://doi.org/10.1080/13674676.2014.950953

Saenz, R., & Waldo, M. (2013). Clients' preferences regarding prayer during counseling. *Psychology of Religion and Spirituality, 5*(4), 325-34. https://doi.org/10.1037/a0033711

Schafer, M. H. (2013). Close ties, intercessory prayer, and optimism among American adults: Locating God in the social support network. *Journal for the Scientific Study of Religion, 52*(1), 35-56. https://doi.org/10.1111/jssr.12010

Schutz, P. J. (2021). "God saw . . . and God knew. . . ." In T. G. Plante & G. E. Schwartz (Eds.), *Human interaction with the divine, the sacred, and the deceased* (pp. 73-88). Routledge.

Skipper, A., Moore, T. J., & Marks, L. (2018). "The prayers of others helped": Intercessory prayer as a source of coping and resilience in Christian African American families. *Journal of Religion & Spirituality in Social Work: Social Thought*, *37*(4), 373-94. https://doi.org/10.1080/15426432.2018.1500970

Smyth, J. M., Nazarian, D., & Arigo, D. (2008). Expressive writing in the clinical context. In I. Nyklíček, A. Vingerhoets, & M. Zeelenberg (Eds.), *Emotion regulation: Conceptual and clinical issues* (pp. 215-33). Springer Science & Business Media. https://doi.org/10.1007/978-0-387-29986-0

Tait, R., Currier, J. M., & Harris, J. I. (2016). Prayer coping, disclosure of trauma, and mental health symptoms among recently deployed United States veterans of the Iraq and Afghanistan conflicts. *International Journal for the Psychology of Religion*, *26*(1), 31-45. https://doi.org/10.1080/10508619.2014.953896

Taylor, J. (2003). *Am I praying?* Kregel Kidzone.

Timbers, V. L., & Hollenberger, J. C. (2022). Christian mindfulness and mental health: Coping through sacred traditions and embodied awareness. *Religions*, *13*(1), 62. https://doi.org/10.3390/rel13010062

Torbjørnsen, T., Pargament, K. I., Stifoss-Hanssen, H., Hestad, K. A., & Danbolt, L. J. (2021). "If you and I and our Lord . . .": A qualitative study of religious coping in Hodgkin's disease. *Archive for the Psychology of Religion*, *43*(1), 3-20. https://doi.org/10.1177/0084672420983482

Tucker, J. (2022). *Breath as prayer: Calm your anxiety, focus your mind, and renew your soul.* Thomas Nelson.

Upenieks, L., & Ford-Robertson, J. (2022). Childhood abuse, goal-striving stress and self-esteem: An explanatory role for perceptions of divine control? *Journal of Religion and Health*, *62*(2), 906-31. https://doi.org/10.1007/s10943-022-01682-7

Walker, A. (1993). *The color purple*. Open Road Media.

Wan, J. (2021). Emotion-focused prayer with an emotion friendly God—My exploration of prayer with EFT techniques as a Chinese Christian counsellor. *Person-Centered & Experiential Psychotherapies*, *20*(3), 214-31. https://doi.org/10.1080/14779757.2021.1938181

Warren, T. H. (2021). *Prayer in the night: For those who work or watch or weep*. InterVarsity Press.

Weld, C., & Eriksen, K. (2007). Christian clients' preferences regarding prayer as a counseling intervention. *Journal of Psychology and Theology*, *35*(4), 328-41.

Wilder, E. J., Garzon, F., & Johnson, E. L. (2020). A Christian multi-modal approach to therapy utilizing inner healing prayer: The life model. *Journal of Psychology and Christianity*, *39*(1), 49-64.

Yancey, P. (2006). *Prayer: Does It Make Any Difference?* Hodder & Stoughton.

Zemeckis, R. (Dir.). (1994). *Forrest Gump* [Film]. Paramount Pictures.

9

HITTING THE WALL

VICARIOUS TRAUMATIZATION

I am old, Gandalf. I don't look it, but I am beginning to feel it in my heart of hearts. . . . I feel all thin, sort of stretched . . . *like butter that has been scraped over too much bread.*

BILBO, IN J. R. R. TOLKIEN, *THE LORD OF THE RINGS*

They made me keeper of the vineyards, but my own vineyard I have not kept!

SONG OF SONGS 1:6

ABOUT THE EIGHTEENTH MILE

I (Tammy) teach a graduate course on trauma. As we traverse the landscape of the sizeable effects of CSA and other forms of trauma, inevitably students experience the heaviness as they bear witness to the material. Hearing about evil in "this dark world" is difficult because we were made for a different world (Eph 6:12 NIV). While all students can experience the weight and freight of angst attached to trauma, the difficulty for some is that they "get" class content all too well due to traumatic experiences in their own lives.

Personal trauma histories are disproportionately high among mental health providers compared with the general population (Keesler, 2018; Thomas, 2016). And not only are trauma histories common among caregivers, but many also even refer to their trauma histories as the reason for their entrance into the helping professions (Lee et al., 2017). However, while trauma histories among mental health care providers may be the impetus for one's calling and occupational pursuit, clinicians with trauma histories may also be more susceptible to mental health concerns (Martin-Cuellar et al., 2018). For example, an examination of thirty-nine studies published over twenty-one years revealed a relationship between clinicians who have personal histories of trauma and disruptions in specific core beliefs about the therapists' view of self, others, and the world. In addition, they experienced an increased likelihood of posttraumatic stress symptoms (e.g., intrusive symptoms, avoidance, hyperarousal) (Leung et al., 2022).

It impacts me when my students hurt. I realize some may be considering personal abuse during their formative years for the first time or at more profound dimensions. And even for those who have not experienced sexual trauma personally, it is hard to listen to the brutality and heartache connected with trauma. Consequently, I work hard to make the class safe so folks can acknowledge that looking at evil is difficult. (See section on developing trauma-informed classrooms in the "Counseling Considerations" section at the end of this chapter.) However, recently, my semester felt extra burdensome. My students were adjusting to the heaviness of the trauma material, but I felt like *I* had loaded my belongings in a white and orange U-Haul truck and moved into Eeyore's Gloomy Place. I was teaching several sections of the Introduction to Trauma class, writing about trauma, working with several clients facing significant burdens, and supporting a loved one in my life who was facing enormous challenges. *I hit the wall.*

The phrase "hitting the wall" is often used by runners to describe what happens between the eighteenth and twenty-fifth miles of a marathon. About that time, a long-distance runner's legs stiffen and hurt, and every ounce of energy is required to lift each leg as muscles scream, "Don't go any farther! Quit now!" The athlete's body is depleted of energy-containing fuel.

Similarly, as trauma therapists listen to the incessant barrage of incest stories and tales of uncles, brothers, sisters, fathers, pastors, and mothers who molest innocent children and trusting teenagers, their very beings may scream, "Don't go any farther! Quit now!" In this chapter, before finishing the final leg of this textbook journey, we focus on you, the trauma caregiver, who may be a little weary from so many trauma stories. This chapter is for you, clinician, not only for the moments in your career when clients' stories weigh you down but for this very moment. May you find some encouragement here on your journey.

In this chapter we emphasize *trauma stewardship* and the dimensions involved in running more sustainable treks alongside survivors. We provide an up-close look at a journey with one individual facing vicarious trauma and offer several considerations for clinicians as they head in the direction of carefully stewarding our bodies, minds, and souls. And all along the way, as trauma therapists run by, we stand on the sidelines, cheering, offering support, and handing out spiritual Gatorade for parched throats.

Several terms exist that describe the consequences of beholding another's suffering.

VICARIOUS TRAUMA, SECONDARY TRAUMATIC STRESS, COMPASSION FATIGUE

We develop so many of the same symptoms that plague our clients, only we are better than they are at denial.

JEFFREY A. KOTTER

McCann and Pearlman (1990) coined the term "vicarious trauma" (VT). The word *vicarious* means participating in an event secondhand. In VT, clinicians are exposed to trauma through empathic engagement with trauma survivors, disrupting a caregiver's frame of reference or worldview. Simply put, VT develops when helpers are harmed from repeated indirect exposure to manifold suffering, resulting in shifts in how we view ourselves, others, the world, and God (Bhagwagar, 2022). For example, a clinician who works with children who have been abused may come to see humankind through a trauma lens and view people dichotomously as either perpetrators or victims.

Ireland and colleagues (2022) underscore two additional terms that are related to VT yet distinct: "secondary traumatic stress" (STS; Figley, 1995) and "compassion fatigue" (CF; Figley, 1995). VT is primarily related to disruptions in cognitive frames of reference. In contrast, STS describes the more observable trauma symptoms that emerge after repeated indirect exposure to trauma (e.g., hypervigilance, patterns of avoidance, intensification of emotions, intrusive thoughts). CF is a more global term for applicable to broader populations (clinicians, lay persons, and loved ones in helping/supportive roles) that combines aspects of secondary traumatic stress with burnout. Bhagwagar (2022) points out that CF and STS are often used interchangeably. Gaboury & Kimber (2022) note that VT alters cognitive perspectives gradually over numerous indirect exposures in empathic relationships, while STS can emerge after a single indirect exposure to trauma.

There is an ongoing debate concerning the nuances of these various terms describing the traumatic consequences of repeated, indirect exposure to trauma. However, there is no controversy about whether there are costs of caring among diverse helping professions. Hitting the wall is a red flag, bringing to attention our limitations. Trauma work is most commonly a marathon and not a sprint. Therefore, for trauma caregivers to press on as they journey with survivors, pacing, refreshment, and restorative activities are vital.

TRAUMA STEWARDSHIP

Restore the sparkle to my eyes.

PSALM 13:3 NLT

"Trauma stewardship" (van Dernoot Lipsky & Burk, 2009) is such a good term; we wish we had coined it. It refers to the idea of bearing witness to trauma, while simultaneously flourishing.

> We know that as stewards, we create a space for and honor others' hardship and suffering, and yet we do not assume their pain as our own. We care for others to the best of our ability without taking on their paths as our paths. . . . To participate in trauma stewardship is to always remember the privilege and sacredness of being called to help. It means maintaining our highest ethics, integrity, and responsibility every step of the way. (van Dernoot Lipsky & Burk, 2009, p. 6)

Viewed through this lens, trauma stewardship is not merely a series of tasks but a way of life. Scripture guides us to steward the life, resources, and gifts entrusted to us (1 Pet 4:10). Canning (2011) further elucidates that stewardship is a journey of freedom, where we manage our valuable resources. Our thoughts, feelings, and actions in this journey are guided by our true north, our benevolent God, who has blessed us with these gifts.

Dear reader, please know that we are uneasy with much of the clinician self-care literature. Too often, we find the North American obsessive, consumeristic, give-me-another-latte-and-a-new-outfit, binge-on-Netflix, take-a-warm-vacation, it's-all-about-me self-care remedies lacking. Jesus gave up food, sleep, time away, and private retreats to love people. So did his disciples. Yet he also called them out to quiet places, praying places, restorative places. Often quick and temporary "solutions" with a central focus on the self, do not provide solutions leading to deep and wide flourishing. Still, many godly trauma clinicians are fatigued people who have difficulty quieting themselves. There is tension here. Frequently, many of us have only momentary glimpses of eating, sleeping, serving, resting, feasting, loving, and laughing as dearly loved children of God.

Moreover, problematically, much of the focus of the literature on remedying VT involves mere activity-based solutions (e.g., exercise more, vary client loads). This inevitably culminates in adding more items to the interminable clinician to-do lists. Referring to medical residents, Pearson (2017) states that they "don't need ice cream and wellness weeks to survive grueling schedules and the deep trauma of patients and families." And, we would add, neither do clinicians. While we believe that proactive, specific action steps to alleviate VT can be helpful, there must be something more involved in the trek toward trauma stewardship and true flourishing.

Over the years, we have reviewed the VT literature, observed colleagues as they, too, endured the marathon pace of trauma work, and considered our own lives to evaluate times when we were overwhelmed versus when we flourished. Just like when we encourage clients to consider some new or different coping skills, perhaps you might decide to try some items listed below during your journey of bearing witness and stewarding trauma stories.

TOWARD A SUSTAINABLE TRAINING SCHEDULE

Taking stock.

Take the first step in faith. You don't have to see the whole staircase. Just take the first step.

MARTIN LUTHER KING JR.

Preparing to run a marathon takes much time, as does navigating new stewarding terrains. As part of this process we, curiously and without judgment, create spaces to explore the impact of accumulated sorrows and exhaustion related to bearing witness. Paradoxically, we open ourselves up to more sorrow by being still and noticing what is going on internally. Yet, while we acknowledge the toll of regularly hearing about the brutality of trauma, we simultaneously marvel at the implacable splendor of a field of sunflowers growing high up in the sky (van Dernoot Lipsky & Burk, 2009).

One way to take stock is to more formally assess and understand the positive and negative aspects of bearing witness to trauma. The ProQOL is a thirty-item self-report scale yielding feedback on compassion satisfaction and compassion fatigue (Stamm, 2010). Two subcategories are associated with compassion fatigue: secondary trauma and burnout. As one of the most widely used measures in the world on the positive and negative effects of helping, the ProQOL is also free, available in various languages, and easily accessed.

Individuals can conveniently take the ProQOL online at any time. I (Hannah) use it for my team and me about once a year. As an organizational leader, I believe that mandating trauma stewardship does not work. But I can take fifteen minutes of a staff meeting every six months and invite our team to take the ProQOL. I can provide a space and help form a culture that says it is okay to pause. It is okay to look inward for a bit. It is okay to say out loud in group or individual supervision that I am exhibiting some signs of VT. And consider ways to work on trauma stewardship so that our supervisees and the clients we serve can flourish.

Taking stock also involves looking at how we are doing spiritually as we journey with survivors. I (Hannah) have learned from working with fellow trauma clinicians that many of us do not pause long enough to do this work. It can be challenging to believe in the value of gazing in when I'm constantly gazing out. One spiritual practice that has helped nurture the "taking stock" skill is the ancient tradition of examen of consciousness or a daily review. Ruth Haley Barton (2006) describes the practice in this way:

> The examen of consciousness involves taking a few moments at the end of each day [week, month, or year] to go back over the events of the day and invite God to show us where he was present with us and how we responded to his presence. We might ask ourselves, How was God present with me today? What promptings did I notice? How did I respond or not respond? (p. 95)

A clinician might add some questions to this practice, such as

- What did I bear witness to today that felt overwhelming?
- What did you see in my client(s), God?
- What did you see in me?
- How did you demonstrate your love through my work today?

Barton (2006, p. 94) reminds us, "The real issue in self-examination is not that I am inviting God to know me (since he already does) but that I am inviting God to help me know me." There are many reasons it is challenging to look inward, and even reasons we think we should not (it is a form of self-absorption, we say). But I am convinced that with God's loving gaze, looking inward becomes a way that my deepest longings of being fully known and fully loved are met, and my capacity to look at suffering only expands.

Trauma-informed supervision. Just as marathoners need wise coaches, clinicians need sensitive supervisors who are attentive to the heaviness related to hearing harrowing trauma narratives hour after hour. Throughout the literature, trauma-informed supervision is deemed a salient protective factor for clinicians working with traumatized clients (Branson, 2019; Padmanabhanunni & Gqomfa, 2022). Strong supervisory alliances can ultimately augment outcomes for survivors too (Berger et al., 2018).

While supervision is not therapy, trauma-informed supervision involves inviting supervisees to be attuned and to acknowledge their emotional and cognitive responses regarding their clients' trauma narratives and their somatic reactions (e.g., jaw clenching, tightness in various parts of the body); to recognize the difference between empathy and countertransference (e.g., awareness when ruminating); to engage with responses fully so they can be completed; and to establish the pattern of engagement with others when more processing is needed (Miller & Sprang, 2017). Moreover, Courtois (2018) noted the importance of discussing the client's shame based on the awareness that client shame can beget therapist shame, and the need to rescue clients from their shame.

As clinicians bear witness to emotionally charged and graphic narratives about violence and anguish related to sexual trauma, we need to have supervision spaces that are attuned to the existential realities of hearing about evil and suffering. Considering where God is amid all the abuse in a respectful, collaborative supervision relationship can facilitate coping. This can furnish opportunities for clinicians to contend with spiritual distress, health, and a sense of calling, promoting meaning making and ways to cope with trauma (Muehihausen, 2021). Delker recommends the importance of having the opportunity to grapple with questions like the following:

- This week, at the end of which days did you feel energized rather than depleted?
- What was different about yourself (what you were doing, thinking, feeling), the relationship between you and the client, or the context itself on this day?
- How are you responding and making sense of the violence and suffering you witnessed today? (Delker, 2019, p. 7)

Trauma-sensitive supervision can include discussions about diversifying client loads and spacing sessions so clinicians can limit the number of survivors they see each day. Looking at examples of when clinicians can increasingly tolerate ambiguity and uncertainty and avoid moving too quickly to pragmatic solutions to rescue survivors from their sorrows can provide rich supervision discussions. Initiating conversations about times when the supervisee overestimated their ability to change client circumstances and its impact on mood can be important terrain to cover (Borders et al., 2022). In addition to sensitive trauma-informed supervision, we also need informal spaces where we can "let down our hair," as we are hard-wired for connection.

Companionship in the marathon.

It's me. It's your Sam. Don't you know your Sam?

SAM, *LORD OF THE RINGS: THE TWO TOWERS*, J. R. R. TOLKIEN (FROM PETER JACKSON'S MOVIE ADAPTATION)

On race day, our coach's voice may only travel so far. It is the fellow runner alongside us who convinces us that we "got this" and to "keep going." You may have seen one of those YouTube videos where a runner becomes injured and a beloved someone from the stadium bursts out onto the track to run side by side with the athlete until they cross the finish line together. We all need companions when we run alongside survivors on the highways and byways of suffering. Elijah had Elisha, David had Jonathan, Mary had Elizabeth, and Frodo had Sam.

A culture of collegial support and peer consultation provides reflective spaces, empathy, and hope. It is not just about sharing experiences but about uplifting each other and fostering a sense of hope. After a tough session, this support can diminish isolation and detachment when it is most needed. Support from peers who share a lived reality can create safe places that allow fellow clinicians to be vulnerable about their clinical and personal concerns. Ultimately, when clinicians sense the support on the front lines from fellow therapists, they can be freed up to express empathy and patience with clients, creating a ripple effect of hope.

Survivors of sexual exploitation staff our drop-in center for women still involved in the sex trade. I (Hannah) regularly observe the positive impact of being greeted by people with shared experiences—people with similar traumas, sometimes from the same people. Recently, one of our peer supporters decided to care for one of our regular guests in a moment of deep pain. The staff person spent hours by the side of a suffering woman. When I checked in with her the following day, she said, "I did for her based on what I needed in the same situation a long time ago." Her smile (we know that smile) convinced us that she was not just okay but somehow filled with joy—that she knew where she ended and the client began, and that somehow she could steward the trauma in front of her without being crushed.

Clinician community support is also a vital component of long-distance clinicians. Pearlman and colleagues (2014, p. 257) explain that the support derived from clinicians' communities helps them to exercise other aspects of their identities, so that in addition to therapist, we engage with the world as partner, pianist, jokester, gardener, and a host of other identities. Our communities hold our values, joys, and sorrows with us and remind us that we are part of an interconnected web, which can counter the isolation of trauma.

PHYSICAL STEWARDSHIP (AKA THE BODY REALLY DOES KEEP THE SCORE)

Get up and eat, or the journey will be too much for you.

1 KINGS 19:7

Clinicians, by and large, work in primarily sedentary settings. Following my (Tammy) annual visit to my primary care physician, who told me I needed to lose weight for the fourth year in a row, I began talking with wise folks and reading about ways that I could better steward my body that the Lord gave me. I engaged in a radical re-evaluation of my Western diet, which includes highly processed foods, sugars, salt, and a lot of meat, and how this is related to a panoply of obesity-related diseases and mental health concerns. I discovered that a growing number of medical experts assert "diet is as important to psychiatry as it is to cardiology, endocrinology, and gastroenterology" (Sarris et al., 2015, p. 271). This awareness began a nine-month journey of radically changing the way I eat.

At the end of my teaching and clinical days, I often put my sneakers on and walk under an umbrella of trees, listening for the sound of birds, and I talk with the Lord about the students, staff, and clients I have encountered. Ancient Romans coined the phrase *solvitur ambulando* (it is solved by walking). They understood the benefits of bilateral stimulation a long time ago. In the aptly named book *Burnout*, physical activity is such an important practice in the battle of burnout (Nagoski & Nagoski, 2019). The authors also discuss the importance of creativity, laughing, crying, physical affection, and deep breathing.

On the other end of the movement continuum, we also need sleep. Few things are more restorative than a good night's sleep. Can we get an amen? As Mark Buchanan stated:

> We can defy slumber only so long—propping ourselves upright with caffeine, manufacturing artificial alertness with drugs—but past a certain point, we collapse. We must submit to sleep's benign tyranny, enter its inescapable vulnerability and solitariness. . . . Unless we do, we die. (2006, p. 60).

You may rely on your counseling office waiting room's Keurig machine to get you through your 2:00 p.m. session. It is okay. But it is also worth looking at your overall sleep hygiene and working with your health provider to improve your sleep habits. There are several technologies available to track and enhance sleep patterns, including several apps with low or no cost to monitor and enhance sleep. Notably, the CBT-i Coach App is one free smartphone app with basic cognitive-behavioral therapy for insomnia education, opportunities to learn relaxation skills, sleep tracking capabilities, and so on.

RESTORATION THROUGH LAUGHTER

Our physical bodies also house two of life's most effective coping mechanisms for completing the stress cycle, or finding a way to let our bodies know we're no longer threatened and we can relax: tears and laughter (Nagoski & Nagoski, 2019). It strikes me (Hannah) how kind God is to design our bodies with these two powerful (and free) gifts to settle our nervous systems. Tears are the language of a therapist, so you have likely observed and experienced the healing effect of a good cry. But as it relates to rest stops for trauma clinicians, when was the last time you had a deep belly laugh?

Those who have run a marathon (or observed one) might know about the cultural phenomenon of hilarious signs by friendly supporters. Family members and friends stand at strategic places along the 26.2-mile course, holding up signs that say things like:

Should I call you an Uber?

Smile. Remember, you paid for this.

Always give 100%. Except when giving blood.

You run marathons. I watch them on Netflix.

Marathon supporters hope their signs might bring some laughter and offer a runner something to think about other than their fatigue. We should be clear that we are not endorsing laughter to avoid pain. We know that laughter can be misplaced. Yet, Scripture reminds us that there is "a time to weep and a time to laugh; a time to mourn and a time to dance" (Eccles 3:4). With this in mind, we recognize and celebrate the gift of laughter. A recent meta-analysis (Stiwi & Rosendahl, 2022) revealed that laughter-inducing interventions positively affected mental health (e.g., positive intra- and interpersonal functioning) and physical health outcomes (e.g., benefits to the muscular, cardiovascular, respiratory, endocrine, immune, and central nervous systems).

Stiwi and Rosendahl (2022) also found that group laughter-inducing interventions were more effective than laughing alone. Another study found that laughing *together*—or even just reminiscing about times we laughed—increases relationship satisfaction (Bazzini et al., 2007). Tammy and I (Hannah) love to reminisce about when we sat in the front row at a conference (a trauma conference, no less!). Somehow, after passing some notes, we began stifling our uncontrollable laughter. Yes, it was likely instigated by some trauma sessions that we were attending. However, it started a cascade of laughter for the rest of the weekend. This is a prime example of poorly timed laughter! It was decidedly *not* "a time to laugh." Yet, telling the story over and over fills our hearts (many years later) with joy. However, you find yourselves caring for your minds, bodies, and souls, may you know the restorative impact of a deep belly laugh with a good friend.

A DEEPER REST

And you will find rest for your souls.

MATTHEW 11:29

I (Hannah) will be a little pastoral here for a second. I'm thinking about all the trauma clinicians I know who regularly bring up a word that is, frankly, frustrating: *productivity*. Is this you? Are you working in an environment where some kind of task master demands of you the creation of more bricks (I mean, notes)? This is not the time for a soapbox about SOAP notes and managed care. Still, it does seem like the time to say that our God is a "Sabbath-giving and Sabbath-commanding God" (Brueggemann, 2014, p. 10) and that it is simply not healthy for us to be in constant caregiving positions. Sabbath is not a burden. It is for the burdened. Sabbath is not so much a task on the checklist as it is a kind invitation to rest. It is a moment to let the soul feel its worth, to rest in our identity as beloved.

Interestingly, some runners experience remarkably faster times when they take walk breaks. During a marathon, periodic pauses allow different muscles to be used, thus allowing greater endurance and improved race times. Even if you have no plans in the next year to do a triathlon or a 26.2-mile marathon, the need for rest times, whether during long-distance competitions or long-term caregiving, is striking.

As with running a marathon, it can be tempting in clinical work to think *keep going* as we have many more miles to go. A runner might start to believe that the only way to get the prize is to run through pain or to pick up the pace despite the body's signals that rest or water is needed. A clinician might start to believe that the only way to feel okay about one's work is to take that section of the calendar they had previously blocked off for some alone time or friend time and give it to the client who is asking for it. Over time, our identity gets entangled with what we produce, whether it's something tangible like a race day PR or the intangible level of healing for someone on our caseload. Sabbath offers a kind of counter-narrative to our identity misunderstanding. As one writer puts it:

> If I do more, I am more. If I have more, I am more. If more people like and recognize me more, I'm more valuable. The idea is subtle, and insidious in its undermining of the Sabbath. What happens to our sense of identity if we stop our activity to observe the Sabbath day? If I am what I do, who am I on a Sabbath day when I do nothing productive? (Fadling, 2013, p. 115)

Rest is also a theme peppered throughout Scripture. Even God rested: "On the sixth day God finished the work that he had done, and he rested on the seventh day from all the work that he had done" (Gen 2:2). God offers rest to his people in his new covenant with them: "I will satisfy the weary, and all who are faint I will replenish" (Jer 31:25). In the New Testament, we see Jesus, God's Son, making similar declarations to his people and to us. He says radical things like, "Come to me, all you who are weary and are carrying heavy burdens, and I will give you rest" (Mt 11:28), and "Let anyone who is thirsty come to me" (Jn 7:37). Rest is important to God. Yet it so often seems unimportant to us.

RADICAL ACCEPTANCE OF SUFFERING IN THIS WORLD

I cannot carry all these people by myself;
the burden is too heavy for me.

NUMBERS 11:14 NIV

No seasoned marathoner embarks on training without an expectation that there will be some pain in the process. For some athletes, the allure of training for and competing in long-distance running events lies in embracing the pain to achieve the fulfillment of not *merely competing but also completing.* Perhaps we might consider approaching our profession with a similar vision for embracing suffering in a long journey toward the satisfaction of completing something worthwhile.

Acceptance-based therapies shed light on the liberating nature of embracing the pain for therapist and client alike. Hayes (2019) notes that avoidance is a natural, human, tragic response to pain. This escapism leads us down a pathway where we increasingly avoid negative and even positive emotions. In contrast, acceptance invites us to turn toward our pain and to fully feel and open ourselves up to lessons and values only gleaned in pain. This is not resignation or tolerance, however. It does not call that which is terrible "good." Instead, it says yes to the totality of our lived experience so that we can be present, aware, and alive.

Every race is run on a different day, climate, and terrain. Some suffering is inevitable along the journey. If we as therapists recognize our tendency to hurt where we care and lean into the pain, it helps us dig down to find conviction and even love. This long-term, suffering-accepting approach to trauma therapy can buffer us from VT because repeated empathic exposures to the suffering of others also invite us to discern our values and remain connected to compassion satisfaction along the journey. Suffering vicariously in this work can yield thoughts such as *I've trained for this hill* versus *I am Sisyphus rolling a rock up a hill.* We are not damned to roll rocks up hills by ourselves; we are liberated to embrace the hill because the hill rests atop the Rock of ages, and the Cornerstone himself equips and empowers us to carry on with meaningful strides.

Pain scoops us out and leaves more room for wisdom, joy, conviction, and gratitude. A posture of acceptance invites a therapist to be less interested in solving or fixing a professional or personal problem and more oriented toward building a meaningful life (and career). Acceptance perceives painful memories, emotions, bodily sensations, and thoughts in this broken world as part of the total package of a life well lived. This approach transcends therapy outcomes or even the subjective experience of compassion satisfaction. Along the way, storms may stir, and the scenery is breathtaking at other times. If we keep our eyes open, we might find beauty in the storm and the sunshine. The joy is not only in the journey and crossing the finish line but also in remembering that the race maker planned the specific trek according to plans we may not fully comprehend this side of eternity.

While serving as a director of psychological health at several military bases or as the director of emotional well-being at a large organization, it was common for me (Adam) to have requests from departments to give a seminar that includes a time for Q&A. Inevitably, in nearly every session, a question arose regarding the potential benefits of "mental health days." This is often a time to provide education about the liberating nature of radical acceptance and the dangers of avoidance. Days off from work can quickly become self-sabotage if they are characterized by avoidance. We don't escape VT by laying in our beds for twelve hours binge-watching streaming services and binge-eating sugar and potato chips. Acceptance allows us to turn away from the day-to-day routine and toward joy, engagement in meaningful activities, artistic expression, and so on.

Imagine a world where people come back to work restored after a day or week of vacation. Imagine a world where Sunday nights are the most restful sleep (versus the worst due to dreaded Monday morning). By the way, simple and nearly cost-free opportunities exist. I've learned that an hour to two of sidewalk chalk or playground adventures with my daughter offers exactly the restorative, joyful respite my soul needs for the marathon that awaits.

Let us turn our attention to how Karmen began to wrestle with some new ideas and how she developed her own sustainable "training schedule."

COUNSELING SCENARIO

Karmen is a lay helper in a religious organization with many caregiver demands. In her professional role, she is regularly confronted with suffering and struggles in the people she seeks to serve. She sought therapy expressing a desire to establish healthier boundaries with a work-life balance due to a self-diagnosed "identity crisis" associated with "losing my joy" in work that was previously deeply rewarding. Karmen describes mild symptoms of depression, recent increases in anxiety and panic symptoms, and a general loss of compassion satisfaction in her work. She also reports a diminished distress tolerance for stresses away from work and a loss of connection and joy at work and in her personal life.

Karmen was agreeable to taking the ProQOL and reviewing the results. Interestingly, orienting Karmen to the ProQOL and the constructs of compassion satisfaction, burnout, and secondary traumatic stress was a powerful intervention to normalize and offer coherence to her circumstances. She said, "It's strangely comforting to know I am not alone." Her results were not surprising, but they offered specific therapeutic targets. She endorsed items on the ProQOL, resulting in a low range of compassion satisfaction, a medium range for burnout, and a medium range for secondary traumatic stress. Using an Acceptance and Commitment Therapy (ACT) approach, our therapy journey together focused on aspects of psychological flexibility to help Karmen reconnect with her values in professional and personal domains. Cognitive defusion, a classic ACT construct, helped Karmen identify her "dictator within" (whom she named Sally) and served as a pathway toward insight and self-compassion when considering the origins of these thoughts. Self-as-context was an aspect of psychological flexibility that also resonated with Karmen. She connected her transcendent self with theological and spiritual beliefs about her identity as a child of God. Toward the end of therapy, many challenging aspects of Karmen's work and caregiver demands were unchanged, but she reported significantly more gratitude, joy, and connection to her values. The ProQOL was administered again in one of the final counseling sessions, yielding significant increases in compassion satisfaction, lower endorsements for items associated with burnout, and low-range endorsements for secondary traumatic stress. Karmen also reconnected with more values-based living, including greater belongingness to friends. She also obtained a spiritual mentor.

During our conversations about trauma stewardship, we also discussed the idea of developing a plan B, meaning that Karmen could plan more options than her current one so that she wasn't stuck. Even if she didn't make a change, her spirit was buoyed by knowing she *could*. We all know that sometimes our best-laid intentions for stewarding in wiser ways do not always go as we hoped. While it may be difficult to envision a plan B, it is a practice worth trying. We can be so overwhelmed by logistics, minutiae, and the perceived constraints in our lives that we see our work as a burden, an imposition, something being done to us. Through creating and re-creating a plan B, we come to understand that it is we who make the fundamental choices about the work we do. While there is great responsibility that comes with this understanding, there is tremendous freedom as well. We always have options to change what we do, where we do it, or how we approach the work at hand (van Dernoot Lipsky & Burk, 2009, pp. 180-183). For Karmen, it was helpful for her to have a plan B so she knew that she was not stuck.

RUNNING WITH PERSEVERANCE

The long and short of it is that "trauma is contagious," and as Oswald Chambers once said, "the sheep are many and the shepherds few, for the fatigue is staggering, the heights are giddy, and the sights awful." In our strength, this marathon is too difficult, too long, and too dangerous. Of this race, Scripture speaks into the trauma caregiver's soul:

> Let us also lay aside every weight and the sin clings so easily, and let us *run with perseverance* the race that is set before us, looking to Jesus, the pioneer and perfecter of faith, who for the sake of the joy that was set before him endured the cross, disregarding its shame, and has taken his seat at the right hand of the throne of God.
>
> Consider him who endured such hostility against himself from sinners, so that you may *not grow weary in your souls or lose heart.* (Heb 12:1-3, emphasis added)

COUNSELING CONSIDERATIONS

Assessment tools.

- *Professional Quality of Life (ProQOL):* The ProQOL is designed to be useful for anyone in a helping role. This free and validated measure helps individuals understand the positive and negative effects of working with suffering individuals. Individual items in the ProQOL load on scales such as Compassion Satisfaction, Burnout, and Secondary Traumatic Stress.
- *Sussex-Oxford Compassion for the Self Scale (SOCS-S):* The SOCS-S measures compassion for the self on five domains: recognizing suffering, understanding the universality of suffering, empathy, tolerating uncomfortable feelings, and acting/being motivated to act to alleviate suffering.

Building protective factors.

- *Acceptance and Commitment Therapy:* As a transdiagnostic approach, ACT outlines psychological flexibility processes such as self-as-context and defusion, which directly address painful thoughts, memories, emotions, and bodily sensations. Specifically, defusion techniques are useful to notice and respond with self-compassion and values to self-criticism. Steven Hayes's book *A Liberated Mind* includes numerous examples of defusion, and his TEDx Talk titled "Mental Brakes to Avoid Mental Breaks" is a helpful resource as well.

- *Emotional agility:* Susan David's model provides another framework to address self-critical thoughts as well as a connection to values and qualities of action aligned with values. Her book titled *Emotional Agility* and her TED talk are excellent resources.
- *Self-compassion resources and books by Kristin Neff:* Kristin Neff (2011) authored an empirically supported treatment program called *Mindful Self-Compassion* and has authored numerous books and workbooks for diverse populations related to self-compassion. Her website is filled with resources for personal and professional use.
- *CBT-i Coach App:* This app is free to download on iTunes (IOS) or Google Play (Android) and is found at The National Center for PTSD (a division of the Veterans Administration).

Developing trauma-informed classrooms. Mental health educators need to be wise in the ways that we teach about trauma to avoid VT in the classroom. Teaching about trauma in trauma-informed ways includes (a) modifying the intensity of topics based on student needs (i.e., wise pacing of course content), (b) encouraging students to avoid late-night trauma textbook reading, (c) providing opportunities for journal writing about course material without requiring personal trauma disclosure, (d) teaching on VT and vicarious resilience, (e) giving opportunities for small-group discussion to develop meaningful self-less self-care beyond activity-based activities alone, (f) teaching emotion-regulation skills and pairing with trauma content exposure, (g) training practicum supervisors to provide space for existential and spiritual questions related to trauma work with clients, (h) encouraging personal counseling when trauma histories may be triggered, (i) teaching on evidence-based hope interventions, posttraumatic growth, transformation, and religious coping strategies (Carello & Butler, 2014; Gilin & Kauffman, 2015).

CHILDREN'S CORNER

- ***The Velveteen Rabbit*** (2023). Over a hundred years ago, Margery Williams understood that people strive to be more loveworthy. Over time, something happens within the rabbit in this book—a quieting and a gradual ceasing to strive as he learns to be real.

- ***The Gift of Nothing*** (McDonnell, 2008). Mooch the cat searched high and low to find a gift for his friend Earl. He was so discouraged until he eventually found the perfect gift where he and Earl stayed still and enjoyed nothing.

REFERENCES

Barton, R. H. (2006). *Sacred rhythms: Arranging our lives for spiritual transformation.* InterVarsity Press.

Bazzini, D. G., Stack, E. P., Martincin, P. D., & Davis, C. (2007). The effect of reminiscing about laughter on relationship satisfaction. *Motivation and Emotion, 31*(1), 25-34. https://doi.org/10.1007/s11031-006-9045-6

Berger, R., Quiros, L., & Benavidez-Hatzis, J. R. (2018). The intersection of identities in supervision for trauma-informed practice: Challenges and strategies. *The Clinical Supervisor, 37*(1), 122-41. https://doi.org/10.1080/07325223.2017.1376299

Bhagwagar, H. (2022). Secondary trauma, burnout and resilience among mental health professionals from India: A review of research. *Asian Journal of Psychiatry, 76,* 1-10. https://doi.org/10.1016/j.ajp.2022.103227

Borders, L. D., Lowman, M. M., Eicher, P. A., & Phifer, J. K. (2022). Trauma-informed supervision of trainees: Practices of supervisors trained in both trauma and clinical supervision. *Traumatology, 29*(2), 125-36. https://doi.org/10.1037/trm0000382

Branson, D. C. (2019). Vicarious trauma, themes in research, and terminology: A review of literature. *Traumatology, 25*(1), 2-10. https://doi.org/10.1037/trm0000161

Brueggemann, W. (2014). *Sabbath as resistance: Saying no to the culture of now.* Westminster John Knox Press.

Buchanan, M. (2006). *The rest of God: Restoring your soul by restoring Sabbath.* Thomas Nelson.

Canning, S. S. (2011). Out of balance: Why I hesitate to practice and teach "self-care." *Journal of Psychology and Christianity, 30*(1), 70.

Carello, J., & Butler, L. D. (2014). Potentially perilous pedagogies: Teaching trauma is not the same as trauma-informed teaching. *Journal of Trauma & Dissociation, 15*(2), 153-68. https://doi.org/10.1080/15299732.2014.867571

Courtois, C. A. (2018). Trauma-informed supervision and consultation: Personal reflections. *The Clinical Supervisor, 37*(1), 38-63. https://doi.org/10.1080/07325223.2017.1416716

Crivatu, I. M., Horvath, M. A., & Massey, K. (2021). The impacts of working with victims of sexual violence: A rapid evidence assessment. *Trauma, Violence, & Abuse.* https://doi.org.10.1177/15248380211016024

Delker, B. C. (2019). When self-care is not enough: Reflections on how to make intensive clinical work more sustainable. *Dignity: A Journal on Sexual Exploitation and Violence, 4*(1). https://doi.org/10.23860/dignity.2019.04.01.06

Fadling, A. (2013). *An unhurried life: Following Jesus' rhythms of work and rest.* InterVarsity Press.

Figley, C. R. (1995). Compassion fatigue as secondary traumatic stress disorder: An overview. In C. R. Figley (Ed.), *Compassion fatigue: Coping with secondary traumatic stress disorder in those who treat the traumatized* (pp. 1-20). Brunner/Mazel.

Gaboury, K., & Kimber, M. (2022). Consequences of vicarious traumatization among mental health service providers with a history of child maltreatment: A narrative review. *Psychological Trauma: Theory, Research, Practice, and Policy, 15*(Supp. 2), S203-12. https://doi.org/10.1037/tra0001298

Gilin, B., & Kauffman, S. (2015). Strategies for teaching about trauma to graduate social work students. *Journal of Teaching in Social Work, 35*(4), 378-96. https://doi.org/10.1080/08841233.2015.1065945

Hayes, S. C. (2019). *A liberated mind: How to pivot toward what matters.* Penguin/Avery.

Ireland, C. A., Keeley, S., Lewis, M., & Bowden, S. (2022). Vicarious trauma and compassion fatigue in residential care workers of traumatized children. *Abuse: An International Impact Journal, 3*(1), 43-54. https://doi.org/10.37576/abuse.2022.030

Keesler, J. M. (2018). Adverse childhood experiences among direct support professionals. *Intellectual and Developmental Disabilities, 56*(2), 119-32. https://doi.org/10.1352/1934-9556-56.2.119

Lee, K., Pang, Y. C., Lee, J. A. L., & Melby, J. N. (2017). A study of adverse childhood experiences, coping strategies, work stress, and self-care in the child welfare profession. *Human Service Organizations, Management, Leadership & Governance, 41*(4), 389-402. https://doi.org/10.1080/23303131.2017.1302898

Leung, T., Schmidt, F., & Mushquash, C. (2022). A personal history of trauma and experience of secondary traumatic stress, vicarious trauma, and burnout in mental health workers: A systematic literature review. *Psychological Trauma: Theory, Research, Practice, and Policy, 15*(Supp 2), S213-21. https://doi.org/10.1037/tra0001277

Martin-Cuellar, A., Atencio, D. J., Kelly, R. J., & Lardier, D. T., Jr. (2018). Mindfulness as a moderator of clinician history of trauma on compassion satisfaction. *The Family Journal, 26*(3), 358-68. https://doi.org/10.1177/1066480718795123

McCann, L. I., & Pearlman, L. A. (1990). Vicarious traumatization: A framework for understanding the psychological effects of working with victims. *Journal of Traumatic Stress, 3*(1), 131-49. https://doi.org/10.1002/jts.2490030110

McDonnell, P. (2008). *The gift of nothing.* Little, Brown.

Miller, B., & Sprang, G. (2017). A components-based practice and supervision model for reducing compassion fatigue by affecting clinician experience. *Traumatology, 23*(2), 153. https://doi.org/10.1037/trm0000058

Muehlhausen, B. L. (2021). Spirituality and vicarious trauma among trauma clinicians: A qualitative study. *Journal of Trauma Nursing, 28*(6), 367-77. https://doi.org/10.1097/JTN.0000000000000616

Nagoski, E., & Nagoski, A. (2019). *Burnout: The secret to unlocking the stress cycle.* Ballantine Books.

Neff K. (2011). *Self-compassion: The proven power of being kind to* yourself. William Morrow.

Padmanabhanunni, A., & Gqomfa, N. (2022). "The ugliness of it seeps into me": Experiences of vicarious trauma among female psychologists treating survivors of sexual assault. *International Journal of Environmental Research and Public Health, 19*(7), 3925. https://doi.org/10.3390/ijerph19073925

Pearlman, L. A., Wortman, C. B., Feuer, C. A., Farber, C. H., & Rando, T. A. (2014). *Treating traumatic bereavement: A practitioner's guide*. Guilford.

Pearson, R. (2017, April 30). When doctors can't afford to feel. *The Daily Beast.* www.thedailybeast.com/when-doctors-cant-afford-to-feel

Sarris, J., Logan, A. C., Akbaraly, T. N., Amminger, G. P., Balanzá-Martínez, V., Freeman, M. P., Hibbeln, J., Matsuoka, Y., Mischoulon, D., Mizoue, T., Nanri, A., Nishi, D., Ramsey, D., Rucklidge, J. J., Sanchez-Villegas, A., Scholey, A., Su, K.-P., & Jacka, F. N. (2015). Nutritional medicine as mainstream in psychiatry. *The Lancet Psychiatry, 2*(3), 271-74. https://doi.org/10.1016/S2215-0366(14)00051-0

Sprang, G., Ford, J., Kerig, P., & Bride, B. (2019). Defining secondary traumatic stress and developing targeted assessments and interventions: Lessons learned from research and leading experts. *Traumatology, 25*(2), 72. http://doi.org/10.1037/trm0000180

Stamm, B. H. (2010). *The Concise ProQOL Manual* (2nd ed.). ProQOL.org.

Stiwi, K. & Rosendahl, J. (2022). Efficacy of laughter-inducing interventions in patients with somatic or mental health problems A systematic review and meta-analysis of randomized-controlled trials. *Complementary Therapies in Clinical Practice, 47.* https://doi.org/10.1016/j.ctcp.2022.101552

Thomas, J. T. (2016). Adverse childhood experiences among MSW students. *Journal of Teaching in Social Work, 36*(3), 235-55. https://doi.org/10.1080/08841233.2016.1182609

van Dernoot Lipsky, L., & Burk, C. (2009). *Trauma stewardship: An everyday guide to caring for self while caring for others*. Berrett-Koehler.

Williams, M. (2023). *The velveteen rabbit*. Read & Co. Children's.

10

FLYING ABOVE THE FRAY

FORGIVING INCALCULABLE SUFFERING

Even stronger than the message of suffering is the message of forgiveness.

LEWIS B. SMEDES

And I have reckoned with what you've taken from me
And I killed that liar in my head
I buried him beneath the maple tree
There's no joy in dancing with the dead
But I forgive you now
Release you from all of the blame I know how

MARCUS MUMFORD, "HOW"

LETTING GRUDGES GO

I pardon him as God shall pardon me.

WILLIAM SHAKESPEARE, *RICHARD II*

Many critics scoff at letting go of grudges for wrongdoings endured. Several reasons for their onslaught of slurs concerning forgiveness seem compelling. One such rationale is revealed in the book and film *A Time to Kill* (Schumacher, 1996), where racism is centerstage. Two white Southern men decided to rape ten-year-old African American Tonya Hailey but were unsuccessful in disposing of her body. The men were drunk and did not cover their tracks. They spent the day after the rape at the local bar, getting a notch above wasted. The courtroom thriller escalates after African American Carl Lee Hailey, father of Tonya Hailey, decides to murder the two white men who raped his daughter. He shoots them in the courthouse on the way to their sentencing for Tonya's rape.

The question of Carl Lee Hailey's level of sanity is not a legal option in the courtroom proceedings due to his declaration that the men deserved to die and he hoped they'd burn in hell. The only debate remained: Did Carl Lee Hailey deserve to be punished for murdering the two men who raped his daughter? In a final statement made by the defense, his Caucasian lawyer asks the jury to close their eyes and listen. He tells a sad story about a girl (i.e., Tonya) walking to the grocery store who gets picked up by two men in a truck. The men take her to a field where they tie her up, strip her clothes, and take turns raping her and then throwing full beer cans at her, tearing her skin from her bones. Finally, after a failed attempt to hang her, they throw her body over a bridge down to a creek. Her body just lay there, raped, beaten, soaked in urine, semen, and blood. The defense rests with the lawyer's final line of this story: he asks the jury to imagine that the girl in the story is white.

Jake Brigance appeals to the hearts of the jury. That place in them and all of us who long for justice. Considering forgiveness for the rape of a little girl seems scandalous. The unseemly prospect of forgiveness for evil acts also appears in various venues like music, books, social media, and trauma literature.

REVENGE IN THE ARTS

Why should the injured, the still bleeding, bear the onus of forgiveness?

DELIA OWENS, *WHERE THE CRAWDADS SING*

A playlist of female pop and country music reveals revenge fantasies on the heels of callous cruelty. The Dixie Chicks' "Goodbye Earl" (1999), Miranda Lambert's "Gunpowder & Lead" (2007), Carrie Underwood's "Church Bells" (2015), Beyoncé's "Sorry" (2016), SZA's "Kill Bill" (2020), Taylor Swift's "Vigilante Sh*t" (2022), and Miley Cyrus's "Flowers" (2023) all tell stories of victims-turned-vigilantes. In the gap between victimization and any realization of justice, these hateful hymns proclaim that some things are unforgivable. These revenge anthems resonated with scores of listeners as these songs climbed the charts.

Forgiveness was not on the Billboard Hot 100 of Friedrich Nietzsche nor Sigmund Freud. Victims forgiving evil people was interpreted as a mask for weakness or a defensive illusion resulting from a fear of condemnation (Shults & Sandage, 2003). Ellen Bass and Laura Davis (1988), authors of the renowned *Courage to Heal* sexual abuse workbook, have this to say about forgiveness:

> Never say or imply that the client should forgive the abuser. Forgiveness is not essential for healing. This fact is disturbing to many counselors, ministers, and the public at large. But it is absolutely true. If you hold the belief survivors must forgive the abuse in order to heal, you should not be working with survivors. (p. 348)

The seminal book *Trauma and Recovery* by Judith Herman (1997) suggests that letting go of torture is the "fantasy of forgiveness."

> Some survivors attempt to bypass their outrage altogether through a fantasy of forgiveness. . . . The survivor imagines that she can transcend her rage and erase the impact of the trauma through a willed, defiant act of love. . . . The fantasy of forgiveness often becomes a cruel torture, because it remains out of reach for most ordinary human beings. (pp. 189-90)

The theme of the unforgivable nature of sexual abuse unfolds in literature too. In the Pulitzer Prize–winning *A Thousand Acres*, Jane Smiley (1991) pens the story of a family living on a large plot of Iowa land. When the aging patriarch decides to hand over his farm to his three daughters, Ginny, Rose, and Caroline, the lavish gift whips up old memories of incest. Eventually, the family scatters, Daddy never admits the abuse, and the farm falls apart. As the saga draws near the end, the oldest daughter, Rose, lies paper-thin, colorless, dying of cancer in a lonely hospital room. She lost her husband, lover, reputation, farm profits, and she weighs her life accomplishments. Rose, speaking to Ginny, lists her failures and then angrily describes her solitary accomplishment: that she saw her father for what he was and that she didn't forgive the unforgivable.

When the #MeToo movement was reignited in late 2017, many women became emboldened to tell their stories of CSA, sexual harassment, and rape. What also followed were more questions regarding the legitimacy of forgiveness. *The New York Times* op-ed contributor Danielle Berrin (2017) queried, "What are the limits of forgiveness?" She concluded that since many perpetrators are adept at prevarication, and thinly veiled victim blaming is pervasive, forgiveness must wait until reparations and debts are paid.

Have Danielle Berrin, Rose, Miranda Lambert, Sigmund Freud, Jake Brigance, Judith Herman, and so many others concluded correctly that some egregious acts of cruelty are *unforgivable*? Perhaps many have a hard time with the notion of forgiveness because many of us in Christendom have not done a very good job defining *or* living it. Too often, we have pummeled forgiveness into denial-based smithereens, avoiding the gated-off section of our souls where bitterness breeds. Alternatively, forgiveness has been weaponized against survivors in the church to dismiss the desire for accountability of church leaders who have abused them. Tim Keller (2022, p. 24) explains,

> How often within the church the idea of forgiveness was used against victims of abuse and injustice. Abusers knew how to use the doctrine of forgiveness to bring about their quick restoration to positions of trust from which they could abuse again. The abused who did not immediately "forgive and forget" were said to be vindictive. The call to forgive was often the way churches or Christian institutions guarded their public image and reputations rather than redressing wrongs.

This chapter discusses pseudo-forgiveness and how this frequently plays a role as a strain of spiritual bypass. We define the three salient forms of forgiveness, unpack the most researched dimension of forgiveness, and review the empirical literature that reveals the association between forgiveness and mental health well-being. We consider how justice and forgiveness stand tall together, how we forgive, and look at courageous portraits of forgiveness.

WHAT FORGIVENESS IS *NOT*

When I (Tammy) was a little girl, the tangled weeds on the side of our house were as high as an elephant's eye. I was embarrassed over our unkempt yard. The unwanted ground cover mirrored my mom's internal angst during the sinking times in her bipolar cycle. She didn't leave her bed much on those days. Her sad soul kept her from engaging in relationships and activities.

One summer day, I decided to rid these blemishes from our yard and our lives. After scouring the basement, I located my artillery: *giant* hedge clippers. With all the moxie an eight-year-old could muster, I brought those handles together, whacking the enemy with each cut. On that warm summer day, like the walls of Jericho, those weeds came tumbling down. All that shame, all that disappointment, all those secrets were chopped away. Or so it seemed because quick fixes are temporary. Hacking off the top of the garden vegetation was only a short-term solution, as those unwanted weeds returned with greater vigor *and* they brought their friends.

Unbeknownst to little Tammy, all those thistles and tares needed to be plucked out by the roots. So do miserable memories. Pseudo-forgiveness merely chops off the tops of traumatic events, leaving the hurt, the anger, and the deep disappointment buried beneath the surface, ready to rise again. Forgiveness was never intended to be the denial of damage.

One common form of pseudo-forgiveness is spiritual bypass. While many draw on strength from God, religious coping practices (e.g., prayer), and meditating on Scripture as a way of grappling with deep-seated hurts and betrayal, spiritual bypass is different. Welwood (1984) was the first to use "spiritual bypass" terminology to describe when individuals avoid unresolved emotions or wounds and incomplete developmental tasks using spiritual language, practices, and worldviews. Problematically, stifling internal realities such as disappointment, shame, and cognitive dissonance by using spiritual clichés or religious activities heightens mental health suffering (Mandelkow et al., 2022). For example, when individuals leap over anger and massive hurt with quick forgiveness, pain reduction's apparent initial benefits give way to extended suffering (Picciotto et al., 2018).

We do not know what Tamar's journey with forgiveness was like. However, we imagine what spiritual bypass might have looked like in her case: going to the temple every day and staying busy with service projects, a sudden interest in memorizing the Torah, or doing whatever it takes to keep moving and not feel.

Sheridan (2017, pp. 359-62) highlights eight manifestations of spiritual bypassing: a quest for perfection, avoidance of painful thoughts/emotions, fear of individuation/personal responsibility, fear of intimacy, obsession with religion, blind faith in spiritual leaders, spiritual narcissism, and a flight into humanitarian work. Hollow holiness strangles true spirituality and ensnares individuals in dogma versus deliverance.

I (Adam) worked with Jackson, who reluctantly entered therapy in response to his pastoral leadership team's directives. Jackson's formative years consisted of a biological father abandoning him and his mother, leaving them impoverished. At school, Jackson was bullied and bore the weight of an onslaught of racial slurs because he was Black in predominately white schools. Vulnerable and alone, Jackson's mother remarried quickly to a Caucasian hot-tempered man with financial resources. Jackson suffered at the hands of his domineering stepfather, who regularly exposed him to pornography. Under the guise of teaching Jackson about sexuality, his stepfather began to sexually abuse him for several years.

Jackson's entrenched shame and longing propelled him to seek out and please father figures. In college, Jackson joined a church and became increasingly involved in ministry activities. All the while, he was reluctant to face the trauma or pain from his past (avoidance of painful thoughts/emotions). Jackson often praised God as a "Father who always loved me . . . who brought me from death to life." He frequently mentioned that he forgave people from his past and that others should do likewise. He binged on podcasts, books, and resources aligned with sanctification as a regular pastime (obsession with religion). He adopted a highly devoted posture with an overbearing mentor. Significant life decisions were based on this counsel (blind faith in a spiritual leader), such as pursuing a seminary degree.

Throughout Jackson's seminary pursuits, he maintained pervasive habits with pornography and masturbation. A deep sense of inadequacy and shame gnawed internally, but Jackson presented as an overconfident leader from the pulpit (spiritual narcissism). Those who worked closely with him in the church knew his critical demeanor and that he tended to keep others at a distance. He abstained from dating for fear of it "distracting him from the Kingdom" and regularly preached about the costs of discipleship (fear of intimacy). After several years, the church leadership staff approached Jackson with concerns and complaints from churchgoers regarding his superficial relationships and spiritual narcissism and strongly recommended therapy.

At the outset of therapy, we discussed our relationship as a white therapist with tangible symbols and artifacts associated with authority (e.g., diplomas, suit/tie) and a Black man seeking therapy. I invited him to reflect and respond candidly, communicating awareness and sensitivity to how these dynamics impacted therapy. He replied, "Most white people are too ignorant/afraid to bring this up with a Black person, and it spoke volumes that you went there." It was important to ground our work together in trust and empathy.

Jackson frequently bypassed deeper emotions with spiritual language and suggestions that he had already forgiven his stepfather. At times, anger and fear were projected onto me in the therapist role for what my skin and power represented to Jackson. Sometimes, it was difficult for me to see some of his responses in context and to refrain from a defensive posture. Ultimately, his increasing willingness to trust a white male clinician was courageous and liberating. It was particularly meaningful for me to enter Jackson's life and story. It was more daunting for Jackson to disclose his sexual abuse history with a white male therapist. We had intentional conversations regarding this dynamic, and he consented to engage in exposure-type therapy related to the details of his abuse. Over time, our relationship proved to be a catalyst for vulnerability and authentic healing. Much farther down the road, Jackson took monumental steps of seeking forgiveness from others and authentic interpersonal forgiveness.

WHAT FORGIVENESS *IS*

Forgiveness is the fragrance the violet sheds
on the heel that has crushed it.

MARK TWAIN

Near the end of the semester, I (Tammy) ask counseling students to draw a picture of forgiveness. Apologies over the lack of artistic abilities abound, yet their creations are remarkable, as one would expect in a room full of counselors-to-be. One young woman drew raindrops and explained that forgiveness is like a cloudburst because it often includes a lot of tears in the process and is life-giving. Others drew people holding hands or making eye contact, things hard to do when forgiveness has been withheld. Another drew a flag, a symbol of "claiming" forgiveness, while one drew a woman on her knees praying, stating that there is just "something about the kneeling posture." Another student attempted to draw something to resemble music, simply and wisely mentioning that "when I am holding onto bitterness, I cannot sing."

The shapes and hues of forgiveness are expansive, multi-layered, complex, ongoing, and fluid. The empirical literature describes three salient dimensions of forgiveness. Self-forgiveness is "a willingness to abandon self-resentment in the face of one's acknowledged objective wrong, while fostering compassion, generosity, and love toward oneself" (Enright et al., 1996, p. 116). Divine forgiveness involves believing that while one has failed, one has been forgiven by God (Sperry, 2022). It is noteworthy that embracing the belief that God has forgiven oneself seems to increase self-forgiveness (Sperry, 2022).

Interpersonal or *other forgiveness* is the most frequently studied type of forgiveness. Webb et al. (2017, p. 221) define other forgiveness as something that occurs over time and is

> a deliberate, volitional process involving a fundamental shift in affect, cognition, and/or behavior in response to negative feelings regarding an acknowledged offensive experience, without condoning, excusing, or denying the transgression(s), at a minimum, an absence of ill will toward an offender.

A growing body of empirical literature is informative regarding the relationship between forgiving others and mental health well-being (Wade & Tittler, 2020; Webb & Toussaint, 2020). For example, Wade and colleagues (2014) conducted a meta-analysis to assess the benefits of therapy interventions in helping people forgive others. They discovered several notable findings, including:

1. Forgiveness interventions are more effective in promoting forgiveness compared to no treatments and alternative treatments.
2. Forgiveness interventions produce other changes, such as hope for the future and a reduction in anxiety and depression (see also Webb & Toussaint, 2020).
3. The longer the duration of treatment or the more time someone works at forgiving, the greater the forgiveness (i.e., forgiveness is dosage-related).

4. The specific type of forgiveness intervention approach (e.g., Enright, Worthington) and modalities (e.g., individual, group) did not make a difference in outcomes.

Thus, the empirical literature repeatedly reveals the possibility of life beyond atrocities and suffering. Forgiveness provides the potential of no longer being a prisoner of moments in the past. Images of forgiveness as a resilient response to trauma are a repeated theme—like a bird in a raging storm cloud, rising higher until it flies above the fray.

JUSTICE *AND* FORGIVENESS

Little girls don't stay little forever. They grow into strong women.

CSA SURVIVOR OF LARRY NASSAR AT HIS SENTENCING HEARING

In *Exclusion & Embrace: A Theological Exploration of Identity, Otherness, and Reconciliation* (2019), Miroslav Volf explains that embracing others via forgiveness is the opposite of exclusion. He calls for a receiving posture as a defining characteristic of Christ followers. Further, he presents a picture for Christians to align themselves with the crucified Messiah, whereby our arms are spread wide to embrace our enemies. However, Volf explains that an embrace does not occur for every person. It requires repentance on the part of the wrongdoer. Reconciliation, therefore, is impeded when individuals who perpetrate abuse continue to engage in abusive and destructive behaviors. Still, sexual abuse survivors can forgive and not be reconciled with the perpetrator (Song & Enright, 2021). Thus, both Song and Enright (2021) and Volf (2019) suggest that individuals can seek justice and practice forgiveness simultaneously.

Many current and former churchgoers remain skeptical, however. Too often, church leadership has aided and abetted perpetrators. Abusive church leaders have adeptly used lies and repeated manipulation, pressuring survivors to forgive. Yet, noticeably absent from the conversation are repentance on the part of the abusing leader, making amends, financial reparation, removing abusing individuals from pastoral leadership, and other actions to prevent the abuse from happening again. Moreover, the pressure to forgive, or forced forgiveness, merely adds another layer of coercion. Lament and forgiveness are messy, and they take time. Even more complicated when those in spiritual authority are not humbled and repentant.

So, how does a survivor seek justice (hold perpetrators accountable) *and* practice interpersonal forgiveness simultaneously? Holding justice involves seeing what is evil and refusing minimizing, excusing, tolerating, or ignoring the harm. Moreover, it involves allowing the offender to experience the appropriate consequences for their actions and desiring that the offender change, reform, repent, and be held accountable for the harm, while holding onto and coming back again and again to forgive the offender.

Rachael Denhollander's story provides a poignant example of the cradling of justice *and* forgiveness. Denhollander, a survivor of CSA at the hands of former US Gymnastics and Michigan State University physician Larry Nassar, was the first to speak out and the last of over 150 young women to give her victim impact statement in Judge Rosemarie Aquilina's courtroom. Nassar was sentenced in 2018 to 175 years in prison after pleading guilty to ten counts of sexual assault; a total of 265 girls accused Nassar of sexual misconduct (Levenson, 2018).

So many things stand out about this story. Denhollander's stance in that courtroom is chief among them, as she spoke directly to Nassar, extended forgiveness to him, asked him to repent, and petitioned the judge to dole out the maximum possible sentence for his actions. In a later interview, she described forgiveness as a personal act: "an individual's decision to let go of bitterness, resentment, and a desire for vengeance. Justice . . . holds the accused to an outside standard" (Woo, 2019).

This narrative also reimagines the role of a judge in the pursuit of justice or, as one reporter stated, "this judge is making a choice about the role the victim should be allowed to play in a courtroom" (Barbaro & Bazelon, 2018, 10:41). Judge Aquilina goes on to make several statements to the women who spoke that day:

> You and your sister survivors are great successes and the magic is in the power of your voice. Thank you for speaking out and breaking your silence. (2018, 4:54)

> Your words are a sign that you are healing—that you are taking your power back, that you're giving him back his kryptonite—that he will fall and you will rise. (2018, 9:34)

Modern-day stories like this cause us to wonder what a journey of forgiveness and justice would have looked like for Tamar. What would Tamar have said in her victim impact statement? What would she say to Amnon? What generous words would a kind judge have to say to Tamar?

Judge Aquilina's example helps us imagine the generous space given to survivors in pursuing justice. The question speaks loud and clear: can it be justice if the *impact* hasn't been stated fully? Denhollander's resilient response to extensive abuse calls us to consider what it looks like to be people marked by forgiveness *and* justice.

HOW TO FORGIVE?

Forgiveness is the giving, and so the receiving, of life.

GEORGE MACDONALD

I (Tammy) counseled Kalyn for a long duration due to years of sexual abuse by her father and his eventual trafficking of her. As a little girl, she recalled men placing paper money in the hands of her father and being forced to go with these men so they could do to her what should never be done to a child. She begged her father not to make her go, yet her father's refusal to hear her cries was firmly etched in her mind.

During therapy, we discussed PTSD and depression and how these pervasive effects impacted her life. We worked on emotional regulation practices that were a good fit for Kalyn. Over time, she established additional supportive, trusted relationships by taking risks with her sister, a neighbor, and survivors in her sexual abuse group (the journey is never quite as easy as it appears on paper). During therapy, we focused on her reoccurring nightmares in which she remained frozen. Kalyn and I decided to use Imagery Rescripting Therapy (IRT) to work with the images in her nightmares rather than simply talk about the specific details. As we walked through the phases together, Kalyn began to rescript the ending of her nightmares, where she became active in escaping the perpetrator and imagining God being with her. Interestingly, as Kalyn started making choices and acting in her reoccurring nightmares, she became more active in her relationships and decision-making. Bravely, she scaled many therapeutic mountains and increasingly developed her strong voice.

Then, one day, Kalyn let me know that she sensed God had been pursuing her and that he wanted her to no longer be barnacled to her hate, but she was unsure *how* to forgive. The task before her loomed large and loud. Kalyn did not appear to be bypassing her rage and sorrow. It had taken her significant time to come to this therapeutic juncture, as the prospect of forgiveness seemed to bring her father emotionally closer, which was terrifying. Still, she seemed ready for this monumental task, absent of forgiveness clichés and glib phrases.

She began a free DIY workbook, *The Path to Forgiveness* (Greer et al., 2014). This evidence-based forgiveness intervention (Kurniati et al., 2020; Toussaint et al., 2020; Worthington, 2020) is called REACH Forgiveness, an acronym for:

- **R**ecall the hurt
- **E**mpathize with the offender
- **A**ltruistically give forgiveness
- **C**ommit to the forgiveness experience
- **H**old on to the forgiveness experience

Eventually, Kalyn bravely completed the REACH workbook and requested that we meet for an extended session. With many of her supportive people praying, this courageous woman verbally stated before God and me the litany of remembered offenses her father and others had done to her. And then, with me as her witness, one by one, she stated, "I forgive________________________." That afternoon, she used a whole box of tissues. That afternoon, I saw a scandalous portrait of freedom.

Kalyn's father had died, and reconciliation of the relationship with her father was no longer an option, nor would it have been, as he had continued a life of violence on this earth and was dangerous (i.e., forgiveness and reconciliation are different). Forgiving her dad was not a one-and-done step. Instead, forgiveness was recursive, and she returned to the hard work of forgiving her dad when memories resurfaced. However, for Kalyn, letting go of her hatred toward her dad was like going from having chronic emotional bronchitis to singing arias and cavatinas. She began to sing the melody of a woman set free.

COUNSELING AND FORGIVENESS WITH SECULAR CLIENTS

Like a symphony without the final movement . . . the ear anticipates and yearns for musical resolution.

ALEXANDER McCALL SMITH

At wise junctures, forgiveness can be presented to clients in secular and faith-based settings as one of several empirically based ways to deal with injustice (ACT and mindfulness alternatives). It can be beneficial to point out that research has demonstrated that forgiveness engagement can help increase forgiveness, decrease depression and anxiety, and increase hope, thus enhancing human flourishing (Wade et al., 2014). As in all therapeutic interventions, sensitive timing is essential, and pressure to forgive is harmful.

The REACH DIY workbooks (available as an adjunct to therapy) are free on Everett Worthington's REACH website. They are available in secular or Christian versions, and repeated randomized control trials (RCTs) reveal they are efficacious (Worthington, 2020). Only six RCT studies have been done with explicitly Christian-adapted REACH materials. Thus, most RCT studies on the efficacy of REACH usage (approximately 25 published studies) have used secular populations (Worthington, personal communication, October 27, 2022).

There are more remarkable portraits of forgiveness on a secular website like *The Forgiveness Project* (see Cantacuzino, 2016)—pictures of individuals surmounting the challenges of seemingly intractable traumatic ruptures and losses. Still, examples of interpersonal forgiveness for heinous crimes remain lean and spare. So, we end this chapter with one more portrait of forgiveness. For the record, clinicians, clients, and all God's people need more of these images. More artwork to hang on the wall. More music to play. The playlist is too short.

RAIN DOWN

In 1994, there was a genocide in a small African country, killing about a million of its citizens (one out of every eight Rwandans), mostly Tutsi minorities. One report claimed that 77 percent of the Rwandan Tutsis were eliminated during this slaughter, primarily by two Hutu militias. Machetes were used to rape and kill people in village after village. Years following this mass genocide in Rwanda, more than 110,000 men and women guilty of these crimes filled their overcrowded prisons. Beginning in 2004, tens of thousands of prisoners were released, and old wounds were reopened. The country was festering with hate (Larson, 2009).

Bishop John Rucyahana, chairman of Prison Fellowship Rwanda, returned to his home country after spending some time in exile in Uganda and studying in the United States. No news report could have prepared him adequately for what he would see when he returned: bodies in shallow graves, corpses in schools and churches. Bishop Rucyahana was filled with bitterness and craved revenge.

Like most Tutsi survivors, Bishop John had lost many members of his extended family in the genocide. As some semblance of order was evolving, Bishop John began preaching to the Hutus in the prisons. And then his niece, Mado, was brutally killed. She was gang-raped, and the torture continued in unspeakable ways. When the bishop received the news, he wept and wept as "his mind replayed the horrible images and rehearsed a thousand if-onlys" (Larson, 2009, p. 70).

Still, Bishop John felt called to forgive the Hutu people and preach Jesus Christ's love to them. He explained that he could not wait for the pain to disappear to forgive his enemy, as Jesus did not wait to forgive until his pain was over. Bishop John and Deo Gashagaza (who also lost more than a dozen family members) used the Umuvumu Tree Project to invite prisoners to repent and survivors to forgive. Deo had prayed and fasted for three days, asking God for strength to overcome his anger and depression. Eventually, these men invited victims, their families, and offenders into the protracted reconciliation process. Bishop John makes clear in prison that he is not meeting prisoners on behalf of prosecutors, who have a file against them.

> "I am not coming here today about that file. I am coming to you about another file—the file of the conscience. The conscience does the secretarial work for God, Mattias. I am coming to tell you that whatever is in this file, the conscience file, I am asking you to put it right today. . . ."
>
> "But these hands . . ." Mattias turned his leathered hands palms upward, fingers spread wide in front of him. The motion had become something of

a ritual for him over the past few months. "These hands killed your family: your brother's wife, her sister, and her children." (Larson, 2009, p. 38)

Overcome by tears, the man could not continue. The bishop refused to join hands with systemic hatred. Instead, he led invitations to forgiveness between his Tutsi people, victims of horrific massacre, and their perpetrators, the Hutus. As if that were not inspiring enough, many of these men displayed remorse and began building houses for their victims. An entire village of thirty houses was built, along with a place of worship. This picture of gathering under the same roof to worship God is an image of the ultimate restoration of the kingdom of heaven. "Our Father in heaven. . . . May your kingdom come. May your will be done on earth as it is in heaven" (Mt 6:9-10).

May we boldly invite the only One who *is* the perfect marriage of justice and grace into our journey so that he might help us to live freely and fully in forgiveness. May we understand that by allowing justice to take its course, we are simultaneously offering grace to all those in need—the ones who are hurting others and need to be stopped, the ones who have been hurt and need to be comforted, and the ones who have been covering the sin and need to be enlightened. May we increasingly come to understand forgiveness as a meaningful choice to heal from grievous harm.

Oh God, rain down your justice and your grace. . . .
We want to want to forgive.

COUNSELING CONSIDERATIONS

- **REACH Model of Forgiveness.** This model can be an adjunctive to various therapeutic approaches. Everett Worthington, Commonwealth Professor Emeritus at Virginia Commonwealth University, developed it. The REACH model found on Worthington's website includes free do-it-yourself workbooks and invites individuals to engage in a deep dive into two forms of forgiveness: decisional and emotional forgiveness.
- **Enright Forgiveness Process Model.** Enright and colleagues created a forgiveness-oriented four-phase model that can be administered in individual or group settings (Freedman & Enright, 2020).

- **Cognitive Processing Therapy (CPT).** In this approach, the client completes a Challenging Beliefs Worksheet multiple times throughout therapy that can be used to address forgiveness. Additionally, self-forgiveness is mentioned briefly in the manual.
- **EMDR.** This approach allows an individual to identify beliefs about forgiveness associated with trauma and desired adaptive beliefs. Barriers to forgiveness (e.g., anger, self-contempt, self-blame, fear) can be reprocessed.
- **Acceptance and Commitment Therapy (ACT).** This transdiagnostic approach utilizes aspects of psychological flexibility, such as mindful acceptance and classic exercises (e.g., Corpus Delicti) to enable clients to engage in forgiveness-oriented, process-based work. Additionally, mindfulness and acceptance-oriented techniques can empower clients to engage in forgiveness with connected authenticity (versus avoidance).

CHILDREN'S CORNER

- ***Rising Above the Storm Clouds*** (2004) by Robert D. Enright tells the story of two sibling rabbits arguing and yelling at each other. Father rabbit asks his children to tell him what forgiveness is like, and the children then tell him that it is the worst idea. It is like eating a liverwurst sandwich with mustard and onions or like falling into a mud puddle and landing on a slimy frog. Father rabbit begins to tell them a story about what it is really like using word pictures, for example, like flying on a plane and rising above the storm.

REFERENCES

Barbaro, M., & Bazelon, E. (2018, January 25). The Doctor and the Judge. *The New York Times.* https://www.nytimes.com/2018/01/25/podcasts/the-daily/larry-nassar-gymnastics-sex-abuse.html

Bass, E., & Davis, L. (1988). *The courage to heal: A guide for women survivors of child sexual abuse.* Harper & Row.

Berrin, D. (2017, December 22). Should we forgive the men who assaulted us? *The New York Times.* www.nytimes.com/2017/12/22/opinion/metoo-sexual-assault-forgiveness.html

Cantacuzino, M. (2016). *The forgiveness project: Stories for a vengeful age.* Jessica Kingsley Publishers.

Cantacuzino, M. (2022). *Forgiveness: An exploration.* Simon & Schuster UK.

Davis, D. E., Yang, X., DeBlaere, C., McElroy, S. E., Van Tongeren, D. R., Hook, J. N., & Worthington, E. L., Jr. (2016). The injustice gap. *Psychology of Religion and Spirituality, 8*(3), 175. https://doi.org/10.1037/rel0000042

Enright, R. D., & Human Development Study Group. (1996). Counseling within the forgiveness triad: On forgiving, receiving forgiveness, and self-forgiveness. *Counseling and Values, 40*(2), 107-26. https://doi.org/10.1002/j.2161-007X.1996.tb00844.x

Enright, R. D., & Kunz Finney, K. (2004). *Rising above the storm clouds: What it's like to forgive.* Magination Press.

Freedman, S., & Enright, R. D. (2020). A review of the empirical research using Enright's process model of interpersonal forgiveness. In E. L. Worthington Jr. & N. G. Wade (Eds.), *Handbook of forgiveness* (2nd ed.; pp. 266-76). Routledge.

Greer, C. L., Worthington, E. L., Jr., Lin, Y., Lavelock, C. R., & Griffin, B. J. (2014). Efficacy of a self-directed forgiveness workbook for Christian victims of within-congregation offenders. *Spirituality in Clinical Practice, 1*(3), 218-30.

Hallam, J. (Prod., Writer), & Lam, K. (Prod., Dir.). (2010). *Staff relations in healthcare: Working as a team* [Film]. Insight Media.

Herman, J. L. (1997). *Trauma and recovery*. BasicBooks.

Keller, T. (2022). *Forgive: Why should I and how can I?* Viking.

Kurniati, N., Worthington, E. L., Jr, Widyarini, N., Citra, A. F., & Dwiwardani, C. (2020). Does forgiving in a collectivistic culture affect only decisions to forgive and not emotions? REACH forgiveness collectivistic in Indonesia. *International Journal of Psychology: Journal International de Psychologie, 55*(5), 861-70. https://doi.org/10.1002/ijop.12648

Larson, C. C. (2009). *As we forgive: Stories of reconciliation from Rwanda*. Zondervan.

Levenson, E. (2018, January 24). *Larry Nassar sentenced to up to 175 years in prison for decades of sexual abuse.* CNN. https://www.cnn.com/2018/01/24/us/larry-nassar-sentencing

Mandelkow, L., Austad, A., & Freund, H. (2022). Stepping carefully on sacred ground: Religion and spirituality in psychotherapy. *Journal of Spirituality in Mental Health, 24*(3), 288-308. https://doi.org/10.1080/19349637.2021.1939834

Metzer, P. L. (2010). What is biblical justice? The theology of justice flows from the heart of God. *Christianity Today.* www.christianitytoday.com/pastors/2010/summer/biblicaljustice.html

Noor, M., & Cantacuzino, M. (2018). *Forgiveness is really strange*. Singing Dragon.

Nudelman, G., & Nadler, A. (2017). The effect of apology on forgiveness: Belief in a just world as a moderator. *Personality and Individual Differences, 116*, 191-200. https://doi.org/10.1016/j.paid.2017.04.048

Picciotto, G., Fox, J., & Neto, F. (2018). A phenomenology of spiritual bypass: Causes, consequences, and implications. *Journal of Spirituality in Mental Health, 20*(4), 333-54. https://doi.org/10.1080/19349637.2017.1417756

Schumacher, J. (Dir.). (1996). *A time to kill* [Film]. Regency Enterprises.

Sheridan, M. J. (2017). Addressing spiritual bypassing: Issues and guidelines for spiritually sensitive practice. In B. R. Crisp (Ed.), *The Routledge handbook of religion, spirituality and social work* (pp. 358-67). Routledge.

Shults, F. L., & Sandage, S. J. (2003). *The faces of forgiveness: Searching for wholeness and salvation*. Baker.

Smiley, J. (2003). *A Thousand Acres*. Random House.

Sperry, L. (2022). Psychotherapy alone is insufficient: Treating clergy sexual abuse and sacred moral injury. *Spirituality in Clinical Practice*. Advance online publication. https://doi.org/10.1037/scp0000291

Song, M. J., & Enright, R. D. (2021). A philosophical and psychological examination of "justice first": Toward the need for both justice and forgiveness when conflict arises. *Peace and Conflict: Journal of Peace Psychology*, *27*(3), 459. https://doi.org/10.1037/pac0000468

Toussaint, L. L., Griffin, B. J., Worthington, E. L., Jr., Zoelzer, M., & Luskin, F. (2020). Promoting forgiveness at a Christian college: A comparison of the REACH Forgiveness and Forgive for Good methods. *Journal of Psychology and Theology*, *48*(2), 154-65.

Volf, M. (2019). *Exclusion and embrace, revised and updated: A theological exploration of identity, otherness, and reconciliation*. Abingdon Press.

Wade, N. G., Hoyt, W. T., Kidwell, J. E., & Worthington, E. L., Jr. (2014). Efficacy of psychotherapeutic interventions to promote forgiveness: A meta-analysis. *Journal of Consulting and Clinical Psychology*, *82*(1), 154. https://doi.org/10.1037/a0035268

Wade, N. G., & Tittler, M. V. (2021). Forgiveness and group therapy: Current research and implications for group psychology research and practice. In C. D. Parks & G. A. Tasca (Eds.), *The psychology of groups: The intersection of social psychology and psychotherapy research* (pp. 207-30). American Psychological Association.

Webb, J. R., Bumgarner, D. J., Conway-Williams, E., Dangel, T., & Hall, B. B. (2017). A consensus definition of self-forgiveness: Implications for assessment and treatment. *Spirituality in Clinical Practice*, *4*(3), 216. https://doi.org/10.1037/scp0000138

Webb, J. R., & Toussaint, L. L. (2020). Forgiveness, well-being, and mental health. In E. L. Worthington Jr. & N. G. Wade (Eds.), *Handbook of forgiveness* (2nd ed.; pp. 188-97). Routledge. https://doi.org/10.4324/9781351123341-18

Welwood, J. (1984). Principles of inner work: Psychological and spiritual. *Journal of Transpersonal Psychology*, *16*(1), 63-73.

Woo, E. (2019, February 21). Rachael Denhollander weighs justice and forgiveness. *The Stanford Daily*. https://stanforddaily.com/2019/02/21/rachael-denhollander-weighs-justice-and-forgiveness

Worthington, E. L., Jr. (2020). An update of the REACH Forgiveness model to promote forgiveness. In Everett L. Worthington Jr. & Nathaniel G. Wade (Eds.), *Handbook of forgiveness* (2nd ed.; pp. 277-87). Routledge.

11

LIVING BEYOND DESOLATE

FORESTS OF FLOURISHING

Freedom is what you do with what's been done to you.

JEAN-PAUL SARTRE

God is always beyond.

MICHAEL CARD

DATE PALMS

It is the nature of the strong heart that, like the palm tree, it strives ever upwards when it is most burdened.

PHILIP SIDNEY

Sleeping Beauty, the Ugly Duckling, Pinocchio—the childhood sagas of characters transformed. A woman trapped in a deep sleep becomes a loved princess, an outcast animal becomes a stunning swan, and a wooden boy becomes real. Movieland is mesmerized by rags-to-riches and hoodlum-to-healed epics. Broken-down horses, cars, toys, and boxers morph into something different, something better. Audiences whoop and holler over the protagonists' ability to prevail over suffering and grasp the depth of character. Perhaps if they can persevere and change, we can too.

Sometimes against-the-odds stories even take place in the world of trees. For example, many years ago, dense eighty-foot-high date palm forests marched across southern Israel, but these towering forests eventually vanished (Kalman, 2005). However, during an archaeological dig in 2005 at Masada, Israel, seven 2,000-year-old date palm seeds were unearthed and later soaked in warm water (Sallon et al., 2020). Growth hormones and enzyme-rich fertilizers were added, and these ancient seeds were planted in an Israeli kibbutz. Expectations were low, but small shoots elbowed their way to the surface. Two-thousand-year-old seeds began developing into Judean date palm trees.

The date palm was a staple in ancient Israel due to its shelter, shade, medicinal properties, and food energy source (Cohen & Glasner, 2015). Palm trees symbolized grace and elegance to the Hebrew nation. Not coincidentally, the daughter of King David was given the Hebrew name for the date palm: Tamar. Princess Tamar was destined to be like a date palm with a commanding presence, providing shelter, shade, and nourishment to those who came near. The dream for Tamar was that she would stand tall in grace and elegance; instead, she was raped and lived a desolate life.

We have wrestled with the biblical narrative of Tamar for an extended time. Her bleak life has permeated our thoughts. Scripture does not provide a front-row seat to the successive years of her life after being sexually assaulted by her half-brother. We continue to grieve over what happened to her. We also know that Tamar is not alone. Countless survivors of CSA are living desolate lives.

The assault of Tamar and countless others prompts an essential question: what enables some survivors of CSA to experience positive personal change eventually and flourish, like buried 2,000-year-old seeds that come bursting to life in the form of graceful Judean date palms, while others experience wide-ranging, lifelong adverse sequelae?

CRUCIAL CAVEATS

> *For a seed to achieve its greatest expression,*
> *it must come completely undone. The shell cracks, its insides*
> *come out, and everything changes. To someone who doesn't*
> *understand growth, it would look like complete destruction.*
>
> CYNTHIA OCCELLI

Before we examine the pathways of CSA healing literature, it is important to highlight some key items. First, focusing on flourishing is not designed to bypass the extensive damage or belittle the remaining scars of CSA. As Rambo (2010) indicates, overlooking the full extent of the shattering in the center where suffering resides results in further damage. Too often triumphalism permeates North American church sermons and songs, whereby we give exclusive rights to those with happily ever after endings. Consequently, this promotes the message to survivors holding suffering narratives that there is no space for you. This "redemptive gloss" (Rambo, 2010, p. 8) conflicts with the initial phases in the biblical practice of lament and underscores cosmetic changes and superficial quick fixes. "Time does not heal all wounds. . . . Scars and wounds persist post-resurrection" (Travis, 2021, p. 52). It is noteworthy that God did not tie a triumphalist bow at the end of Tamar's story recorded in Scripture. Indeed, Jesus' wounds remained when he appeared to the disciples in the upper room (Jn 20:27). We must neither negate nor elevate suffering (Rambo, 2015).

Second, examining flourishing following CSA does not mean some survivors are coping failures. The literature reveals multiple environmental-systemic factors (e.g., supportive families and social environments that wrap themselves around aching individuals) that foster positive coping despite egregious interpersonal trauma (Domhardt et al., 2015; Yoon et al., 2019) and factors that impede recovery processes (e.g., lack of educational opportunities) (Domhardt et al., 2015). Thus, the context surrounding survivors of CSA matters. Supportive caregivers and other protective factors give some individuals a leg up toward healing amidst significant suffering.

With these cautions in mind, it is important to note that the previous three decades of empirical study have revealed that a subpopulation of CSA survivors experience growth and proclaim a counter-testimony that there *is* life beyond desolation (Yoon et al., 2019). Thus, examining the factors that lead to growth and flourishing following CSA can provide a theoretical understanding of the factors that facilitate healing trajectories, inform clinical practice, and prompt clinicians to be on the lookout for inchoate beauty in the lives of survivors.

This chapter unpacks the dimensions of flourishing, resiliency, posttraumatic growth, and meaning making and includes clinical examples. We discuss the work of envisioning the future in the later stages of trauma work emphasized in several front-line trauma approach lenses and highlight the importance of finding the *and*. In addition, we present the "how" of this therapeutic future focus. Throughout the chapter, we include generous servings of quotes and images of trees as symbols of flourishing.

PATHWAYS TO HEALING

In a forest of a hundred thousand trees, no two leaves are alike. And no two journeys along the same path are alike.

PAULO COELHO

Despite the corrosive impact of CSA, there is a growing consensus that many survivors heal, experience meaningful lives, and grow from their ordeals (Domhardt et al., 2015; Haffejee & Theron, 2017; Hartley et al., 2016; Kaye-Tzadok & Davidson-Arad, 2016, 2017; Kirkner & Ullman, 2020; van der Westhuizen et al., 2022; Vilenica et al., 2013). In the aftermath of CSA, growth is more nuanced than simply doing well or poorly (Hamby et al., 2022). Binary approaches lack awareness of the complexity and ambivalence many survivors experience during the healing trajectory (Roebuck et al., 2022).

Researchers have used various terms to describe what helps individuals recover and thrive following adversity (e.g., flourishing, resilience, posttraumatic growth [PTG], meaning making). The *American Psychological Association Dictionary of Psychology* (2022) holistic definition of health is instructive: "A state of mind characterized by emotional well-being, good behavioral adjustment, relative freedom from anxiety and disabling symptoms, and a capacity to establish constructive relationships and cope with the ordinary demands and stresses of life." What is particularly noteworthy is that health is not defined merely as symptom reduction or the *absence* of distress. Instead, it involves the *presence* of myriad factors, including the ability to adjust and develop meaningful relationships amid common stressors.

Etymologically, the Latin roots of *flourishing* mean to bloom, blossom, and flower (Lomas & Vander Weele, 2022, p. 10). This concept of flourishing, deeply rooted in philosophy and now emerging within the mental health field, is a complex and interdisciplinary construct (Seligman, 2011). Still, there needs to be more conceptual clarity and consistency in defining flourishing from a multidisciplinary vantage point (Willen et al., 2022).

Lomas and Vander Weele (2022) argue that health is explicitly concerned with individuals while flourishing includes (a) individuals (positive emotion, engagement, relationships, meaning, and purpose) (Seligman, 2011, p. 27) *and* (b) their contexts (e.g., access to food, safety, structural oppression) (Willen et al., 2022). Thus, flourishing is multifaceted and encompasses a broad spectrum from languishing to flourishing on individual and contextual levels. Let us examine several concepts in the empirical literature centered specifically on growth aspects related to the rootedness and flourishing of CSA survivors.

RESILIENCY

Trees can be contorted, bent in weird ways, and they're still beautiful.

ALICE WALKER

Various professionals have considered the concept of resiliency from differing lenses (e.g., resilience in healthcare, business, and educational institutions). Masten (2011, p. 494) defines resilience as "the capacity of a dynamic system to withstand or recover from significant challenges that threaten its stability, viability, or development." Withstanding is analogous to a ball pushed underwater that ultimately pops above the surface, and the Timex watch commercial slogan: "It can take a licking and keep on ticking" (Southwick et al., 2014, p. 3).

From a mental health perspective, approaches that consider whether an individual *is or is not* resilient (i.e., binary viewpoint) appear limited. Instead, resilience from a dimensional lens is the capacity for individuals to experience varying degrees of resiliency across multiple domains (Pietrzak & Southwick, 2011). For example, a survivor may adapt well to stress in the workplace using several resources to cope (e.g., deep breathing exercises and social support) while struggling to adapt successfully to stress within a friendship. Moreover, diverse families, cultures, and organizations may view resilience differently (Southwick et al., 2014).

In contrast to focusing on the stress-related impact of a particular stressor/trauma, resilience research focuses on various protective factors that buffer individuals and reduce the impact of adversity (Kalisch et al., 2017). According to Bronfenbrenner's ecological model of human development (1979), there are three salient categories of protective factors: (a) internal factors related to the survivor, (b) external factors related to the survivor's family, and (c) external factors within the survivor's broader social environment.

In a systematic review of the literature (37 articles) examining the resiliency levels of survivors of CSA, Domhardt and colleagues (2015, pp. 479-87) reveal that resiliency ranges between 15% to 47%. Moreover, they indicate the most evidenced-based protective factors on resilience levels:

1. *Internal factors:* Optimism/hope/expectancy, internal locus of control, active/nonavoidant problem-solving coping approaches, externalizing versus internalizing blame, academic performance, the ability to work with others, secure attachments, ability to think well of oneself, religiosity, law-abiding behavior, engagement in leisure activities. For example, I (Hannah) think of several women on the street who might as well have PhDs in solving specific problems, such as obtaining food and housing while struggling with other family dynamics.
2. *Family factors:* Social support satisfaction, maternal attachment, familial support and stability, quality of partner relationships, satisfaction with oneself as a parent, partner SES. For example, Nicole was sexually abused by her father and didn't speak about it for years. When she finally shared what was happening with her mother, her mom believed Nicole, and she began taking the necessary steps to protect Nicole. While Nicole went on to experience some collateral damage from the abuse, she regularly points to the support of her mom and other loving family members who got her through this time (see her autobiographical book *Hush*; Bromley, 2008).
3. *Community factors:* Community social support and the quality of peer relations in adolescence. For example, Aliyah was sexually abused by her older brother for several years. When Aliyah began to get help, she recalled the caring service providers and youth workers who regularly attuned to her. In her darkest years, she pointed to her peers and adults who saw her and heard her, which made a monumental difference.

Domhardt and colleagues' (2015) findings reveal a wide range of individual and environmental protective factors associated with resiliency among adult survivors of CSA. They further explain that the number of protective factors survivors draw on is also pivotal.

Applying this to therapy, clinicians have the opportunity to assess the negative impact of CSA (e.g., ACEs) *and* the presence of protective factors. For example, based on decades of extensive developmental research, Hays-Grudo and Morris (2020) developed a ten-question assessment of relationship and resource protective factors (PACEs) that survivors can complete. The PACEs protective factors (e.g., having a best friend, belonging to a healthy group) can foster hope despite adversity. Providing psychoeducation regarding lament (see the "Indomitable Hope" chapter) can also bolster resiliency. Thus, resiliency is like a bald cypress tree in a hurricane, defiantly standing firm with each gust of wind, anchored by its long roots and thick trunk.

POSTTRAUMATIC GROWTH (PTG)

The tree is more than first a seed, then a stem, then a living trunk, and then dead timber. The tree is a slow, enduring force straining to win the sky.

ANTOINE DE SAINT-EXUPÉRY

In contrast to resiliency, posttraumatic growth (PTG) involves experiencing positive change as potential health pathways after traumatic experiences (Tedeschi & Calhoun, 1996). These domains of healing include self-perceptions, relationships, spirituality, new possibilities, and gratitude. PTG is *not* bouncing back to pretrauma experiences, as in resiliency. Instead, Tedeschi and Calhoun explained that a notable aspect of PTG involves seismic cognitive processing (i.e., reflection) of the trauma material and making positive adjustments based on these intentional considerations. Thus, for survivors of CSA, PTG stems from grappling with the trauma. Moreover, survivors who report PTG are not necessarily resilient or free of distress (Kaye-Tzadok & Davidson-Arad, 2016), as PTG and PTSD frequently coexist.

Hartley and colleagues (2016, pp. 207-15) conducted in-depth interviews with six adult female CSA survivors to explore PTG. They discovered three salient themes regarding the growth experienced by these survivors following CSA:

1. *Making sense of the abuse:* Accepting that it happened versus maintaining denial, wrestling with the "why" of the CSA, finding comfort

through religion, forgiveness, and growth related to contending with cultural dynamics that played a role in the CSA. For example, I (Hannah) have loved watching Adam grow mightily through his story. It seems especially common for men to deny or repress their CSA stories, but Adam has dared to be honest and contended with the "why" and the "why me."

2. *Relating to the self in a new way:* Developing new ways of perceiving themselves versus believing they were damaged and different and the cause of the abuse. This theme also includes the openness to dream, the possibility of achieving goals, and taking new risks. For example, I (Hannah) have seen Tammy return again and again to the loving gaze of her heavenly Father and ask him again to share what he saw—what he sees—and what he sees for her future. A woman not necessarily bent toward risk-taking, she has taken them, holding tight to the grip of her Father.
3. *Experiencing growth through relationships with others:* Given that the CSA affects the ability to establish relationships, growth involves learning to trust and develop secure attachments. Learning to form and navigate boundaries with significant others is another important aspect. I (Hannah) entered marriage wearing some of the tattered robes of being abused, thinking still that my existence was for the pleasure of the man in front of me—in this case, my husband. I grew small and passive under his leaning toward control. In one of the hardest growth spurts of my life, I separated from him for a short time until we both were re-committed to showing up in pursuit of staying connected but differentiated from one another. This painful and ultimately healing journey did not happen overnight.

While PTG is frequently explained as individuals wrestling with shattered assumptions about the self, others, and the future, Hartley and colleagues (2016) clarify that among the adult survivors of CSA that they interviewed, the CSA impacted the very *formation* and shaping of their beliefs. In another study, Kaye-Tzadok and Davidson-Arad (2016) explain that familial factors, self-blame, the degree of hope experienced, and levels of resiliency primarily explain PTG variance.

So, what does bolstering PTG look like in therapy? Clinicians can help survivors navigate the complex PTG cognitive process involved in transforming beliefs by teaching emotional relation strategies to bear the distress. Psychoeducation regarding soothing breathing retraining, progressive muscle relaxation, and grounding techniques (i.e., bottom-up endeavors) can foster activation of the parasympathetic nervous system (i.e., the body's braking system). These practices can also provide the foundation for deliberate thinking about assumptions (top-down endeavor) in a PTG approach (Tedeschi & Moore, 2021).

Therapists can provide safe spaces to process the complex existential questions regarding reasons to live and to grapple with fairness and justice issues (Calhoun & Tedeschi, 2013). Metaphors and images from nature can provide pictures of perseverance in the wake of suffering. For example, tree roots that grow against sizeable rocks may have their growth interrupted, causing roots to grow around. It can be helpful when therapists acknowledge the innumerable impediments survivors have faced *and* inquire about how clients can keep growing like tenacious roots. Other examples of paradoxical growth in nature can prompt additional growth queries. For example, lodgepole pine tree cones are glued shut with resin. Only with extreme heat (e.g., fires) will the resin surrounding the cones melt, allowing the scorched scales to separate and seeds to be released. Following blistering blazes, new life sprouts. At wise junctures, clinicians can invite consideration: what kept you alive during the scorching flames in your life? And where is new life sprouting in you?

In Stephen Joseph's book *What Doesn't Kill Us: The New Psychology of Posttraumatic Growth* (2013, pp. xiii-xiv), he discusses a shattered vase metaphor:

> Imagine that a treasured vase sits in a place of prominence in your house. One day, you accidentally knock it off its perch. It smashes. Sometimes when vases shatter, there is enough left intact to provide a base from which to start the process of reconstruction. In this case, however, only shards remain. What do you do? Do you try to put the vase back together as it was, using glue and sticky tape? Do you collect the shards and drop them in the garbage, as the vase is a total loss? Or do you pick up the beautiful colored pieces and use them to make something new—such as a colorful mosaic?"

In my trauma class, at the end of the semester, I (Tammy) discuss the shattered vase metaphor with my students, and we talk about the paradoxical reality that some items in life intensify in beauty *after* being broken. I invite students to gather in groups and develop a list of broken items that are enhanced in beauty or are better *after* being broken (e.g., composts, piñatas, a contrite spirit, kintsugi, well-loved books with cracked spines, the glass ceiling, students breaking into my office and pulling pranks, Jesus). The list is long. At a wise juncture, clinicians too can invite clients to pen such a list or paint an image as well. Not all brokenness is healed on this earth (Heb 11:13). However, *some* people and *some* items can become more beautiful on this side of heaven.

A severely damaged pear tree with burned and broken branches was discovered at Ground Zero in October 2001 after the attack on the Twin Towers located in the financial district of Lower Manhattan in New York City. The fires exacted extensive damage. The New York City Department of Parks and Recreation removed this broken-down tree from the rubble and cared for it for nine years. And over time, healing occurred. In 2010, they returned this tree with growing limbs extending from gnarled stumps, now standing tall. Aptly named the Survivor Tree, it is a visible, living reminder that new life can rise from the flames of trauma. Not only has the Survivor Tree withstood the toll of trauma, but each year, the 9/11 Memorial gifts seedlings from the Survivor Tree to devastated communities that have also endured tragedy (National September 11 Memorial & Museum, 2021).

MEANING MAKING

The creation of a thousand forests is in one acorn.

RALPH WALDO EMERSON

Meaning making involves the combination of items (e.g., emotions, cognitions, existential and spiritual factors, and motivational factors) that help survivors make sense of their lives and the world around them, develop beliefs that their lives hold inherent value, and work toward highly regarded, long-term pursuits (Steger, 2021; van der Westhuizen et al., 2022).

Through meaning making, individuals attempt to "[restore] meaning in the context of highly stressful events" (Park, 2010, p. 257). This process involves nonjudgmental appraisals versus meanings of blame and negative evaluation (Park, 2010). When meaning making is constructive and adaptive, it can foster PTG (Wang et al., 2015). Specifically, meaning making could look like coming to grips with the reasons a survivor used self-harm and substances to avoid internal shame and contempt stemming from believing that the survivor was the cause of the abuse.

A scoping review of fifty-seven articles that discussed meaning making mechanisms that CSA survivors employ reveals four central themes (van der Westhuizen et al., 2022, pp. 14-17):

1. *Being benevolent or helping others:* These types of meaning making behaviors include engaging in altruistic acts, volunteering, encouraging, and advocating for other survivors. For example, the survivors of sex trafficking employed at the Sanctuary Night drop-in center serving women still involved in the sex trade regularly highlight the value of sharing their lived experiences with others. Kalisha frequently says, "it feeds my soul" to do this work.
2. *Restoring and empowering the inner self:* This theme entails survivors prioritizing self-care and externalizing the responsibility of the abuse on the perpetrator, minimizing personal shame. In addition, obtaining education opportunities and developing academic skills confirmed an internal awareness of personal value among survivors. For example, Shawn's negative cognition identified in setting up an EMDR target around abuse was *It's my fault*, and *I am bad.* Once he was doing the reprocessing work, he was finally able to release personal responsibility as he was flooded with anger toward his perpetrator—appropriately placing the blame where it needed to go. Eventually, he effectively installed the positive belief that *I am lovable.*
3. *Mobilizing external and social resources:* Focus and support groups are seen as empowering places of safety, and beneficial in helping survivors better understand their own experiences through hearing the stories of other survivors. Survivors also mentioned finding meaning through religious and spiritual support. For example, Sarah has benefited from various interventions (e.g., group therapy, individual trauma therapy, and equine therapy); however, she regularly states that she has been able to heal and stay sober because of her faith community and her growing relationship with God. Her faith

community is a safe space for people who have experienced extensive trauma. She has found solidarity and sweet friendship there.

4. *Actively integrating the trauma narrative:* The processing, reframing, and establishing lessons learned are identified as a way of making sense of the abuse. Specifically, survivors indicated that accepting that the abuse happened and that the abuse will always be a part of their story was essential. However, realizing that the abuse no longer defined who they were was particularly meaningful. For example, it was an important day in Evan's life when he decided to stop introducing himself as a "survivor," even though he was regularly in spaces where he was invited to share his story. It's not that the label survivor wasn't accurate anymore, but he realized that he had value—and so did his story—outside of that identity marker. He still tells the story and sometimes uses the survivor verbiage. It is his story, and he gets to decide.

For some survivors, meaning making involves wrestling with the question of theodicy (i.e., why a good God permits evil in this world). For others, while meaning is frequently construed by sifting through perspectives and beliefs, deeper understandings are also "anchored in our attachment to significant others" (Neimeyer et al., 2002, p. 248). And most specifically through our deepening attachment with God (Lewis Hall, 2016) (i.e., "Are you there?" "Are you fair?" and "Do you care?"). Pargament (1997) describes this transformative perspective of God arising through wrestling with his sovereignty and paradoxical gifts that come in the aftermath of abuse:

> When the sacred is seen working [his] will in life's events, what first seems random, nonsensical and tragic is changed into something else—an opportunity to appreciate life more fully, a chance to be with God, a challenge to help others grow, or a loving act meant to prevent something worse from taking place. (p. 223)

Ultimately, resiliency, PTG, and meaning making describe pathways for survivors toward flourishing in the aftermath of abuse. In their purest form, they are not growth guilt trips. They do not involve rushing people to the front of the testimony line, bypassing pain. In contrast, the thrust of these factors is more like *kintsugi*, the centuries-old Japanese art of repairing cracked pottery. Here, the artist rejoins broken pieces with powdered gold instead of hiding the cracks. These pathways help us to understand, in more nuanced ways, the Canadian songwriter Leonard Cohen's anthem: "There is a crack in everything, that's how the *light gets in*."

A GLIMPSE OF TRANSFORMATIVE GROWTH

Good timber does not grow with ease. The stronger wind, the stronger trees.

DOUGLAS MALLOCH

I (Tammy) spoke in a small, impoverished town in another part of the world. Following the seminar, a woman in her forties, Liliia, waited, shifting her weight from foot to foot like a child outside the principal's office. A heaviness was wedded to her like an illness that would not heal. In a hushed voice, Liliia asked if we could talk. There was no access to licensed mental health therapists in this area. With the aid of a quiet room and a translating friend, she voiced a secret that had never previously found its way to spoken words.

When Liliia was eleven years old, she walked home after school down an unfrequented road, past an abandoned building where a group of teenage boys was milling about in the distance. Before this young girl's fear burst into flames, the teenagers grabbed and dragged her down a back alley. Weeping through each word, she recalled a brutal rape on the cold ground and sounds of harsh laughter in the background. The raping voices proclaimed her dead and then disappeared. Yet Liliia survived.

Over the years, hardships continued to stockpile, like stacks of bricks at a construction site, but somewhere along the way, Liliia came to know Jesus. With conviction and tears streaming down her face, she told me Jesus did not allow her to die that night in that cold back alley. Liliia was now working with pregnant and unwed mothers, and her fervent passion was to care for the women and help save babies' lives. After spending an extended time listening to her sordid story, with tears on both of our faces, what came next in our conversation is difficult to put words to. It was like a collective watershed God moment that rained down and drenched us. We realized that her devout passion for caring for these women and unborn babies arose out of the ashes of the rape, as she knew what it was like to be left to die and what it was like to be given the opportunity to live.

That day this dear woman wept and wept as she realized this. Where was God when Liliia was raped? In Genesis 28:16, Jacob said, "Surely the LORD is in this place—and I did not know it!" Jacob was never out of God's presence, but for a time, his surroundings shouted God's absence. So too, the Lord was there amid Liliia's darkest hour. Without ironing away every wrinkle and placing suffering neatly in its proper drawer so that the mysteries are smoothed away, Liliia realized he was there. He was there in her anguish over the evil done to her, and his Son was interceding on her behalf.

Amid Liliia's great grief, as the truth of God's love and purpose for her life embedded into the substance of her soul, she started smiling not only with her mouth but with her eyes and the upright angle of her shoulders. She resembled a red poppy opening wide to the sun as she grasped the truth that he never left her. For a sizeable part of her life, she embraced the belief that she was the sum of that discarded and crumpled little girl left to die in that alley. That day, in the tiny room, God impressed on her very being that he never left her, he loved her, and he had purposed her to protect little ones from evil.

She embraced her life calling, birthed in her painful past, growing into his redemptive future. Rarely have I witnessed a timespan of a couple of hours like this where God saw fit to supernaturally bring meaning and PTG transformation before my eyes. Yet, it was evident that day. Perhaps, our gracious Holy Spirit, aware of the lack of counseling resources in that context, decided to speed up the process and do what only he could do. More work was needed in Liliia's life. But that day, he was mending the wounds of a little girl, planting new meaning, growing this beautiful and courageous woman in the broken places.

FINDING THE *AND*

To really feel a forest canopy one must use different senses, and often the most useful one is the sense of imagination.

JOAN MALOOF

Creativity and imagination can be challenging and, for many survivors, even seem dangerous. It can feel a little like playing with matches. Hypervigilance, a common response to trauma, can prompt survivors to hold protective stances in their body, mind, and soul versus seeing the surroundings as places of possibility. However, there is evidence that creativity can be a protective factor from trauma (Metzl & Morrell, 2008; Thomson & Jaque, 2018). God is the ultimate Creator, and given that we are made in his image, we too can create through imagination. As van der Kolk (2015, p. 17) explains, "Without imagination, there is no hope, no chance to envision a better future, no place to go, no goal to reach."

The twelfth and final module in Cognitive Processing Therapy (CPT) welcomes survivors to become their own therapists and form a new, transformed identity. Placing particular emphasis on this new identity is central. The trauma impact statement (i.e., a written account of the identified traumatic event) is revisited using a CPT approach. Individuals are then encouraged to take a here-and-now focus on trauma from the perspective of a person completing a healing journey (Resick, Monson, & Chard, 2017). The first version of the written trauma impact statement is often raw and filled with vivid sensory details. Therapy draws to a close with a second attempt at the written trauma impact statement that typically still includes references to detailed experiences; however, it also displays an evolution in meaning, attributions, and present/future realities. In some senses, the first written trauma account is typically written by a courageous survivor who writes, "CSA happened to me." The rewritten trauma impact statement is undertaken by a flourishing survivor who writes, "CSA happened to me, *and* . . ." Transformational therapy for CSA survivors helps them find the *and*.

EMDR can also assist clients in processing future scenarios. Utilizing bilateral stimulation (alternating right and left stimulation using eye movements, tactile or auditory stimulation, or tapping on the knees/shoulders) while recalling specific images/details associated with future themes, a survivor engages in a powerful exposure exercise that includes distress and the potential for meaning making. An EMDR approach with a future scenario could invite a survivor to imagine an upcoming situation that would have previously prompted distress before processing. Clients are invited to describe that scenario from beginning to end. Then, they process disturbances that arise. For example, a CSA survivor may have a pattern of distress when experiencing physical touch from a physician at a typical office visit. EMDR can assist the client in imagining the process of entering the building, waiting in the waiting room, going to the exam room, and so on. Just as a world-class athlete or performer can visualize a looming competition, EMDR empowers clients to envision the signature strengths they can call on to face future circumstances (Shapiro, 2017).

Another approach, Written Exposure Therapy (WET), invites survivors to write about details associated with a traumatic event during initial sessions. However, as treatment progresses, survivors are prompted to write about the present and future realities. By the fourth and especially the fifth sessions of Written Exposure Therapy, survivors spend writing time focused on the present and future contemplation (Sloan & Marx, 2019). For example, with the WET approach, a survivor is invited to write about the traumatic event and how it relates to the present and the future. This future orientation invites survivors to forecast a future with agency. Here, processing is slowed to the speed of writing when authoring sentences about the past, present, and future with a careful selection of words and the development of ideas.

When someone is lost in the forest, it can be challenging to visualize a way out. Each of these first-line trauma therapies provides a rough blueprint to explore themes associated with safety, interpersonal effectiveness, and the wisdom accrued from enduring and emerging from the rubble of traumatic circumstances. Moreover, imagination exercises can include envisioning a world overseen by a loving, attentive God. A world where they are a child under God's care.

COUNSELING SCENARIO

Your imagination is your preview of life's coming attractions.

ALBERT EINSTEIN

David initially began counseling with me (Adam) to discuss a break-up with a long-term girlfriend and stresses at work. Over time, as trust was built, he eventually disclosed CSA. He said he had never verbalized the details of performing oral sex on a man from his neighborhood. We discussed various therapeutic approaches, and he decided to pursue Written Exposure Therapy (WET), as he felt it would be preferential for him to engage in exposure via writing versus verbal disclosure.

During the first two WET sessions, David was startled at how emotional and intense the writing time was. He became tremulous and noticed his sweaty palms, increased heart rate, and hypervigilance. He was also surprised by his vivid dreams and recollections experienced on multiple days after the first two sessions. By the third writing session, he reported fewer symptoms of distress during and between sessions, and I invited him to explore how the CSA impacted him in the present. The fourth and fifth sessions allowed David to explore through writing the most graphic details of the CSA and how these events impact him in the present and the future. David remarked, "I was surprised how vividly I could think about these things at the speed of my handwriting." Both David and I felt that WET was effective because it allowed him not only to reap the benefits of exposure therapy related to his CSA memories but also to intentionally focus on the present and future with a greater sense of distance from the CSA memories and bolstered his sense of agency.

One of the foremost pivots in David's therapy journey was realizing that he could continue to author his beliefs in the chapters of his life. Tragedy befell his past and was likely to revisit his future. He became increasingly convinced that he could embrace the sorrow with an unyielding commitment to finding the *and joy*, *and friends*, *and God*, *and now*.

We have the privilege of helping our clients find the *and*. CSA survivor *and* beloved child of God. CSA survivor *and* person with hope and a future. CSA survivor *and* instrument of change in the world. CSA survivor *and* loving parent. And. And. And.

They flourish in the courts of our God.

PSALM 92:13

COUNSELING CONSIDERATIONS

- **Adverse childhood experiences (ACEs) *and* protective and compensatory experiences (PACEs).** Using the brief, free ACEs ten-question measurement can help clients understand the pervasiveness of trauma in their lives. However, too often in therapy, we focus on what hurts and fail to highlight what protects. Zeroing in on some of the protective and compensatory factors can foster hope. Based on decades of developmental research, Hays-Grudo and Morris (2020) developed a brief, free ten-question assessment of protective factors (PACEs) to give individuals a sense of relationships and resources that may have buffered them from difficult circumstances and provide a sense of where there is room for growth. Giving both the brief ACEs and the PACEs measurements together can provide a springboard to clinical discussions that, despite the presence of adversity, the presence of protective factors can provide buffers.

- **Posttraumatic growth (PTG).** Incorporating a PTG lens in trauma therapy is not a new form of treatment. Rather, it involves graduate awareness of the PTG paradox that frequently, "gains may come from losses" (Calhoun & Tedeschi, 2006, p. 303). Absent of formulaic interventions, explorations of both the impact of pain and growth out of pain at wisely timed junctures can be beneficial.
- **Posttraumatic Growth Inventory (PTGI).** The PTGI is a free, twenty-one-item scale measuring the five domains of PTG defined by Tedeschi and Calhoun (1996). Translated into more than twenty languages, this inventory provides a snapshot of the degree to which an individual identifies with and endorses the domains, and it can be a helpful way to measure initial levels of PTG and changes over time.
- **Resiliency.** Resources abound. Reviewing the work of one of the pioneers in the field of resiliency, Emmy Werner (2005), who published a study tracking how 698 children born on the Hawaiian island of Kauai handled adversities for thirty-two years. The Harvard University Lee Kum Sheung Center for Health and Happiness also contains a repository of resilience measures and conceptual papers.

CHILDREN'S CORNER

- ***The Tale of Three Trees*** (Hunt, 1989). This gorgeous book tells the story of three trees that stood and dreamed of what they would be someday. One tree wanted to become a chest to hold treasure, one wanted to become a mighty ship, and the last one wanted to grow as tall as possible and "point to God." As the story goes, they are each chopped down and turned into things they did not want to be: a small feeding trough, an insignificant fishing boat, and a beam. Eventually, they realized their dreams came true: the feeding trough was used to hold baby Jesus, the insignificant fishing boat holds the Messiah who calms the storm, and the beam is carried on the back of our Savior to Calvary and will always "point to God." This parallels Tamar's story of wanting to be a certain kind of "tree" but being wounded and then transforming into a new tree.

REFERENCES

American Psychological Association. (2022). Mental Health. In *APA dictionary of psychology*. https://dictionary.apa.org/mental-health

Brison, S. J. (2002). *Aftermath: Violence and the remaking of a self*. Princeton University Press.

Bromley, N. B. (2008). *Hush: Moving from silence to healing after childhood sexual abuse*. Moody Publishers.

Bronfenbrenner, U. (1979). *The ecology of human development: Experiments by nature and design*. Harvard University Press.

Calhoun, L. G., & Tedeschi, R. G. (2006). *Handbook of posttraumatic growth research and practice*. Lawrence Erlbaum Associates.

Calhoun, L. G., & Tedeschi, R. G. (2012). *Posttraumatic growth in clinical practice*. Routledge.

Cohen, J. A., Mannarino, A. P., & Deblinger, E. (Eds.). (2012). *Trauma-focused CBT for children and adolescents: Treatment applications*. Guilford.

Cohen, Y., & Glasner, B. B. (2015). Date palm status and perspective in Israel. In J. M. Al-Khayri, S. M. Jain, & D. V. Johnson (Eds.), *Date palm genetic resources and utilization* (pp. 265-98). Springer. https://doi.org/10.1007/978-94-017-9707-8_8

Domhardt, M., Münzer, A., Fegert, J. M., & Goldbeck, L. (2015). Resilience in survivors of child sexual abuse: A systematic review of the literature. *Trauma, Violence & Abuse, 16*(4), 476-93. https://doi.org/10.1177/1524838014557288

Haffejee, S., & Theron, L. (2017). Resilience processes in sexually abused adolescent girls: A scoping review of the literature. *South African Journal of Science, 113*(9/10), 9. https://doi.org/10.17159/sajs.2017/20160318

Hamby, S., Taylor, E., Segura, A., & Weber, M. (2022). A dual-factor model of posttraumatic responses: Which is better, high posttraumatic growth or low symptoms? *Psychological Trauma: Theory, Research, Practice, and Policy, 14*(S1), S148-56. https://doi.org/10.1037/tra0001122

Hartley, S., Johnco, C., Hofmeyr, M., & Berry, A. (2016). The nature of posttraumatic growth in adult survivors of child sexual abuse. *Journal of Child Sexual Abuse, 25*(2), 201-20. https://doi.org/10.1080/10538712.2015.1119773

Hays-Grudo, J., & Morris, A. S. (2020). Protective and compensatory experiences: The antidote to ACEs. In J. Hays-Grudo & A. S. Morris, *Adverse and protective childhood experiences: A developmental perspective* (pp. 23-40). American Psychological Association. https://doi.org/10.1037/0000177-002

Hunt, A. E. (1989). *The tale of three trees*. Lion Publishing.

Joseph, S. (2011). *What doesn't kill us: The new psychology of posttraumatic growth*. Basic Books.

Kalisch, R., Baker, D. G., Basten, U., Boks, M. P., Bonanno, G. A., Brummelman, E., Chmitorz, A., Fernàndez, G., Fiebach, C. J., Galatzer-Levy, I., Geuze, E., Groppa, S., Helmreich, I., Hendler, T., Hermans, E. J., Jovanovic, T., Kubiak, T., Lieb, K., Lutz, B., . . . Kleim, B. (2017). The resilience framework as a strategy to combat stress-related disorders. *Nature Human Behaviour*, *1*(11), 784-90. https://doi.org/10.1038/s41562-017-0200-8

Kalman, M. (2005, June 12). *Seed of extinct date palm sprouts after 2,000 years*. SFGATE. www.sfgate.com/cgi-bin/article.cgi?f=/c/a/2005/06/12/MNGJND7G5T1.DTL

Kaye-Tzadok, A., & Davidson-Arad, B. (2016). Posttraumatic growth among women survivors of childhood sexual abuse: Its relation to cognitive strategies, posttraumatic symptoms, and resilience. *Psychological trauma: Theory, research, practice, and policy*, *8*(5), 550-58. https://doi.org/10.1037/tra0000103

Kaye-Tzadok, A., & Davidson-Arad, B. (2017). The contribution of cognitive strategies to the resilience of women survivors of childhood sexual abuse and non-abused women. *Violence Against Women*, *23*(8), 993-1015. https://doi.org/10.1177/1077801216652506

Kirkner, A., & Ullman, S. E. (2020). Sexual assault survivors' post-traumatic growth: Individual and community-level differences. *Violence Against Women*, *26*(15-16), 1987-2003. https://doi.org/10.1177/1077801219888019

Lewis Hall, M. E. (2016). Suffering in God's presence: The role of lament in transformation. *Journal of Spiritual Formation and Soul Care*, 9(2), 219-32. https://doi.org/10.1177/193979091600900207

Lomas, T., & Vander Weele, T. J. (2022). The garden and the orchestra: Generative metaphors for conceptualizing the complexities of well-being. *International Journal of Environmental Research and Public Health*, *19*(21), 14544.

Masten, A. S. (2011). Resilience in children threatened by extreme adversity: Frameworks for research, practice, and translational synergy. *Development and Psychopathology*, *23*(2), 493-506. https://doi.org/10.1017/S0954579411000198

Metzl, E. S., & Morrell, M. A. (2008). The role of creativity in models of resilience: Theoretical exploration and practical applications. *Journal of Creativity in Mental Health*, *3*(3), 303-18. https://doi.org/10.1080/15401380802385228

National September 11 Memorial & Museum (2021). *The Survivor Tree*. 9/11 Memorial & Museum. https://www.911memorial.org/visit/memorial/survivor-tree

Neimeyer, R. A., Prigerson, H. G., & Davies, B. (2002). Mourning and meaning. *American Behavioral Scientist*, *46*(2), 235-51. https://doi.org/10.1177/000276402236676

Pargament, K. I. (1997). *The psychology of religion and coping*. Guilford.

Park, C. L. (2010). Making sense of the meaning literature: an integrative review of meaning making and its effects on adjustment to stressful life events. *Psychological Bulletin*, *136*(2), 257-301. https://doi.org/10.1037/a0018301.

Park, C. L., & Ai, A. L. (2006). Meaning making and growth: New directions for research on survivors of trauma. *Journal of Loss and Trauma, 11*(5), 389-407. https://doi.org/10.1080/15325020600685295

Park, C. L., & Fenster, J. R. (2004). Stress-related growth: Predictors of occurrence and correlates with psychological adjustment. *Journal of Social and Clinical Psychology, 23*(2), 195-215. https://doi.org/10.1521/jscp.23.2.195.31019

Pietrzak, R. H., & Southwick, S. M. (2011). Psychological resilience in OEF-OIF Veterans: Application of a novel classification approach and examination of demographic and psychosocial correlates. *Journal of Affective Disorders, 133*(3), 560-68. https://doi.org/10.1016/j.jad.2011.04.028

Rambo, S. (2010). *Spirit and trauma: A theology of remaining*. Westminster John Knox Press.

Rambo, S. (2015). Spirit and trauma. *Interpretation, 69*(1), 7-19. https://doi.org/10.1177/0020964314552625

Resick, P. A., Monson, C. M., & Chard, K. M. (2017). *Cognitive processing therapy for PTSD: A comprehensive manual.* Guilford.

Roebuck, B. S., Sattler, P. L., & Clayton, A. K. (2022). Violence and posttraumatic change (PTC). *Psychological Trauma: Theory, Research, Practice, and Policy*. Advance online publication. https://doi.org/10.1037/tra0001222

Sallon, S., Cherif, E., Chabrillange, N., Solowey, E., Gros-Balthazard, M., Ivorra, S., Terral, J.-F., Egli, M., & Aberlenc, F. (2020). Origins and insights into the historic Judean date palm based on genetic analysis of germinated ancient seeds and morphometric studies. *Science Advances, 6*(6), eaax0384. https://doi.org/10.1126/sciadv.aax0384

Seligman, M. E. (2011). *Flourish: A new understanding of happiness, well-being—and how to achieve them.* Nicholas Brealey.

Shapiro, F. (2017). *Eye movement desensitization and reprocessing (EMDR) therapy: Basic principles, protocols and procedures* (3rd ed.). Guilford.

Sloan, D. M., & Marx, B. P. (2019). *Written exposure therapy for PTSD: A brief treatment approach for mental health professionals.* American Psychological Association. https://doi.org/10.1037/0000139-000

Southwick, S. M., Bonanno, G. A., Masten, A. S., Panter-Brick, C., & Yehuda, R. (2014). Resilience definitions, theory, and challenges: interdisciplinary perspectives. *European Journal of Psychotraumatology, 5*(1), 25338. https://doi.org/10.3402/ejpt.v5.25338

Steger, M. F. (2021). Meaning in life: A unified model. In C. R. Snyder, S. J. Lopez, L. M. Edwards, & S. C. Marques (Eds.), *Oxford handbook of positive psychology* (3rd ed., pp. 679-88). Oxford University Press.

Tedeschi, R. G., & Calhoun L. G. (1996). The Posttraumatic Growth Inventory: Measuring the positive legacy of trauma. *Journal of Traumatic Stress, 9*(3), 455-71. https://doi.org/10.1002/jts.2490090305

Tedeschi, R. G., Calhoun, L. G., & Cann, A. (2007). Evaluating resource gain: Understanding and *misunderstanding* posttraumatic growth. *Applied Psychology, 56*(3), 396-406. https://doi.org/10.1111/j.1464-0597.2007.00299.x

Tedeschi, R. G., & Moore, B. A. (2021). Posttraumatic growth as an integrative therapeutic philosophy. *Journal of Psychotherapy Integration*, *31*(2), 180. https://doi.org/10.1037/int0000250

Thomson, P., & Jaque, S. V. (2018). Childhood adversity and the creative experience in adult professional performing artists. *Frontiers in Psychology*, 9, 111. https://doi.org/10.3389/fpsyg.2018.00111

Travis, S. (2021). *Unspeakable: Preaching and trauma-informed theology*. Wipf and Stock.

Van der Kolk, B. A. (2015). *The body keeps the score: Brain, mind, and body in the healing of trauma*. Penguin Books.

Van der Westhuizen, M., Walker-Williams, H. J., & Fouché, A. (2022). Meaning making mechanisms in women survivors of childhood sexual abuse: A scoping review. *Trauma, Violence, & Abuse, 24*(3). https://doi.org/10.1177/15248380211066100

Vilenica, S., Shakespeare-Finch, J., & Obst, P. (2013). Exploring the process of meaning making in healing and growth after childhood sexual assault: A case study approach. *Counselling Psychology Quarterly*, *26*(1), 39-54. https://doi.org/10.1080/09515070.2012.728074

Wang, Y., Gan, Y., Miao, M., Ke, Q., Li, W., Zhang, Z., & Cheng, G. (2016). High-level construal benefits, meaning making, and posttraumatic growth in cancer patients. *Palliative and Supportive Care, 14*(5), 510-18. https://doi.org/10.1017/S1478951515001224

Werner, E. E. (2005). Resilience research. In R. D. Peters, B. Leadbeater, & R. J. McMahon (Eds.), *Resilience in children, families, and communities: Linking context to practice and policy* (pp. 3-11). Kluwer Academic/Plenum. https://doi.org/10.1007/b102741

Willen, S. S., Williamson, A. F., Walsh, C. C., Hyman, M., & Tootle, W. (2022). Rethinking flourishing: Critical insights and qualitative perspectives from the US Midwest. *SSM-Mental Health*, 2, 100057.

Yoon, S., Howell, K., Dillard, R., McCarthy, K. S., Napier, T. R., & Pei, F. (2019). Resilience following child maltreatment: Definitional considerations and developmental variations. *Trauma, Violence & Abuse,* 22(3), 541-59. https://doi.org/10.1177/1524838019869094

EPILOGUE

They will be called oaks of righteousness,
the planting of the Lord*, to display his glory.*

ISAIAH 61:3

Tamar put ashes on her head and tore the long robe that she was wearing;
she put her hand on her head and went away, crying aloud as she went.

2 SAMUEL 13:19

We began *Freedom to Heal* with the story of Tamar, a woman who now feels like a beloved friend. We end by returning to her story one last time. Earlier we made note that Tamar's name meant "date palm," signifying that she would one day provide shelter, shade, and nourishment to those in her life. It was the original imagination for her life until she was raped and lived in desolation.

Wearing ashes in the ancient world was a visual picture of a soul devastated by the fires of life. It was an expression of violation, deep sorrow, grief, repentance, humiliation (Eager, 1913), or a symbol of the death of someone or something. Ashes expressed grief when words were found wanting. As Tamar left the one who violated her, she not only wore ashes and a ripped royal robe, but she also wept aloud. Her tears seemed endless; it is the sobbing the violated understand. There is a time to grieve (Eccles 3:4). We need to wear our grief, like Tamar's ashes, when we have been violated.

Over time, as we have sat with Tamar's story, we began to imagine a new kind of future: the *and* we mentioned in the last chapter. Tamar may have imagined a different type of future—we cannot be sure. What we can see, of course, is that Tamar's story, like those 2,000-year-old date palm seeds, has been planted in each of our hearts and is bearing fruit. Tamar would not get to see it in her lifetime, but her story has provided a kind of nourishment that she didn't imagine. Instead of a date palm life, Tamar's legacy points us to oaks of righteousness.

Isaiah 61 paints a vivid picture of the great exchange made available to us all because of Jesus. Verse 3 gives us a prophetic imagination for the Tamars in this world:

> to provide for those who mourn in Zion—
> to give them a garland instead of ashes,
> the oil of gladness instead of mourning,
> the mantle of praise instead of a faint spirit.
> They will be called oaks of righteousness,
> the planting of the LORD, to display his glory. (Is 61:3)

Tamar put ashes on her head *and* God offers a beautiful garland instead.

Tamar wept aloud *and* God offers the oil of gladness.

Tamar ripped her royal robes *and* God offers a mantle of praise instead.

Tamar was meant to be a date palm *and* God offers a new picture: a mighty oak. A new identity.

Forrester Peter Wohlleben's perspective of trees transformed from viewing them as commodities (lumber) to something far more wonderful. He details his treasure trove of findings in the book *The Hidden Life of Trees* (2015). He describes a walk through the forest he manages, where he discovers oaks in distress, often competing for light with beech trees and the like. He writes,

> In its time of need, perhaps in the face of rising panic, it does something that goes against all the rules: it grows new shoots and leaves way down at its base. . . . And what if an oak gets a deep wound or a wide crack in its trunk as a result of a lightning strike? That doesn't matter to the oak, because its wood is permeated with substances that discourage fungi. . . . Even severely damaged trees with major branches broken off can grow replacement crowns and live for a few hundred years longer. . . . In the forest I manage, oaks show they are made from very stern stuff. (pp. 70-71)

Dead trees in the forest become a "culinary relay race" for around six thousand different animal and plant species, Wohlleben further explains (pp. 133-34). Death is not the final answer. Even the trees remind us of our calling as resurrection people. One final theme from Wohlleben's work worth mentioning is his repeated emphasis on the social connections within a forest—the ways, for example, that they supply nourishment to one another:

> A tree is not a forest. On its own, a tree cannot establish a consistent local climate. It is at the mercy of wind and weather. But together, many trees create an ecosystem that moderates extremes of heat and cold, stores a great deal of water, and generates a great deal of humidity. And in this protected environment, trees can live to be very old. To get to this point, the community must remain intact no matter what. If every tree were looking out only for itself, then quite a few of them would never reach old age. Regular fatalities would result in many large gaps in the tree canopy, which would make it easier for storms to get inside the forest and uproot more trees. The heat of summer would reach the forest floor and dry it out. Every tree would suffer. Every tree, therefore, is valuable to the community and worth keeping around for as long as possible. (p. 4)

Significantly, this passage in Isaiah says, "*they* [plural] will be called oaks of righteousness," rather than "she/he [singular] will be called an oak of righteousness." Transformation is unlikely in isolation.

We are part of Tamar's legacy. You are part of Tamar's legacy. We are the seeds that have been planted, beginning to emerge. And so are your clients. Together, may we be oaks of righteousness, the planting of the Lord, that he might be glorified. May it be so.

I am making everything new!

REVELATION 21:5 NIV

REFERENCES

Eager, G. B. (1913). Ashes. In J. Orr (Ed.), *International Standard Bible Encyclopedia*. (2007, April 1 ed.). www.blueletterbible.org/search/Dictionary/viewTopic.cfm?type=GetTopic&Topic=Ashes&DictList=4#ISBE

Wohlleben, P. (2015). *The hidden life of trees.* Greystone Books.

APPENDIX

EVIDENCE-BASED PRACTICES AND CLINICAL PRACTICE GUIDELINES RECOMMENDATIONS FOR CLINICIANS WORKING WITH CLIENTS WITH PTSD

Evidence-based practices (EBPs) integrate the most well-researched treatment approaches, therapist experience and clinical wisdom, and client preferences and values (Hamblen et al., 2019; Lang et al., 2023). **Clinical Practice Guidelines (CPGs)**, specifically PTSD CPGs, recommend particular PTSD interventions based on rigorous systematic reviews of the empirical evidence, safety, acceptability, and feasibility of interventions (Guerra-Farfan et al., 2023; Hamblen et al., 2019; Lang et al., 2024).

Panels of experts (e.g., American Psychological Association [APA], Department of Veterans Affairs and the Department of Defense [VA/DOD], International Society for Traumatic Stress Studies [ISTSS]) develop CPGs to provide summaries of large bodies of research that help therapists make prompt and wise decisions regarding interventions for clients. While PTSD CPGs are tools designed to improve client care with CSA survivors, client preferences, histories, values, individual differences, and cultural considerations, therapist expertise and clinical wisdom are vital in determining wise therapeutic pathways. CPGs are neither the standard of care nor legally binding. They are subject to biases (Guerra-Farfan et al., 2023). Moreover, CPGs must be regularly updated as more research is achieved. Thus, in a few years, the list of EBPs and CPGs for CSA survivors will change.

Thus, EBPs and client-centered care involve reviewing the research on specific approaches for working with survivors of CSA, therapists' clinical wisdom and experience, and therapists collaborating with clients to determine the treatment approach that best meets their values and preferences (Lang et al., 2024). A meta-analysis of 53 studies revealed a relationship between client preferences, lower drop-out rates, and improved therapeutic outcomes (Swift et al., 2018). In another study, Zoellner et al. (2019) discovered that clients with PTSD who received their requested treatment approach were more likely to follow through and respond to treatment and more likely to lose the PTSD diagnosis. Therefore, it is helpful when therapists use understandable language when explaining the various treatments to survivors so that they can work collaboratively to determine the best approach for the specific client. Lang and colleagues (2024, p. 25) provided an example of a nonjargon way therapists can discuss various PTSD treatments with clients:

> We have a few options among the most effective treatments for PTSD. I would like to tell you a little about each and answer any questions you may have. I'm also happy to share web-based resources where you can learn more about treatments and hear from people who have been through them talk about their experiences. Trauma changes the way that people look at themselves, other people, and the world. Some of those changes may be helpful, but some may not. Even though they are meant to protect you, they may actually not be realistic and keep your symptoms going. . . . Each of these treatments reduces PTSD symptoms. What questions could I answer that would help you to select a treatment approach?

In this appendix, we include a look at the following researched EBPs discussed in the CPGs:

- **Evidence-based practices (EBP)** in alphabetical order recommended in at least one PTSD CPG to inform therapists working with CSA survivors (see Burback et al., 2024) (i.e., Cognitive Processing Therapy [CPT], Eye Movement Desensitization and Reprocessing [EMDR], Narrative Exposure Therapy [NET], Prolonged Exposure [PE], and Trauma-Focused Cognitive Behavioral Therapy [TF-CBT]).
- **Emerging Trauma-Focused Approaches** (i.e., Somatic, Body-Oriented Therapies, Written Exposure Therapy [WET])
- **Emerging Non-Trauma-Focused Psychotherapies** (i.e., Acceptance and Commitment Therapy [ACT] for Trauma, Spiritually Oriented Interventions)
- **Sleep Interventions** (i.e., Cognitive Behavioral Therapy for Insomnia [CBT-I], Imagery Rehearsal Therapy [IRT] for PTSD-related Nightmares)

- **Trauma Approaches with Comorbid SUD** (i.e., Seeking Safety, Concurrent Treatment of PTSD and SUDs using Prolonged Exposure [COPE])

TRAUMA-FOCUSED APPROACHES

1. Cognitive Processing Therapy (CPT) is a specific type of manualized cognitive behavioral therapy that helps individuals learn how to modify unhelpful beliefs related to the trauma. It centers on reprocessing major posttraumatic cognitive themes such as safety, avoidance, shame, trust, power, control, self-esteem, and intimacy.

Survivors who might benefit are individuals

- with significant shame and/or confusion about their responsibility for a traumatic event
- who are ready and able to challenge and modify unhelpful beliefs related to the CSA
- who appreciate a skills-based approach with regular assignments between sessions to continue processing

CPT may be less *helpful for survivors*

- with literacy difficulties, as it involves written homework
- who are unlikely to complete regular worksheets/written assignments

Therapist tips

- The use of a manual with this approach can help beginning therapists learn about it and provide structure for survivors. Homework is an essential component.
- Clients learn about the connection between thoughts, feelings, and behaviors. They use progressive worksheets to learn about the effects of CSA on their beliefs about themselves, others, and the world. A homework assignment may involve the client writing a full account of the most traumatic incident of CSA and reading it to themselves daily.
- You can find a plethora of manuals and workbooks on Religiously Integrated Cognitive Behavioral Therapy (RCBT) at Duke University's website, Center for Spirituality, Theology and Health.

- CPT has helpful virtual/online resources that can be accessed easily by therapists and clients. See:
    - The National Center for PTSD for more information on CPT
    - The Center for Deployment Psychology FAQs for Cognitive Processing Therapy (CPT) and Cognitive Processing Therapy for Group (CPT-G)
    - Apps such as CPT Coach

2. Eye Movement Desensitization and Reprocessing (EMDR) is a structured approach that invites individuals to use a dual-attention task. With this task, individuals briefly focus on the trauma memory while simultaneously experiencing bilateral stimulation (e.g., eye movements, tapping, etc.), which can reduce the vividness and emotionality of the trauma memories.

Survivors who might benefit are individuals

- who had very recent exposure to trauma
- who prefer to be minimally verbal and mostly engage in exposure nonverbally
- who are not a good fit for other evidence-based psychotherapies that require verbalizing the details of trauma events

EMDR may be less *helpful for survivors*

- who are hesitant to engage in bilateral stimulation
- when there are challenges to offering EMDR (particularly bilateral eye movement) via virtual/online platforms

Therapist tips

- EMDR is not a one-size-fits-all approach. Some survivors can move through the phases at a faster pace, while others need more extended processing time.
- During the preparation phase, therapists can invite clients to learn resources and tools to help manage triggers outside the therapy session.
- During the desensitization phase, therapists will ask clients to recall specific disturbing memories while the therapist uses bilateral stimulation (BLS).
- A helpful resource for therapists working with children that is filled with handouts is Mark-Griffin, C. (2023). *EMDR workbook for kids: A*

collection of EMDR handouts & worksheets to help kids process trauma, stress, anger, sadness and more. PESI.

*3. **Narrative Exposure Therapy (NET)*** is a culturally inclusive, short-term, trauma-focused approach for survivors of multiple traumatic events, including organized violence, torture, war, rape, and interpersonal childhood abuse.

Survivors who might benefit are individuals

- including children, adolescents, and adults
- who are refugees in group settings
- in low-resource settings

NET may be less *helpful for survivors*

- who have difficulty with intensive exposure. NET involves a detailed reliving of trauma can be challenging for some individuals and potentially escalate negative emotions, thoughts, and behaviors.

Therapist tips

- Clinicians and other professionals (e.g., health and social workers, teachers, and community members) can be trained to use NET in various contexts and crisis and emergency settings.
- Clients are helped to establish a coherent life narrative (including traumatic and positive events). Therapists invite clients to develop a lifeline by laying a piece of rope (or ribbon if ropes have unhelpful connections). Clients indicate one end of the rope when they were born; the other end represents the life yet to come. Stones are used to represent traumas, and flowers indicate positive people in their lives. These items are placed in chronological order to demarcate specific events.
- Therapists can obtain online training from the founders of NET through NET The Institute.
- A key instructional manual is Schauer, M., Neuner, F., & Elbert, T. (2025). *Narrative Exposure Therapy (NET): For survivors of traumatic stress.* Hogrefe & Huber.

*4. **Prolonged Exposure (PE)*** is a manualized CBT approach that teaches individuals to gradually approach their trauma-related memories, feelings, and situations. In contrast to avoiding reminders of trauma, PE helps clients process the CSA and learn that CSA memories are not dangerous and do not need to be avoided. It includes psychoeducation, breath training, in vivo exposure, repeatedly recounting traumatic memories during sessions, and listening to recordings of these recollections.

Survivors who might benefit are individuals

- who can commit to 10-12 intensive sessions in a specific, regimented schedule. I (Adam) have found that military members and first responders value this approach because it is well-researched in these populations and a gold-standard approach. Additionally, it is highly structured, and this appeals to some clients.
- who values research-informed approaches to trauma therapy
- who are willing to engage in intensive exposure

PE may be less *helpful for survivors*

- who have difficulty with intensive exposure. Between sessions, therapists instruct clients to listen to exposure exercises from therapy between appointments, and this may increase drop-out rates from therapy.

Therapist tips

- PE helps clients gradually approach CSA memories, feelings, and situations. This approach embodies the "face your fears" adage. Thus, the client and therapist collaborate on a hierarchy of real-world exposure exercises, and clients are invited to consistently face objects or situations that prompt anxiety throughout the therapy journey.
- Therapists can gain PE training online. We also recommend consultation with a seasoned clinician to ensure fidelity to the approach. See
  - The National Center for PTSD for more information on PE
  - PE Coach, a helpful app for clients and therapists
- I (Adam) have found that PE can result in vicarious traumatization potential of all therapies outlined in this session because of the length of time in sessions assisting a client to process trauma memories.

*5. **Trauma-Focused Cognitive Behavioral Therapy (TF-CBT)*** includes CBT principles and trauma processing for children and adolescents affected by trauma and their parents or caregivers. A central focus involves helping children and adolescents to address trauma-related distorted and distressing beliefs and learn skills to help cope.

Survivors who might benefit are individuals

- including children, adolescents, and their parents (or other caregivers) to overcome the impact of CSA using this specific form of Cognitive Behavioral Therapy (CBT) that includes psychoeducation, challenging beliefs about the CSA, and reinterpreting the CSA
- who have distorted or upsetting beliefs to learn skills to help them cope with life stressors
- such as parents and caregivers to cope with the distress of abuse happening to their children/adolescents

TF-CBT may be less *helpful for survivors*

- who have severe behavioral problems (e.g., aggressive or destructive behaviors) that occurred before the CSA
- who have not developed the capacity to engage in distress tolerance skills

Therapist tips

- During the stabilization phase, survivors and caregivers learn the difference between "bad things" and "bad kids" (i.e., bad things happen; this does not mean the child is "bad").
- During the trauma narrative and processing phase, the child or adolescent survivor may create a narrative that includes written expression and/or drawing of what happened.
- During the integration and consolidation phase, the clinician, child, and parent develop a hierarchy of fear scenarios and rank them from one to ten (least to most). To build tolerance, the child/adolescent begins with the least fearful scenario and works through them all.

EMERGING TRAUMA-FOCUSED APPROACHES

While PE, CPT, EMDR, NET, and TF-CBT are recommended psychotherapies for clients with PTSD in at least one CPG for PTSD (Burback et al., 2024), Yunitri et al. (2023) explained that meta-analyses are biased by design according to psychotherapies that have accumulated more clinical information and studies. Norcross and Wampold (2019) wisely noted that in CPGs, highlighting the importance of the rapport between the therapist and client appears missing, while Lang and colleagues (2024) further emphasized the importance of therapist/client collaboration and client choice when determining the best approach for a specific client. Moreover, Captari and colleagues' (2018) metanalysis revealed that religiously accommodated interventions have mental health outcomes that are at least as effective as carefully matched secular interventions and better outcomes than less well-matched interventions or no treatment (see also Bouwhuis-Van Keulen et al., 2024 meta-analysis). Thus, the following section includes current emerging approaches with variable evidence for the treatment of clients with PTSD (Burback et al., 2024):

1. ***Somatic, Body-Oriented Therapies*** (Somatic Experiencing [SE]) and Sensorimotor Psychotherapy [SP]) emphasize focusing on how the body is affected by trauma. These approaches involve experiencing bodily states such as sensation, posture, and defensive motor patterns and mindful ways to regulate bodily arousal.

Survivors who might benefit are individuals

- who have pent-up emotions in their body. For example, during SP, therapists invite clients to identify fight, flight, freeze responses and alternate ways to release this tension.
- who are disconnected from their bodily sensations and then teach survivors how to feel safe in their bodies so that they can connect with their emotions, memories, and thoughts
- who are adults; however, it has been adapted for children and adolescents as a standalone approach or as an adjunct with other trauma-focused evidence-based approaches

Somatic, body-oriented therapies may be less *helpful for survivors*

- who struggle with mindfulness, as it relies on the survivor's capacity to be attuned to their physical state
- who find re-experiencing memories of trauma overly taxing

Therapist tips

- In this individualized bottom-up approach, therapists help survivors foster awareness of how their body communicates emotions and how the CSA has impacted the survivor physically (e.g., noticing how a survivor cringes and becomes very quiet during specific discussions).

- Clients can use body movements to develop a more empowering relationship with their memories. For example, therapists can ask clients to notice their bodies when discussing a specific memory. What is happening in their body that helps them know they are upset (e.g., quieter voice, tightening in the stomach, back of their head pounding)? The therapist might then ask the client to focus on these sensations, observe their body posture, and consider what movement the client would have liked to have made but couldn't at the time of the CSA (e.g., standing up tall, expressing a message with a loud voice).
- A helpful resource: McBride, H. L. P. (2024). *Practices for embodied living: Experiencing the wisdom of your body*. Brazos.

2. ***Written Exposure Therapy (WET)*** is a manualized, five-session, exposure-based approach developed through systematic evaluations of expressive writing interventions. It requires limited client and therapist time and does not require homework assignments in between sessions.

Survivors who might benefit are individuals

- preferring a shorter cognitive approach to therapy (four to five sessions total)
- who are willing to write the details of a traumatic event as the only means of exposure
- who have a higher likelihood of dropping out of therapy

WET may be less *helpful for survivors*

- with literacy difficulties, as it involves written exercises
- who may benefit from beginning with a bottom-up approach first before this more top-down, cognitive approach

Therapist tips

- WET follows a manual (*Written Exposure Therapy for PTSD: A brief treatment approach for mental health professionals* by D. M. Sloan and B. P. Marx), which can help beginning therapists learn about it and provide structure for survivors. It also has a low drop-out rate.
- This approach is perhaps the most cost-effective and efficient evidence-based trauma therapy, as licensed mental health professionals

are solely required to purchase the manual and read it prior to administration (see Sloan et al. 2019).

- See the National Center for PTSD for more information on WET.
- WET provides a writing prompt for clients to focus their written exercises on how the client felt when the CSA happened, when they felt safe again, and what triggers those memories currently. After a specified time of writing, the therapist processes the experience of writing with the client.
- I (Adam) have found that while WET may not be the preferred form of therapy for all clients, it comes with a much lower potential for vicarious traumatization for therapists.

EMERGING NON-TRAUMA-FOCUSED PSYCHOTHERAPIES

*1. **Acceptance and Commitment Therapy (ACT) for Trauma*** is a cognitive approach that focuses on experiential avoidance of distressing or unwanted thoughts, feelings, and experiences. ACT for Trauma invites survivors to learn to acknowledge and accept these thoughts, emotions, and experiences instead of avoiding them. It also emphasizes psychological flexibility through mindfulness and value-based actions to build meaningful lives.

Survivors who might benefit are individuals

- with comorbid depression and anxiety in addition to posttraumatic stress
- who might benefit from a process-based, skills-building approach to therapy
- who resonate with the broad themes of ACT, including awareness, openness, and engagement based on values

ACT may be less *helpful for survivors*

- seeking therapy for a single traumatic exposure. A targeted, exposure-based approach (e.g., EMDR or WET) in fewer sessions may be more beneficial.

Therapist tips

- Therapists introduce clients to elements of mindfulness, perspective taking, and openness/acceptance to break the cycles of avoidance. For example, an ACT therapist could invite a client to engage in experiential mindfulness of a breath exercise to develop the ability to *rest into* uncomfortable sensations. This can pave the way to practicing psychological flexibility and engaging in valued activities while making room for distressing internal experiences.

- Praxis Continuing Education and Training provides live and online workshops by peer-reviewed trainers on ACT and other approaches.
- There is no official certification progress for ACT therapists; however, joining the Association for Contextual Behavioral Science is a great place to network and seek resources/consultation/supervision.
- A helpful resource: Knabb, J. J., & Hayes, S. C. (2023). *Faith-based ACT for Christian clients: An integrative treatment approach*. Routledge.

2. ***Using expressive art in therapy*** involves artistic endeavors (e.g., drawing, music, poetry, dance, drama, sand tray) to communicate self-expression, emotions, and thoughts, cultivating well-being and fostering change.

Survivors who might benefit are individuals

- including children, adolescents, and adults in individual or group sessions
- in a range of settings, such as hospitals, private practice, and residential centers
- needing a safe place to express complex emotions such as ambivalence, fear, shame, and anger

Creative art therapies may be less *helpful for survivors*

- who have difficulty with the activation of unresolved emotions
- if the therapist is not skilled

Therapist tips

- Clinicians who are art therapists (a protected term) have a master's-level or higher degree trained in art and therapy. This contrasts with using expressive art (expressive painting, drawing, photography, collage, whatever medium) in therapy.
- Creative art interventions are formalized through the disciplines of art therapy, music therapy, dance/movement therapy, drama therapy or psychodrama, poetry therapy, play therapy, and sand tray therapy.

- Therapists can invite clients to use multiple forms of creative expression to convey the unspeakable and aim toward greater integration between the body and mind using art as language. For example, therapists can invite clients to engage in mask making using various materials (e.g., tissue paper, magazines, or clay).
- A client can be invited to develop a series of self-portraits using a range of materials (e.g., drawing, painting, sculpture). This process can demonstrate how a client's view of their self is transforming over time.

*3. **Spiritually oriented interventions*** focus on the client's connection with the sacred and how this positively and/or negatively affects mental health well-being. Using a holistic perspective, treatment may emphasize the mobilization of hope, forgiveness, and meaning making through religious or spiritual resources (e.g., lament, prayer).

Survivors who might benefit are individuals

- who are religious or spiritual and desire that their religious and spiritual experiences, language, and worldviews be acknowledged and addressed (Bouwhuis-Van Keulen et al., 2024)

Spiritually oriented interventions may be less *helpful for survivors*

- who are not interested in religious or spiritual interventions. Also, individuals who have been abused by faith-based perpetrators or have had a negative experience with the church may be opposed to spiritually oriented interventions.

Therapist tips

- The Everett Worthington website offers free workbooks, videos, and other resources on forgiveness for clinicians and clients.
- The Center for Spirituality, Theology, and Health at Duke University website has numerous resources (e.g., Religiously-Integrated Cognitive Behavioral Therapy [RCBT] manuals, workbooks, and training videos). This website also contains a free video educational series designed to train health professionals to integrate spirituality into client care.

SLEEP INTERVENTIONS

1. ***Cognitive Behavioral Therapy for Insomnia (CBT-I)***

   Survivors who might benefit are individuals

   - who are reticent to start exposure/trauma-specific therapy while also enduring insomnia symptoms
   - who are willing to use behavioral approaches to sleep enhancement
   - who are building rapport with a therapist

   CBT-I may be less *helpful for survivors*

   - who have poor sleep quality/quantity due to sleep-wake issues different from insomnia. Careful evaluation and possible referral for a sleep study may be warranted.

   Therapist tips

   - Insomnia is a prevalent concern. Learning CBT-I can be a helpful add-on to other approaches for many clients.
   - I (Adam) have found that assisting a client with insomnia in only one to two sessions has the potential to dramatically increase rapport and credibility for the therapy process and future trauma-related work.
   - CBT-I is a straightforward technique to learn, and there are numerous free, easily accessible apps and resources available online to aid both therapists and clients. See the app Insomnia Coach.

2. ***Imagery Rehearsal Therapy (IRT) for PTSD-related nightmares***

   Survivors who might benefit are individuals

   - who have recurring nightmares related to the CSA. Nightmares are a central feature for many individuals with PTSD (Standards of Practice Committee et al., 2010).
   - in group sessions, as an inexpensive, flexible, and short-term intervention
   - who are not ready yet to discuss the CSA experiences that may have initiated the nightmares. Instead, clients focus on changing the content of their dreams by rewriting the dream (one scene) and then practicing imagining the new dream during the daytime.

IRT may be less *helpful for survivors*

- who are significantly stressed by the content of their nightmares, which can prompt drop-out rates. Thus, it is important for therapists to monitor stress levels to minimize drop-out rates (Romier et al., 2024).

Therapist tips

- The combination of CBT-I *and* IRT for PTSD-related nightmares can be particularly beneficial.
- During therapy, therapists invite clients to rewrite a specific nightmare scene. It can be helpful to recommend active solutions, whereby clients confront the threat in some way instead of a passive solution (e.g., hiding), as passive solutions can foster a sense of helplessness. In addition, simple and easy-to-remember endings can be beneficial.

TRAUMA APPROACHES WITH COMORBID SUD

*1. **Seeking Safety*** is a present-focused approach for clients with co-occurring PTSD and SUD that emphasizes coping skills, safety from trauma, education, and grounding interventions.

Survivors who might benefit are individuals

- who do not desire or are not ready to talk at length about the details of their CSA
- who value a present-focused, cognitive-behavioral approach that helps clients attain safety from trauma and substance abuse by highlighting coping skills, grounding techniques, and education
- who desire an integrated approach to dealing with substance abuse *and* CSA since substances (e.g., alcohol, food, drugs) can be used to numb the pain of the abuse
- or groups, adolescents, or adults in various levels of care and settings (e.g., outpatient, inpatient, residential, home care, schools) for CSA and SUDs

Seeking Safety may be less *helpful for survivors*

- who are veterans. In some studies, Progressive Exposure (COPE), which integrates PE for clients struggling with PTSD and SUD, has outperformed Seeking Safety for veteran populations (Norman et al., 2019).

Therapist tips

- Seeking Safety addresses 25 topics along with a safe coping skill (e.g., learning to ask for help, setting boundaries) germane to *both* PTSD and SUD.
- Safety is the overarching goal of this approach (i.e., coping with life without substances and developing safe relationships who are supportive). For example, therapists provide a list of dozens of Safe Coping Skills and invite clients to explore what safety means to them.
- Therapists could invite clients to review the "Climbing Mount Recovery" handout and engage in an experiential exercise to consider preparation for giving up substances.

2. ***Concurrent Treatment of PTSD and SUDs using Prolonged Exposure (COPE)*** is a manualized, TF-CBT approach using PE for clients with PTSD and relapse prevention for SUD.

Survivors who might benefit are individuals

- who value an evidence-based approach to CSA and addiction treatment
- who value a structured style of therapy steered by manualized treatment
- who desire an integrated approach to dealing with substance abuse *and* CSA since substances (e.g., alcohol, food, drugs) can be used to numb the pain of the CSA
- or groups, adolescents, or adults in various levels of care and settings (e.g., outpatient, inpatient, residential, home care, schools) for CSA and SUD

COPE may be less *helpful for survivors*

- who are not ready to commit to both trauma and addiction treatment. Careful informed consent may increase the likelihood of treatment completion.

Therapist tips

- Like PE, COPE is a manual-based form of TF-CBT with concurrent content and interventions related to substance use disorders.

- CSA and addiction therapy co-occur every session in this approach.
- Therapists invite clients to participate in 3 broad areas:
    - Education on trauma and substance use disorders
    - Imaginal and real-world exposure related to the CSA
    - Relapse prevention for SUD

REFERENCES

Bouwhuis-Van Keulen, A. J., Koelen, J., Eurelings-Bontekoe, L., Hoekstra-Oomen, C., & Glas, G. (2024). The evaluation of religious and spirituality-based therapy compared to standard treatment in mental health care: A multi-level meta-analysis of randomized controlled trials. *Psychotherapy Research*, *34*(3), 339-52. https://doi.org/10.1080/10503307.2023.2241626

Captari, L. E., Hook, J. N., Hoyt, W. T., Davis, D. E., McElroy, S. E., & Worthington, E. L., Jr. (2018). Integrating clients' religion and spirituality within psychotherapy: A comprehensive meta-analysis. *Journal of Clinical Psychology: 74*(11), 1938-51. https://doi.org/10.1002/jclp.22681

Guerra-Farfan, E., Garcia-Sanchez, Y., Jornet-Gibert, M., Nuñez, J. H., Balaguer-Castro, M., & Madden, K. (2023). Clinical practice guidelines: The good, the bad, and the ugly. *Injury*, *54*, S26-S29. https://doi.org/10.1016/j.injury.2022.01.047

Hamblen, J. L., Norman, S. B., Sonis, J. H., Phelps, A. J., Bisson, J. I., Nunes, V. D., . . . & Schnurr, P. P. (2019). A guide to guidelines for the treatment of posttraumatic stress disorder in adults: An update. *Psychotherapy*, *56*(3), 359. https://doi.org/10.1037/pst0000231

Knabb, J. J., & Hayes, S. C. (2023). *Faith-based ACT for Christian clients: An integrative treatment approach*. Routledge.

Lang, A. J., Hamblen, J. L., Holtzheimer, P., Kelly, U., Norman, S. B., Riggs, D., . . . & Wiechers, I. (2024). A clinician's guide to the 2023 VA/DoD clinical practice guideline for management of posttraumatic stress disorder and acute stress disorder. *Journal of Traumatic Stress*, *37*(1), 19-34. https://doi.org/10.1002/jts.23013

Mark-Griffin, C. (2023). *EMDR workbook for kids: A collection of EMDR handouts and worksheets to help kids process trauma, stress, anger, sadness and more.* PESI.

McBride, H. L. P. (2024). *Practices for embodied living: Experiencing the wisdom of your body*. Brazos.

Norman, S. B., Trim, R., Haller, M., Davis, B. C., Myers, U. S., Colvonen, P. J., . . . & Mayes, T. (2019). Efficacy of integrated exposure therapy vs integrated coping skills therapy for comorbid posttraumatic stress disorder and alcohol use disorder: A randomized clinical trial. *JAMA Psychiatry*, *76*(8), 791-99. https://doi.org/10.1001/jamapsychiatry.2019.0638

Romier, A., Clerici, E., Stern, E., Maruani, J., & Geoffroy, P. A. (2024). Therapeutic management of nightmares: Practice guide for Imagery Rehearsal Therapy (IRT). *Current Sleep Medicine Reports*, 1-16. https://doi.org/10.1007/s40675-024-00287-8

Schauer, M., Neuner, F., & Elbert, T. (2025). *Narrative Exposure Therapy (NET): For survivors of traumatic stress.* Hogrefe & Huber.

Sloan, D. M., & Marx, B. P. (2019). *Written Exposure Therapy for PTSD: A brief treatment approach for mental health professionals.* American Psychological Press. http://dx.doi.org/10.1037/0000139-001

Standards of Practice Committee, Aurora, R. N., Zak, R. S., Auerbach, S. H., Casey, K. R., Chowdhuri, S., . . . & Morgenthaler, T. I. (2010). Best practice guide for the treatment of nightmare disorder in adults. *Journal of Clinical Sleep Medicine*, *6*(4), 389-401. https://doi.org/10.5664/jcsm.27883

Swift, J. K., Callahan, J. L., Cooper, M., & Parkin, S. R. (2018). The impact of accommodating client preference in psychotherapy: A meta-analysis. *Journal of Clinical Psychology*, *74*(11), 1924-37. https://doi.org/10.1002/jclp.22680

US Department of Veterans Affairs/Department of Defense. (2023). VA/DoD clinical practice guidelines: Management of posttraumatic stress disorder and acute stress disorder 2023. www.healthquality.va.gov/guidelines/MH/ptsd/

Yunitri, N., Chu, H., Kang, X. L., Wiratama, B. S., Lee, T. Y., Chang, L. F., . . . & Chou, K. R. (2023). Comparative effectiveness of psychotherapies in adults with posttraumatic stress disorder: a network meta-analysis of randomised controlled trials. *Psychological medicine*, *53*(13), 6376-88. https://doi.org/10.1017/S0033291722003737

Zoellner, L. A., Roy-Byrne, P. P., Mavissakalian, M., & Feeny, N. C. (2019). Doubly randomized preference trial of prolonged exposure versus sertraline for treatment of PTSD. *American Journal of Psychiatry*, *176*(4), 287-96. https://doi.org/10.1176/appi.ajp.2018.17090995

GENERAL INDEX

SCRIPTURE INDEX